Energy

Energy

JOSEPH M. DUKERT

GREENWOOD GUIDES TO BUSINESS AND ECONOMICS
Wesley B. Truitt, Series Editor

GREENWOOD PRESS
WESTPORT, CONNECTICUT · LONDON

Library of Congress Cataloging-in-Publication Data

Dukert, Joseph M.
    Energy / Joseph M. Dukert.
        p. cm. — (Greenwood guides to business and economics,
ISSN 1559–2367)
    Includes bibliographical references and index.
    ISBN 978–0–313–34877–8 (alk. paper)
    1. Energy policy—United States.   2. Power resources—United States.   3. Energy
conservation—United States.   4. Renewable energy sources—United States.   I. Title.
    HD9502.U52D828   2009
    333.790973—dc22   2008032968

British Library Cataloguing in Publication Data is available.

Library of Congress Catalog Card Number: 2008032968
ISBN: 978–0–313–34877–8
ISSN: 1559–2367

First published in 2009

Greenwood Press, 88 Post Road West, Westport, CT 06881
An imprint of Greenwood Publishing Group, Inc.
www.greenwood.com

Printed in the United States of America

The paper used in this book complies with the
Permanent Paper Standard issued by the National
Information Standards Organization (Z39.48–1984).

10   9   8   7   6   5   4   3   2   1

Contents

Series Foreword

Scanning the pages of the newspaper on any given day, you'll find headlines like these:

"OPEC points to supply chains as cause of price hikes"

"Business groups warn of danger of takeover proposals"

"U.S. durable goods orders jump 3.3%"

"Dollar hits two-year high versus yen"

"Credibility of WTO at stake in trade talks"

"U.S. GDP growth slows while Fed fears inflation growth"

If this seems like gibberish to you, then you are in good company. To most people, the language of economics is mysterious, intimidating, impenetrable. But with economic forces profoundly influencing our daily lives, being familiar with the ideas and principles of business and economics is vital to our welfare. From fluctuating interest rates to rising gasoline prices to corporate misconduct to the vicissitudes of the stock market to the rippling effects of protests and strikes overseas or natural disasters closer to home, "the economy" is not an abstraction. As Robert Duvall, president and CEO of the National Council on Economic Education, has forcefully argued: "Young people in our country need to know that economic education is not an option. Economic literacy is a vital skill, just as vital as reading literacy."[1] Understanding economics is a skill that will help you interpret current events playing out on a global scale or in your checkbook, ultimately helping you make wiser choices about how you manage your financial resources—today and tomorrow.

It is the goal of this series, Greenwood Guides to Business and Economics, to promote economic literacy and improve economic decision making. All books in the series are written for the general reader, high school and college student, or the business manager, entrepreneur, or graduate student in business and economics looking for a handy refresher. They have been written by experts in their respective fields for nonexpert readers. The approach throughout is at a "basic" level to maximize understanding and to demystify how our business-driven economy really works.

Each book in the series is an essential guide to the topic of that volume, providing an introduction to its respective subject area. The series as a whole constitutes a library of information, up-to-date data, definitions of terms, and resources, covering all aspects of economic activity. Volumes feature such elements as timelines, glossaries, and examples and illustrations that bring the concepts to life and present them in historical and cultural context.

The selection of the titles and their authors has been the work of an Editorial Advisory Board, whose members are the following: Alan Carsrud, Florida International University; Alan Reynolds, Cato Institute; Wesley Truitt, Pepperdine University; Walter E. Williams, George Mason University; and Charles Wolf Jr., RAND Corporation.

As series editor, I served as chairman of the Editorial Advisory Board and want to express my appreciation to each of these distinguished individuals for their dedicated service in helping bring this important series to reality.

The volumes in the series are as follows:

The Corporation by Wesley B. Truitt, School of Public Policy, Pepperdine University

Entrepreneurship by Alan L. Carsrud, Florida International University, and Malin Brännback, Åbo Akademi University

Globalization by Donald J. Boudreaux, George Mason University

Income and Wealth by Alan Reynolds, Cato Institute

Money by Mark Dobeck and Euel Elliott, University of Texas at Dallas

The National Economy by Bradley A. Hansen, University of Mary Washington

The Stock Market by Rik W. Hafer, Southern Illinois University–Edwardsville, and Scott E. Hein, Texas Tech University

Demography by Robert I. Lerman, American University and Urban Institute; and Stephanie Riegg Cellini, George Washington University

Energy by Joseph M. Dukert, Center for Strategic and International Studies

Real Estate by Mark F. Dobeck, Cleveland State University

Special thanks to our original editor at Greenwood, Nick Philipson, for conceiving the idea of the series and for sponsoring it within Greenwood

Press, and many thanks to our current senior editor, Jeff Olson, for skillfully steering the continuation of the series.

The overriding purpose of each of these books and the series as a whole is, as Walter Williams so aptly put it, to "push back the frontiers of ignorance."

Wesley B. Truitt, Series Editor

NOTE

1. Quoted in Gary H. Stern, "Do We Know Enough about Economics?," *The Region*, Federal Reserve Bank of Minneapolis, December 1998.

Preface

Energy worldwide is at least a seven *trillion* dollar a year business and expanding—not least because of energy prices that have defied conventional economic thinking. Energy profoundly affects our economy, society, and environment. The energy outlook in the United States is shaped ultimately by a host of people—including consumers, producers, business leaders, entrepreneurs, and investors, along with many types of government officials across the country. The principles spelled out in this book apply in most cases to anyone and everyone, although the responses and actions they stimulate will vary a lot. That isn't because there was a sly effort to please everybody, but because people act ultimately in what *they see* as their own self-interests—even when their intentions are objectively laudable as high-minded. The book should help readers figure out what their own best interests are. That might help us all!

This is not your "ordinary" energy book. It is not an advocacy work. It is neither a history nor a mere snapshot of the present, although it contains aspects of each. It is a good book to read if you are concerned about the future, and it will help you pose questions to yourself and others that will help us all to get from where we are now to where we'd like to be.

While erasing energy myths and demystifying some complex but critical energy technologies, it won't burden the reader with too many statistics. Numbers change. One of its chief aims, however, is to clarify what the numbers you hear every day mean.

The book doesn't either glorify or dismiss *any* of our current or prospective energy sources. Instead, it explains how each fits into a kaleidoscope that changes continually for many reasons. This small volume, *Energy*, addresses "efficiency" throughout—in terms that allow successive interlocking chapters to put new insights into everyday conversation, investment discussions, or seminars among experts.

It also stresses and explains the value of consensus without trying to impose it in a specific way. Consensus is needed to formulate and implement a *balance* that is inevitably required.

The first chapter is a reference base for the rest of the book, setting out some terms and concepts. The second chapter explores what we can count on from various energy resources—including energy efficiency—and why we *need* "all of the above." Chapters 3, 4, and 5 are compact but meaty examinations of cost, reliability of supply, and effects on human environment, respectively. These facets give rise to the most common questions about energy, but the answers given most often have come from commentators with some bias or another and thus don't tell the more fully rounded story that can be helpful. Chapter 6 deals with something that is missing almost entirely from most public discussions of energy—how time affects all other factors, either positively or negatively. The seventh chapter defines "energy policy" in a way that this is rarely done, but which is crucial to understanding the business and economics of U.S. and global energy . . . and why a call for "energy independence" is generally a scam. The final chapter proposes a sober, adaptive approach to a sustainable energy future that just might work.

All the chapters intentionally mesh with each other and occasionally restate a point or two. This volume dispenses with the glossary that is customary in this series because a special effort has been made instead to define terms that are likely to be unfamiliar *in context*. This is important because some of these terms and distinctions among categories (e.g., primary energy vs. end-use energy, energy demand vs. energy consumption) are often indispensable in judging the extent to which claims being made for a policy, a product, or a potential investment may be valid. For those seeking a conventional and authoritative glossary of energy terms that is far more comprehensive than eight to ten pages here could have provided, the one at http:www.eia.doe.gov is only a couple of mouse-clicks away.

Overall, the approach this book takes can lead to a somewhat meandering text, which insists that a serious reader take a look at the whole thing rather than just shuttle between the index and a few paragraphs here and there. Sorry . . . no apologies! This mirrors real-life, in which everything is connected to everything else.

Unless otherwise cited, statistics about the U.S. and world energy economies are drawn from the latest figures published by the Energy Information Administration, a semi-autonomous arm of the U.S. Department of Energy.

Acknowledgments

This book was more than 30 years in the making. I first compared the sensitive balancing of goals in energy policy to a mobile when offering suggestions for a public television program in Washington during the mid-1970s. I later stressed the balance theme (using the very elements featured in this book) in a letter to Dr. James R. Schlesinger on March 12, 1977. Unfortunately, I doubt that he ever saw the letter, deluged as he was with correspondence in his role as White House energy advisor. Dr. Schlesinger became our first Secretary of Energy, and I still consider him the best thus far, although he has chided me for introducing him as such. He accuses me of damning him with faint praise.

Since then I have tried (repeatedly but unsuccessfully) to include the mobile image in the periodic issuances of the document usually referred to as our "national energy policy" and which I have been privileged to help produce on five occasions in administrations representing both major parties. Gradually, parts of the basic idea have become "conventional wisdom," but so far it has never become effective overall policy.

All this is by way of saying that I have devoted so much time to analyzing energy in changing circumstances over many years that there isn't room here to name the hundreds of people who have helped me to learn—or forced me to learn—about energy economics and technology along the way. Nevertheless, I would be remiss not to mention the institutions (past and present) where colleagues helped shape the thinking expressed in this brief book: The Martin Company and Martin's Research Institute for Advanced Study, the U.S. Atomic Energy Commission, the Energy Research and Development Administration, the Department of Energy and the incomparable Energy Information Administration, Resources for the Future, the Wilson Center, the Center for Strategic and International Studies, the U.S. Energy Association, the U.S. Association for Energy Economics, Washington Policy and Analysis, Edison Electric Institute, the Electric Power Research Institute, the Aspen Institute, and the Johns Hopkins School of Advanced International Studies.

Particular thanks go to Professor Wil Kohl, who recommended to Greenwood Publishers and Wes Truitt, the very helpful series editor, that I finally write this book, and to Jeff Olson, Greenwood's patient senior editor. Also to the busy experts who did me the honor and favor of reviewing chapters: Adam Sieminski, John Felmy, Branko Terzic, Tom Cochran, David Knapp, Bill Martin, and Mike Telson. Their combined critiques protected me from some errors and omissions. As for those failings that may have slipped past their scrutiny, I accept full responsibility.

Finally I thank my wife, Betty Cole Dukert, for putting up with the schedule that enabled me to complete this work more or less on time . . . and my sister, Cecilia Finley, whose faith and prayers made it impossible for me *not* to finish.

One

Energy in the Balance

We make choices about energy every day. Some are small and others large, but collectively they affect where the U.S. economy and environment will be a quarter-century from now.

We may fit into the energy picture ourselves as customers, producers, suppliers, or officials, but all of us help determine (directly or indirectly) the relative roles for energy sources such as coal, wind-turbines, and nuclear power in each given region. Attitudes toward energy efficiency count just as much, if not more.

As individuals, we may finally resolve to replace incandescent light bulbs at home with our own selections from among the numerous new "energy saver" varieties. Corporate boards may be asked to approve, postpone, or cancel projects that would commit vast resources for years into the future. In many ways, those disparate actions are similar—or at least can draw on similar principles.

Although energy has become a hot topic for discussion, surprisingly many decisions are made on the basis of habit, impulse, or incomplete information, with disappointingly little careful thought—sometimes even by professionals in the field.

A huge range of choices in regard to energy sources and energy applications touches private lives and livelihoods, whether or not we are in the energy business.

Shall I vote for that politician who promises that our country can be "energy independent"? Could I save money by trading in my car for a hybrid? Is Company X a good stock investment because (besides being on what I consider "the right side" in moving toward a "green" environment) its commercials about biofuels sound like the wave of the future? Thinking back to how a storm once left us without power for close to a week, would my business be better off if we installed our own generating equipment? If we do, what type should it be?

It doesn't matter whether someone is choosing among ways to provide energy to others or deciding what kinds of energy and how much energy we ourselves will use. If we look more closely at the multitude of options, most decisions face dilemmas on both the supply side and the demand side.

This book does not propose ideal solutions for any of those dilemmas, because there are no sweeping, perfect answers. But there usually is a range of sensible responses—although even sincere, well-informed people will differ in their exact choices of action among them. The energy situation in this country and the world is dynamic, and it will stay that way.

If this were being written more than a few months ago, it would have been harder to resist including more specific examples of actual costs. Yet those numbers change so often and so violently (think about the quick run-up in 2008 oil prices to well beyond $100-a-barrel before backing off) that price comparisons among competing energy sources risk becoming anachronistic between the time a text is complete and the earliest it can be published. That's why the successive chapters stick to principles, which you should be able to apply for yourself. Changes are inevitable in technology, social attitudes, government regulation, and geopolitics; a reader who comes to understand which of these will make a difference (and how much) can modify choices accordingly. After all, energy is still a *commodity* within our economy. Informed decisions are a personal matter in a basically free-enterprise environment.

A FREE MARKET'S RIGHT TO BE WRONG

One of several reasons why projections of our energy future have turned out so often to be wrong is that free will—for better or worse—plays a large role. The "invisible hand" of energy markets doesn't always produce what many economists would call rational behavior, although each separate input may be perfectly explicable. Another reason is that decisions about energy by individuals, corporations, organizations, and governments are often founded on their failure to comprehend adequately all the factors involved—ranging from fundamental realities to unintended consequences. The latter reason is something this book hopes to help minimize.

Our overall attitudes toward energy are not dictated by a central authority, although executive leadership and legislative commitment are both essential for public policies to be effective. One thing that *is* certain, however, is that optimized responses that can achieve public consensus must to some extent include "all of the above," from solar energy to nuclear reactors. This may seem like an inconvenient solution, and it will still be imperfect. It will also involve adjustments, but it is the path to the future that looks least rocky. And it is achievable.

GETTING OUR ARMS AROUND THE SUBJECT

What *is* energy? It was only in the 1970s that we generally began to use that term as it is broadly used today, embracing many sources that are sometimes interchangeable. A search of publication directories such as the *New York Times Index* and *Reader's Guide to Periodical Literature* issued before then shows entries referring to coal or oil or electricity or atomic power, but not often to energy in the more generic sense. The same is true of the word *environment* in the way most people now use it. Yet it would be out of the question at this point to write a book like this about energy without devoting at least one chapter entirely to "environmental factors."

Nowadays, people talk about energy all the time. Sometimes they even ask questions relating to energy, but not always to get information. Often these are merely rhetorical questions, for which nobody actually expects satisfying answers. For example, why don't we have a national energy policy? When is the United States going to become "energy independent"? Where do the oil companies get off raising gasoline prices again? What can we do about global warming? Will we have enough natural gas to heat the house next winter? Why don't we use more solar energy? Or shale oil? Or something like fuel cells?

This book will supply answers to some of those questions directly. But it will also prompt you to ask more meaningful questions (and react thoughtfully to the answers you find or the ones you are offered). In the long run, this can help you shape energy policy yourself. National energy policy is produced, after all, by bottom-up as well as top-down processes.

Each part of this book builds on those that precede it, and it does so with a continuing underlying theme: Decisions about buying, selling, using, or investing in energy are invariably related to *balance* of one sort or another. Many of the numerous interrelationships are hard to figure out, but some are dangerous to ignore for too long.

Even if you happen to be something of an energy expert already, you may view energy issues in a new light after a few chapters. On the other hand, if all you know about energy is what you read in the papers or hear on TV, this should help you spot many of the careless errors that even some good energy writers make every day. Along the way, you may win some bets with friends.

This first chapter involves some tough going, especially when it wades right into part of the "numbers business"—the many different ways in which energy is *measured*, here and abroad. Widely quoted statistics may be purposely or innocently misleading. Without some understanding of all this, discussions of energy dribble into meaningless comparisons of apples, oranges, and rutabagas.

Nobody expects anybody to memorize all the equivalencies among barrels of oil, kilowatt hours, and tons of coal. That's what tables and calculators are for, although nonengineers in most cases will only need those occasionally. They may be essential to double-check a feeling of suspicion about something one may have seen in the press. But anybody who thinks or talks about energy in broad terms should have at least a general impression of what a "megawatt" or "a trillion cubic feet of natural gas" *means*. This helps us sense whether claims about new energy developments should be taken as credible.

Some of these underlying concepts are keys to finding answers. What this book cannot promise is that you will be pleased with all the answers.

SUPPLY, DEMAND, AND VARIOUS KINDS OF BALANCE

Like any commodity, energy reacts to the forces of supply and demand. Their interaction is one of several sorts of *balance* this book addresses. Energy prices are only one of the aspects of energy that may cause problems for individuals, economies, and societies; but it is fundamental to recognize that prices in a free market are determined by the balance between (1) what the whole chain of energy producers and sellers on the supply side are collectively willing to accept for delivering given amounts of energy in some form to customers and (2) what people who wish to consume energy are willing and able to pay for that amount at a given time, and in the form being offered (see Figure 1.1).

So far this seems simple, or at least as simple as any basic principle of economics can be made. But for energy there can also be complicating factors, even in a largely free market economy such as the United States. Many of those will be treated in Chapter 3. Each of the various sources of energy is also more multifaceted than a commodity like wheat or potatoes. There are factors on both the supply side and the demand side of energy that control the *slopes* of those two lines in the diagram, and that affects the point at which they intersect:

1. *Energy may be supplied by different "primary" sources, such as coal, oil, gas, wind, or water behind a dam. Both the nature and the relative costs of fuels or other energy sources vary more between one part of the country and another than most people realize.* Consider coal: Texas burns lots of very-low-grade coal with so little potential energy per ton that it wouldn't be worth shipping to most other parts of the country. Or consider gas: This country's first gas utility was founded in Baltimore in the early part of the nineteenth century, and what it sold then was gaseous fuel produced *synthetically* from coal, pine tar, and other materials. Natural gas pumped directly from the ground is the cooking-and-heating fuel used there now, but it wasn't generally available in the middle Atlantic states until after World War II. That's when a wartime pipeline used originally to bring crude oil from the Gulf Coast to refineries along the Atlantic was converted to carry gas instead. The point

FIGURE 1.1
Supply (S) and Demand (D): It Seems Simple

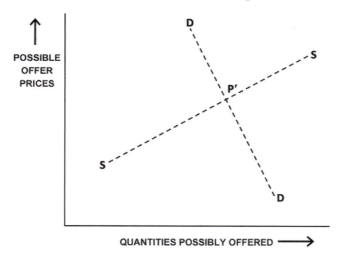

In a free market, energy prices and the amounts of each type of energy exchanged are both determined by the point at which buyers and sellers agree—whether they are completely happy about it or not. But there are stories inside this story.

is that some fuels don't come close to competing in some regional markets at a given time, while supplies of those that do may be affected by many different and sometimes unrelated conditions. Drought may limit the ability of power-dams to function. A strike by miners or employees of a railroad may cut off coal deliveries to generating stations.

2. *On the other side of the supply-and-demand balance, why do users* want *energy anyway? They are interested mainly in what it does for them. Among other things it provides light, controls temperatures within buildings, propels automobiles, operates machinery, or carries out chemical processes in industry. But not all sources and forms of energy are equally suited for such dissimilar tasks.* Demand doesn't apply evenly to all *types* of energy either, and the requirements of energy-users may change with the weather or with personal habits and overall economic conditions. Americans drive more during the summer, and that's certainly when they use air conditioners most; so gasoline and electricity prices routinely change with the seasons. The price of natural gas rises during a cold winter, and temporary shortages may even develop then in some regions for this particular fuel. About 35 percent of the natural gas used in the United States goes into space heating within buildings.

3. *As an additional complication, the various forms of energy—such as heat, motion, physical and chemical change, electricity, and so on—can be converted* into *one another (see Figure 1.2). In fact, we sometimes find it convenient to switch back and forth between forms to accomplish our purposes.* For example, burning pulverized coal to

heat water can produce steam. In coal-fired power plants, the steam expanding from boilers spins the blades of turbo-generators to turn out about half of all U.S. electricity. Yet some of that electricity will be converted back into heat, boiling water *once again* so that a coffeemaker can transform ground-up beans into the flavorful brew you drink at Starbucks. This seems at first glance like a mindless circle, but think about it. My grandmother burned chunks of coal directly in a cast-iron stove to make her coffee in a big blue-and-white pot on top of it, but my wife would never think of mussing up her kitchen that way when all she has to do instead is flick an electric switch. Electricity is both a consumer and a source of useful energy. It has many desirable characteristics, and convenience is one of the most important. It fits on *both* the supply side *and* the demand side in our energy picture. That's important to the overall energy portrait!

4. *Finally, various sources of energy can often be substituted for one another, and there are many factors that determine whether or not they will be.* Some of the turbine-generators that produce electricity are capable of using either oil or natural gas as their fuel. A "flex-fuel" automobile can switch back and forth between gasoline and a mixture of 15 percent gasoline and 85 percent ethanol. A home owner may decide to change from an electric range in the kitchen to one using gas. But, besides being able to do the job at hand, any form of energy is evaluated by actual and potential end-users (and investors) according to multiple criteria—not just base price. More and more, for instance, Americans are becoming aware that the production and use of *any* energy resource affects the natural environment—although those effects differ from case to case in kind, extent, and gravity.

FIGURE 1.2
One Form of Energy Leads to Another

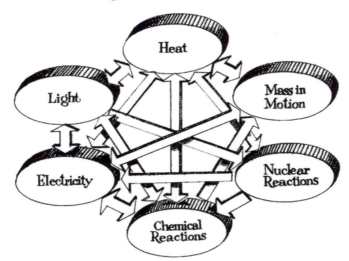

Conversion always involves some loss, with the efficiency of conversion measured in percentage.

All this may seem confusing to keep in mind at once, even though we may have already known these facts or could have figured them out. However, there are three reasons for mentioning and emphasizing these interrelated basics right up front: (1) The supply-demand *balance* in energy is the final resultant of numerous subordinate factors, any of which can be determinative; (2) the United States has come for good reason to depend on a "diversified energy portfolio"—thus, for instance, enabling us to *balance* the ready availability of hydropower in one state with cheap and abundant coal in another; and (3) any attempt to "solve" our energy problems needs to weigh *both* supply and demand for *all* fuels, as well as the opportunities to make both the production and the consumption of energy more efficient. So we wind up *balancing* positive and negative attributes, according to a long wish list as we put together a composite national recipe of energy ingredients that changes over time—more about this shortly.

ALL THE SOURCES, PLUS EFFICIENCY

Efficiency should be more than a buzzword in discussions of energy. Efficiency is not an energy source, but it isn't stretching too much to call it an energy *resource*. At times it is fair to treat it as an extra fuel option. Improved efficiency, on the supply side *or* the demand side, enables us to accomplish what we need and wish to do while suffering less risk of running short of the right amounts and kinds of energy to get those things done.

On the supply side, efficiency applies to the way fuels and energy are produced, stored, transformed, and delivered. On the demand side it includes of course the "efficiency ratings" of energy-using equipment such as cars, computers, and light bulbs; but it also involves the way in which energy is utilized. Avoiding unnecessary energy use by recycling some materials is only one of many possibilities. Others, which are often urged by electric utilities in their "demand side management" campaigns, include the regulation of thermostats and the timing of some household chores that use lots of electricity to avoid periods of peak demand when less efficient generation units have to be pressed into service. Often—although not always—saving energy also helps to cut costs and reduce undesirable environmental effects. The rest of this book will explain some of the subtleties in choices among energy sources and various efficiency options.

For reasons that should become increasingly clear in subsequent chapters, the most troubling energy *supply* problem facing the United States today is not energy in general but oil. In 2007 we imported nearly two-thirds of the oil we consumed, and much of the oil supply in the world market comes from politically troubled countries whose total oil production and exports could plunge at almost any time. Simultaneously, "conventional oil" is hard-pressed to meet fast-growing demand in developing countries around the world. This is most notably obvious in populous China and India. Industry is booming in both countries, living standards are rising, and the numbers of gasoline- or diesel-fueled motor vehicles are multiplying. The *definition* of conventional oil changes from time to time, and that will be addressed more specifically in Chapter 2.

Table 1.1 is worth looking at carefully. Saudi Arabia and Russia are the two largest oil producers, but they are even more important in the global oil market because they are also the two largest exporters. By contrast, the United States and China are significant oil producers, but their production each year falls far short of the amount they are consuming annually, so they must *import*. Furthermore, U.S. and Chinese "proved reserves" of oil (a term to be explained later) are dwarfed by those in several Middle Eastern countries.

U.S. dependence on imports of oil and refined petroleum products is substantial enough to cause concern, although statistics and recent trends have sometimes been exaggerated or misrepresented for effect. After a long series of almost uninterrupted increases, net imports have actually appeared to stabilize since 2004, despite continuing growth in population and economic output. Nevertheless, with gross imports representing about 65 percent of total U.S. petroleum consumption in both 2007 and 2008, maintaining overall

TABLE 1.1
World's Leading Oil Producers, with Related Data (global rankings in parentheses)

Country	Production	Exports	Consumption	Reserves
(1) Saudi Arabia	10,655	(1) 8,525	(10) 2,139	(1) 264
(2) Russia	9,677	(2) 6,866	(4) 2,811	(8) 60
(3) United States	8,330		(1) 20,687	(12) 21
(4) Iran	4,148	(5) 2,462	(15) 1,686	(3) 136
(5) China	3,845		(2) 7,201	(13) 16
(6) Mexico	3,707	(10) 1,710	(11) 1,997	12
(7) Canada	3,288	(15) 1,024	(7) 2,264	(2) 179
(8) UAE	2,945	(3) 2,564		(6) 98
(9) Venezuela	2,803	(7) 2,183		(7) 87
(10) Norway	2,786	(4) 2,551		7
(11) Kuwait	2,675	(6) 2,340		(5) 102
(12) Nigeria	2,443	(8) 2,131		(10) 36
(13) Brazil	2,166		(8) 2,217	12
(14) Algeria	2,122	(9) 1,842		(15) 12
(15) Iraq	2,008	(12) 1,438		(4) 115

Production, exports and consumption are in millions of barrels per day for 2006; reserves are rounded to billions of barrels, as estimated by *Oil and Gas Journal* at the end of 2007.

adequate supply would rapidly pose problems if foreign sources were cut off and/or domestic production could not at least be maintained.

A U.S. shortfall of oil—or any other source of energy—might be alleviated in several ways: by increasing production, by reducing consumption, and/or by substituting other energy sources. Those who champion any *single* energy source exclusively as the sole answer to all of our problems, however, are part of the underlying problem. So are the cynics who spend all their time condemning one source or another. Those who think energy efficiency will take care of everything by itself are unrealistic. Almost any energy decision we make will involve some internal contradictions among the many results we would like it to achieve.

We in the United States need every significant source that exists. So do countries in the developing world, which will soon be consuming more energy jointly than the entire roster of nations that have already industrialized. For the stability of the global economy and the health of the planet, we also need greater efforts everywhere to improve the efficiency of energy production and energy consumption. All energy sources have pluses and minuses, and we individually assign different values to the various characteristics we wish to see in a "perfect" energy source.

Figure 1.3 represents the situation graphically. Our energy goals interact like the arms of a dangling mobile, so that by emphasizing any *one* we affect the others. If we try to insist on *absolutely* secure supplies we will pay a price, often in dollars and cents, but just as possibly in the volume of that type of energy that is readily available to us. All energy sources involve *some* disturbances to our environment. If we forgo using much of what we have and wait for some future technology that promises to be more gentle but isn't quite ready, we may have to accept a great deal of expense, discomfort, and inconvenience in the meantime. Time is a factor that is most often downplayed in energy discussions, but this book will devote all of Chapter 6 to this.

It's sometimes hard to tell in advance how arms of the mobile will react to each other, positively or negatively. This delicate balance is even more complicated than that between supply and demand. Also, it changes constantly, since we live in a global economy influenced by evolving technology and geopolitics.

Ideally, we want *affordable* energy
   to be available in *ample quantities*
      from *reliable* sources
         that are *safe* and *environmentally benign*
            when we want it!

FIGURE 1.3
Our Energy Goals Are Always in a Delicate, Changing Balance

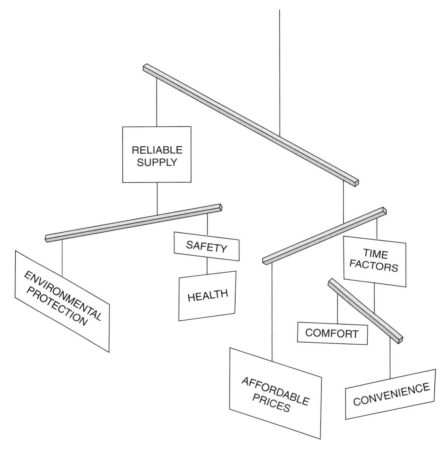

Major elements interact continuously with one another—often unpredictably.

The sum of all those good attributes is what we really mean by "energy security." That, too, is a relative term.

Like the elements in Figure 1.3, all the chapters of this book interact. A reasonable place to start its explanations is with a picture of where U.S. energy comes from now, and what we do with it. This is depicted in Figure 1.4 as a "spaghetti chart"—the latest one available among those that have been produced by Lawrence Livermore Laboratory periodically since before the U.S. Department of Energy was established in 1978.

FIGURE 1.4
Where U.S. Energy Came
from and How It Was Used
in 2006 ~99.8 Quads

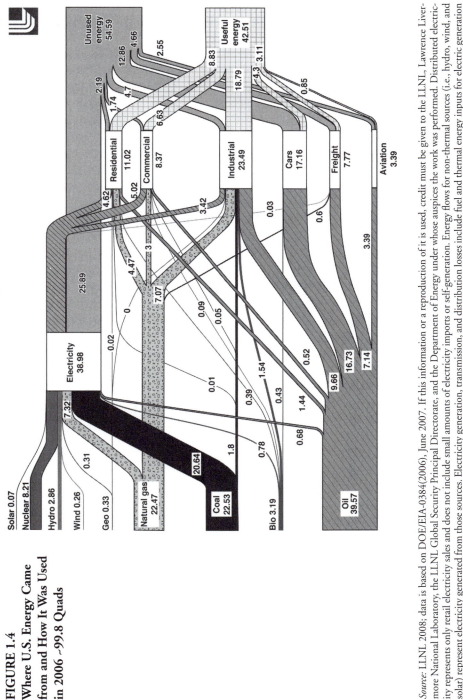

Source: LLNL 2008; data is based on DOE/EIA-0384(2006), June 2007. If this information or a reproduction of it is used, credit must be given to the LLNL, Lawrence Livermore National Laboratory, the LLNL Global Security Principal Directorate, and the Department of Energy under whose auspices the work was performed. Distributed electricity represents only retail electricity sales and does not include small amounts of electricity imports or self-generation. Energy flows for non-thermal sources (i.e., hydro, wind, and solar) represent electricity generated from those sources. Electricity generation, transmission, and distribution losses include fuel and thermal energy inputs for electric generation and an estimated 9% transmission and distribution loss, as well as electricity consumed at power plants. Total lost energy includes these losses as well as losses based on estimates of end-use efficiency, including 80% efficiency for residential, commercial, and industrial sectors, 20% efficiency for light-duty vehicles, and 25% efficiency for aircraft. LLNL-MI-402223

The chart is more user-friendly than it appears at first. It's easy to see, for instance, that our major uses of primary energy (lined up on the left, from solar and nuclear through coal, biofuels, and oil) are

1. to generate electricity, and
2. to supply transportation fuels for cars, freight, and aviation.

Electricity is an intermediate form of energy, converting various kinds of primary inputs into energy that has convenient end-uses in many different consuming sectors of the economy.

Technically, what is shown here is "commercial energy." It does not include the energy supplied free by our sun that permits vegetation to grow and us to survive within a tolerable temperature range on Earth. It *does* display those relatively small amounts of solar and wind energy that enter our economy directly because we manage to concentrate their effects—at additional cost—in a way that substitutes for fuels.

As points are made throughout the book, you will probably wish to look back at this chart repeatedly. In the long run, you'll spot other informative features for yourself. You may also find it useful to glance again occasionally at Figures 1.2 and 1.3. They are reminders that most of our day-to-day interest in energy depends on what we want it to do for us.

The "spaghetti chart" makes it evident that more than half of all primary energy normally goes unused, that is, it is not being put to *any* end-use. Some loss is unavoidable, because no system exists for perfectly converting one form of energy (for example, heat or solar rays) into another that may be more convenient to use (such as electricity). But there are ways to boost conversion efficiency. Most of the improvements in vehicle mileage that have been introduced since the 1970s have taken place through engine, tire, and body modifications; but it is clear that a great deal of the primary energy-input to autos is still wasted—regardless of what fuel is being utilized. Techniques for further improving efficiency in other end-use sectors range from replacing incandescent light bulbs with compact fluorescents to introducing "tri-gen" systems for large buildings. The latter can produce electricity, heating, and cooling while reducing the annual costs of all three. Footnote references will guide the reader to more information about these and other detailed aspects of energy that can't be fully explored in a book of this length, but the richest bibliography imaginable is available on the Internet through careful use of a good search engine. One goal of this book is to help the reader-turned-browser sense when information on the computer screen is potentially useful and when to exercise caution or just dismiss it.

Take another look at Figure 1.4. Are there any surprises? Did you notice, for example, that oil is now a relatively insignificant fuel in generating electricity?

Before the "energy crisis" of the early 1970s, petroleum rivaled natural gas and hydro in supplying the primary energy input to generate electricity, with each accounting for roughly one-sixth. That changed pretty quickly when concerns arose about the nation's dependence on imported fuel, because the global market can be squeezed by political moves such as the Arab oil embargo (see Chapter 3). Electric utilities weaned themselves off oil, especially as new generating equipment was installed to satisfy this country's continued growth in demand for electricity. By the turn of the century the United States was using approximately twice as much electricity as it had in the early 1970s, but in 2007 petroleum's proportional share in supplying it was only about one-tenth what it had been then. Currently, oil provides much less than 2 percent of the total primary energy input for the electricity sector.

Note that this chart compares quantities of various kinds of energy in "quads." A quad is a very large unit of measurement that can be applied equally to the energy content of oil, gas, coal, nuclear fuel, or electricity. It is far easier at times to use a common unit such as this than to juggle tons of coal versus barrels of oil, cubic feet of gas, kilowatt hours, and so on. Measuring energy in this simplified way makes direct comparisons possible. It involves some conventional assumptions, but those details generally need not concern us. They do not affect the basic thread of this chapter or this book.

Quad is shorthand for "one quadrillion British thermal units." That is the equivalent of what is contained in the supply or consumption of about half a million barrels of oil each day for a whole year. A quadrillion, incidentally, is 10^{15}—or a "1" followed by fifteen zeroes. British thermal units themselves are abbreviated Btu, and Btu is another unit you should get used to seeing. Its own definition, however, is arbitrary and not especially helpful in visualizing much of anything: A Btu is the amount of heat-energy used to raise the temperature of one pound of water by 1°F under specified conditions.

Isn't it ironic that the British have largely accepted the metric system while we in the erstwhile colonies stick pretty much to the hard-to-manage old English units? It might be easier if everybody in the world used a pure metric system, and there *is* one for energy content. It uses a very small unit called a joule and multiples thereof. The joule links directly to metric units of volume and weight, which simplifies the arithmetic. But the U.S. public decided resoundingly a long time ago *not* to switch to the metric system entirely, so we use a mixture of measurements. We generally think in terms of pounds rather than kilograms, cubic feet rather than cubic meters, and gallons rather than liters. Fortunately, an exajoule—which is 10^{18} joules—is very close to the same amount of energy as a quad; exajoules are a large unit of energy that Europeans are more likely to use. My view is that when one is dealing with such large numbers it is almost unnecessary to distinguish between quads and exajoules when trying to make a general point. Those very large numbers may merely be estimates anyway, subject to revision when the yearly totals are cross-checked a few months later. If you know that one exajoule is *about* the same as one quad, you will be as close as anybody in your carpool to understanding relationships at that level.

Measuring energy supplies and requirements in quads has become surprisingly common in general circulation newspapers and magazines, especially in North America. Above all, this provides a convenient way to compare large quantities of distinct sources of energy (such as oil, coal, or the electrical output of a wind farm). But it is far less helpful when one gets down to cases of what sort of automobile to buy . . . or how much a new port facility that brings in cargoes of liquefied natural gas (LNG) from Trinidad and Tobago will mean in terms of heating homes in New England and thus how valuable it might be to a community. Among other things, this calls for a table that converts various units of measurement into one another, like the multipage Table 1.2. Once again, however, it's often sufficient to keep only rough equivalencies in mind. As already noted and in the table, for instance, a "quad" is *about* the same as half a million barrels of oil per day for a year. That's close enough for most general discussions and comparisons.

MORE SPECIFIC DEFINITIONS ALSO MATTER

There is some justification for using a variety of measuring units in referring to specific energy sources, and that practice is not going to change. It seems reasonable to talk about coal in terms of tons and oil in terms of barrels. It is surely more graphic, and those are the units in which production levels and prices are most commonly expressed. When one talks about overall energy requirements, it can't be emphasized too often that "tons of coal" or "barrels of oil" are not all homogeneous either. For instance, a typical ton of coal from deep-underground coal mines in the Eastern United States usually contains about 30 percent more Btus than most coal from India, no matter where or how each is burned. That makes the former far more valuable as an energy source. Most U.S. "deep coal" also has a higher energy content than an average ton of the "surface coal" that is excavated from open pits in states such as Wyoming, which produces about 40 percent of all U.S. coal. But coal from east of the Mississippi tends at the same time to contain more sulfur, and sulfur is an undesirable contaminant. Burning any fuel loaded with sulfur releases air pollution unless it is removed somewhere along the line. Thus, besides taking into account the costs of shipping coal from mines to a point of use, the relative market price of "Eastern" and "Western" coal in the United States cranks in the expense of adapting electricity generating stations to strict regulatory limits on how much sulfur dioxide may be allowed to escape into the air as a plant operates.

TABLE 1.2
Measuring Energy: A Quick Reference Table—Enough to Give a "Feel" for Energy Statistics

General

1 British thermal unit (btu) = the energy required to raise the temperature of one pound of water, at its maximum density, by one degree Fahrenheit.

1 quad (1 quadrillion btu) = about 470,000 barrels of crude oil per day for a year or 50 million tons of average U.S. steam coal, as burned by electric utility generators. (But if you use the rough equivalency that one million barrels per day works out to around 2 quads per year you'll get the general idea.)

1 btu = 1,055 joules

1 quad = 1.055 exajoules

It's helpful to remember that in 2006 the United States consumed *approximately* 100 quads of primary energy. Thus, the number of quads shown for any element on the spaghetti chart (Figure 1.4) also represents almost exactly the *percentage share* of total U.S. consumption—which that chart shows as about 99.8 quads. In fact, many sources—including the tables in EIA's *Monthly Energy Review*—list 2006 energy consumption as within a few tenths of a quad of 100. In case you wish to be finicky, the explanation appears in the section of this table dealing with electricity.

Metric Unit Prefixes

kilo (as in kilowatt of electricity) = 1,000—or 10^3

mega = 1 million (1,000,000)—or 10^6

giga = 1 billion (1,000,000,000)—or 10^9

tera = 1 trillion (1,000,000,000,000)—or 10^{12}

peta = 1 quadrillion—or 10^{15}

exa = 1 quintillion—or 10^{18}

deci = One-tenth—or 10^{-1}

centi = One-hundredth—or 10^{-2}

milli = One thousandth—or 10^{-3}

micro = One millionth—or 10^{-6}

nano = One billionth—or 10^{-9}

pico = One trillionth—or 10^{-12}

(Continued)

TABLE 1.2 (Continued)

Common Abbreviations (as used in this book)

kwh—kilowatt hour

mw—megawatt

mcf—thousand cubic feet (the "m" comes from the Roman letter "M" for 1,000)

mmcf—million cubic feet (of gas)

bcf—billion cubic feet

tcf—trillion cubic feet

bbl—barrel

mmbd—millions of barrels per day

mmbdoe—millions of barrels per day of oil equivalent

bcfd—billions of cubic feet per day

(You can figure out other combinations for yourself. But be warned that some publications may capitalize certain letters or use other variations of these abbreviations. If in doubt, check the first use in an article or chapter—which should spell out the full word or phrase and add the abbreviation in parentheses)

Weights

1 U.S. (or "short") ton = 2,000 pounds

1 long ton = 2,240 pounds

1 metric ton = 2,200 pounds, or 1,000 kilograms

1 kilogram = 2.2 pounds (the weight of one liter of water—a bit more than a quart—under specified conditions)

1 barrel of crude oil weighs about 200 pounds (but see the caveats below).

Petroleum

1 barrel = 42 U.S. gallons (But, after a barrel of crude oil has been refined, the yield of various products is greater in volume—in many cases about 44 gallons. This is because some of the less dense refinery products, including gasoline, fill a larger volume.)

1 Imperial gallon (used in Canada and UK) = 1.20095 U.S. gallons. Countries that use the imperial gallon usually sell vehicle fuel such as gasoline or diesel by the liter (with four liters to each gallon).

16

Crude oil is like a raw mineral ore, and thus by no means uniform in chemical content or heat energy; but the contents of a barrel of crude are normally equivalent to about 6 million btu. Once crude is refined, the useful (but less dense) products it yields typically have slightly less energy in a given volume. Aviation gas, for instance, may contain about 5 million btu per barrel. Home heating oil is somewhat over 5.8.

1 billion barrels of producible reserves = 1 mmbd for two years and about nine months

Europeans frequently specify large quantities of oil in millions of metric tons. One metric ton of crude usually contains somewhat more than 7 barrels, so if you divide a certain number of metric tons by seven you will know the approximate number of barrels involved. If the number applies to annual production or consumption, just divide by 365 to get the number of barrels per day. (Use a calculator; that isn't cheating.)

1 barrel of crude oil per day = about 50 tons of crude oil per year (That's close enough to gauge what's being talked about.)

Natural Gas

1 cubic foot of U.S. pipeline quality gas contains slightly more than 1,100 Btu

1,000 cubic feet (a quantity used often in comparisons) is roughly equivalent in energy content to 1 million Btu (the unit used most often in quoting the price of natural gas—e.g., $7.00 per mmBtu)

1 billion cubic feet of natural gas per day (bcfd) = somewhat more than 0.37 quads during a year

1 trillion cubic feet (tcf) = 28.3 billion cubic meters

1 billion cubic meters (bcm) = roughly 0.04 tcf

1 cubic meter = about 35 cubic feet

Liquefied natural gas (LNG) has been refrigerated to below about 260 degrees below zero, Fahrenheit (–160 Celsius), so a given amount occupies only one six-hundredth of the space it would take up at ambient temperature. A modern LNG tanker may carry 70,000 tons or so of gas in liquid form, but this will swell to several billion cubic feet when regasified. Since some sources may cite quantities of LNG by weight rather than btu content or regasified volume, here are some rough equivalents:

1 million metric tons of liquefied natural gas = 0.05 tcf, or 1.4 billion cubic meters.

1 metric ton of LNG represents 0.05 mmcf (50,000 cubic feet), or a bit more than 50 billion btu of energy content.

Coal

1 short ton of steam coal, as consumed on average by U.S. utilities, yields about 20.5 million btu. Thus one billion tons of coal (the amount this country has used each year to generate electricity in recent times) contributes more than 20 quads of primary energy—or about one-fifth of total national energy consumption.

(Continued)

TABLE 1.2 (Continued)

Electricity

1 kwh = 3,413 btu

1 kw = 1,000 watts; 1 mw = 1,000,000 watts, or 1,000 kw; 1 gw = 1,000 mw

U.S. production and consumption of electricity each year is sometimes stated in billions of kilowatt hours (bkwh), or in terawatt hours (twh)—which is the same thing.

To calculate how much primary energy for the generation of electricity comes from sources whose weight and volume is problematic to measure (such as hydro), it has long been conventional in the United States to assume a "heat-input rate" similar to that of a typical fossil-fueled steam-electric plant—slightly more than 10,000 btu input for each kilowatt hour of output. Nuclear power systems and geothermal plants generally operate at lower conversion efficiency, and that is taken into account in estimating comparable numbers for them. This produces some inconsistencies between U.S. and Canadian statistics, because Natural Resources Canada (the counterpart of the U.S. Department of Energy) assumes zero primary energy input for hydroelectric generation. In the case of wind and solar, the primary energy input has been taken to be the heat equivalent of the electricity they produce. Total generation from these sources has been so small that tiny discrepancies went unnoticed and were really too small to matter, but the increase in wind generation may force official energy statisticians to take note of them in future tables. As the generating capacity—and total output—of wind turbines grows nationally, future spaghetti charts may involve rethinking how best to suggest how much conventional primary energy wind is replacing, as well as how much electricity it is feeding into the grid.

Global Warming

Some discussions of potential climate change refer to emissions of carbon dioxide, while others deal in "carbon emissions." So it's good to know that: 1 ton of carbon dioxide gas contains 545 pounds of carbon.

A rule of thumb is that burning coal releases about 1.8 times as much carbon dioxide as deriving a similar amount of heat through the combustion of natural gas. Petroleum falls in between these two—about 1.5 times as much as natural gas.

Various gases other than carbon dioxide contribute to the "greenhouse effect" as well. In fact, methane (the primary constituent of natural gas) is usually described as being about 20 times more potent in this respect than CO_2. Methane and CO_2 both stay active in the atmosphere for many years, and different estimates of their respective contributions to warming depend on the time-horizon considered.

Similarly, a barrel of West Texas Intermediate oil is worth more to most refiners than a barrel of the "heavy" crude that comes from most of Mexico's oil fields, even though each is measured as 42 U.S. gallons. In the case of these two types of crude oil, the difference lies not only in the amount of sulfur and other contaminants each contains, but also in viscosity. The petroleum refining process (see Chapter 3 for more detail) separates crude into many different fractions that have different densities—weight per unit of volume. Such lighter fractions as gasoline and home heating oil are more valuable than the heavy gunk near "the bottom of the barrel"—which might be processed into fuel suitable primarily for ocean vessels, or possibly sold as asphalt for paving roads.

Of course, petroleum is no longer handled in barrels, and we may also need to remember that a U.S. gallon is about 20 percent smaller than an imperial gallon—the measurement used at filling stations in Canada and elsewhere. One way to eliminate that particular source of confusion would be to use the international convention of measuring quantities of petroleum in thousands or millions of tons, but this fails to take into account either density differences or variations in energy content among different kinds of crude oil and refined petroleum products. For that matter, a "ton" is normally defined in the United States as weighing 2,000 pounds, whereas global statistics for coal are more commonly given in metric tons—which are about 10 percent heavier. It simplifies matters if we stick to Btus and quads, or joules and exajoules, whenever we can.

Is it frustrating to have to think about all this? Sure! But, even after getting a grip on systems of measurement, one should also be wary of the many ways both energy advocates and energy critics *misuse* statistics to support highly questionable conclusions. Table 1.3 lists my "favorite" dozen.

Right at the top of the list is one that shows up clearly on the spaghetti chart a few pages back (Figure 1.4). In 2006, the United States consumed close to 100 quads of "primary energy" as commonly calculated. That is, we more or less took that much energy out of circulation and tried to put it to work. Almost all of the primary energy came from nonrenewable sources such as coal and oil, so we might say that for practical purposes planet Earth's supply of roughly this much fuel energy vanished forever. Yet less than half of that primary energy (about 43 percent) really wound up being put to end-uses such as operating machinery, hauling freight and passengers, or maintaining a comfortable temperature inside buildings. The rest was unused, or "rejected," as shown on the right side of the chart.

Energy statistics are easy to mix up unless we differentiate clearly between "primary energy" and "end-use energy." For the purpose of public understanding, it doesn't matter whether this is done innocently or consciously. The residential and commercial sectors are sometimes lumped together in statistical

TABLE 1.3
A Dozen Ways to Confuse People with Energy Statistics

 1 Mix up "end-use energy" with "primary energy"
 2 Cite "generating capacity" as if it were the same as "electricity supply"
 3 Exaggerate or minimize the significance of change by choosing certain time periods or playing with percentages
 4 Ignore the time value of money and such items as opportunity cost
 5 Pretend that all "resources" will some day be "proved reserves"
 6 Don't bother with "life cycle costs"
 7 Forget about "transaction costs" (including transportation expense)
 8 Be selective in taking account of "externalities"
 9 Overlook offbeat categories such as "nonenergy use" and "natural gas liquids"
10 Aggregate or disaggregate statistics (whichever supports your argument)
11 Be vague about definitions
12 Hide your underlying "assumptions"

presentations such as this because they both take place largely within similar types of buildings. However, that makes energy consumption in the combination of the two appear to be less significant than in either the industrial sector or the transportation sector. That's *true* for "end-use" energy, but *not* necessarily for primary energy. Both residential and commercial energy use involves a great deal of electricity, and it takes a lot of primary energy to generate electricity. There are also "line losses," largely in the form of heat, during delivery of electricity along transmission and distribution wires. Thus, the distinction between primary and end-use energy can be important when we look for policies and practices that will help balance supply and demand over time in a way that keeps the goals of availability, reliability, affordability, and environmental acceptability all in mind.

A very large portion of the primary energy we consume is rejected as "waste heat" in the conversion process of generating electricity, and Chapter 2 explores some ways this loss of energy can be reduced. Another big chunk disappears in much the same way during industrial operations. Many people are surprised to learn how much of the primary energy that is expended in transportation also goes for no direct useful purpose. Fairly large energy losses in driving a car or truck come via the tailpipe in the form of environmental pollutants such as unburned or only partly combusted fuel, through the friction of internal moving parts as well as tires on the road surface, *and* via engine heat.

Other chapters will refer to other of these "easy ways to confuse statistics" in appropriate contexts, but—in addition to distinguishing between primary and end-use energy—one more is so fundamental that it needs to be addressed here. That is the common practice of mixing up "electricity generating *capacity*" with "generation *output*." The first term usually refers to the maximum amount of electricity that a generating unit such as a wind turbine can deliver at any given moment in time, and you might compare it to the top speed of an automobile. It can be measured in watts, kilowatts, or any other multiple of those metric units of measurement. (The metric prefixes are given in Table 1.2.) By contrast, "generation output" is used to indicate how much electricity the unit really delivers over a substantial given period of time—say, a year. This is comparable to the distance an auto actually travels, thus providing useful transportation. It is the number related to total energy supply.

Notice that not all the blades of the wind turbines pictured on the cover of this book are turning, because variations in air movement are often highly localized. The average wind speed at a site that is carefully chosen for a wind farm should be fairly brisk and steady overall, yet a group of wind generators can be counted on typically to produce only something like 35 percent of their combined capacity. Electricity is very difficult to store, however; and during periods when *demand* for electricity is at or near its peak wind farms supply as little as 10 percent and usually no more than 20 percent of their rated capacity.[1]

Electricity output delivered to an individual home or business is usually measured on a utility bill in kilowatt-hours, and for broader comparisons it is more commonly reported in successively larger metric units—each 1,000 times the smaller one. Thus, the supply of electricity for a large region is customarily expressed in megawatt-hours or gigawatt-hours. The average residential customer's household consumes approximately 920 kilowatt hours per month on a year-round basis; but this number fluctuates seasonally. Thus, some utilities face demand peaks in summer while others are "winter peakers." It generally depends on whether air conditioning or electrical-resistance heating predominates.

Don't be embarrassed if it takes a while to get a feel for the significance of various metric units as used in energy systems:

- An electric *kilowatt* is the same as 1,000 watts. Think of the power needed to switch on ten 100-watt light bulbs—or a single electric hair dryer—for an instant.
- A *megawatt* equals 1,000 kilowatts, or 1 million watts.
- A *gigawatt* is 1000 times that big, and a *terawatt* is equivalent to 1,000 gigawatts. The generating capacity in the entire United States in 2007 was about 1,000 gigawatts (1 terawatt), and there are 8,760 hours in a year, yet all the units together produced only about 4,000 *terawatt hours* of electric power during 2007. That was less than half of full capacity, so obviously they weren't all going full-blast all the time. They can't, for a variety of reasons that this book will help explain. The important thing to remember is the difference between a kilowatt (kW) and a kilowatt hour (kWh). Each is important, but for different reasons.

Why would anybody fudge the difference? It happens often when people are touting a source of generation that for practical purposes operates only intermittently. Some old fossil-fueled plants are so inefficient that they are called on to perform only when supply is so scarce that it is deemed all right to accept their extra operating expense or pollution burden. Although it's true that even efficient, directional wind turbines produce electricity that is equivalent to only about one-third of their rated capacity at best, they can still fill useful niches in our national energy portfolio. On the other hand, some types of generation are especially adapted to almost full-time operation. These are called *baseload* plants. They are complemented by *intermediate* systems that can be turned on and "throttled up and down" quickly. Some hydro installations are especially valuable for such assignments. The aptly named *peaking* units complete the roster. They are called on as available to satisfy *peak* demand.

The prototype of a large baseload unit is a nuclear power plant. The ones in the United States now typically operate at more than 95 percent capacity, which means they operate economically 24 hours a day, seven days a week, for months at a stretch. Does that mean that nuclear power is the answer to all our worries about reliable and adequate supplies of energy? Sorry! More than 100 U.S. reactors now supply commercial power; but no new ones have been added for decades, and any new ones ordered by 2010 will probably not be ready for half a dozen years or more to supply electricity. Even with improved designs and more streamlined regulation, advanced nuclear plants take at least several times as long as most other types of generating systems to plan and build, and the timeliness of an energy solution is one of its basic criteria. It is one of the arms of the policy mobile. "Nukes" are also capital-intensive. Their heavy initial costs can be balanced by relatively low operating costs, so they can produce decent returns—but only over decades of operation. And there are still public concerns about safety and ultimate nuclear waste disposal. These are perhaps overblown, but they are still troublesome. Keep in mind that consensus, as difficult as it may be to achieve, is needed in order to move in any direction with energy at any level.

We can't afford to give up in despair. We just need to recognize that legitimate policy goals interact, and that there is no single answer. This applies not only to electricity but across the board. It is true for energy uses in homes, businesses, transportation, and industry.

Even the most appealing programs of energy efficiency will probably see our country increasing its appetite for energy, thanks to a growing population and a traditionally vibrant economy with rising living standards. A national "budget" of roughly 100 quads of energy consumption might easily grow to 120 or more by 2025 without strenuous national and individual efforts that might come in the quest for energy security, reliability, or protection against the possible problems of climate change. It's safest to project that we will need *all* of the energy inputs alluded to above. Those who control capital resources must decide when, where and how to invest in the future, and prudence insists that they consider multiple factors simultaneously.

Since you, the reader, will help decide what path we *all* take, please read on!

NOTE

1. Personal communication from Adam Sieminski, chief energy economist of Deutsche Bank, resulting from his inquiries in Germany—perhaps the world's most dedicated and experienced national exponent of wind energy.

Two

How Much Is Enough?

Addressing our energy balance in terms of the various popular goals cited in Chapter 1 is an offbeat technique, but it leads to a more pragmatic way of understanding energy than the usual approach of shuffling through energy sources (coal, oil, wind, etc.) in encyclopedic style. Dealing with energy sources and their interrelationships from the standpoint of what we expect of them forces us from the start to *think* and to *question*.

Consider "adequacy." How much electricity do we need to get along? How much (and what sort of) fuel for heating and transportation—including what trucks, buses, ships and planes use? Regardless of how we measure it or what form it is in, how much energy do farms and factories (and even such applications as recreation) require?

In other words, how much energy of various types gives us "an adequate supply" to provide what we consider a reasonable degree of personal comfort and convenience, besides maintaining the commercial and industrial infrastructure our economy depends on? Mineral resources are finite, and we tend to extract them at an increasing pace, so could we literally be running out of some natural fuels that are nonrenewable?

Having access as a nation to adequate supply is a different matter from whether the energy is available at what we consider affordable prices; we'll get to that issue in Chapter 3. Nor is an adequate supply necessarily a reliable supply; the topic of reliability will be treated separately in Chapter 4.

The question of how much energy people need is subjective; most residents of Minneapolis will estimate these quantities quite differently from people in Mumbai, India. Furthermore, as the spaghetti chart in Chapter 1 (Figure 1.4) showed, the mix of end-use energy we expend in this country each year varies among the major consumption sectors (residential, commercial, industrial, and transportation of all kinds). Abstractly, having "enough" energy really means having enough of the right kind, in the right place, and at the right time to satisfy what potential consumers feel they ought to be *able* to acquire in the way of goods and services.

In the strictest sense, a nation's access to supplies of energy may be "adequate" even when some or all of it is so expensive that many people cannot afford as much as they would like. The consequences of such high prices range from annoyance to tragedy; that is why we'll also analyze the process of price formation in the next chapter. This chapter considers the potential for shortfalls in the types of energy we call on most. Think of a power blackout or filling stations that must close because they simply couldn't get gasoline from their wholesale suppliers *at any price*. Some serious analysts insist that we will face such situations in this country routinely before long unless a massive restructuring of the energy economy takes place, involving actions on both the supply side and the demand side. There is enough fact in such projections to give us pause, although we should realize that pessimists and optimists are both prone to exaggeration. The purpose of a book such as this is to help readers begin with informed questions and then form their own opinions.

THE END IS NEAR . . . AGAIN!

There have been numerous previous predictions of an imminent end to the availability of oil, the largest primary source of energy for the United States. So far, all have proved premature. *National Geographic Magazine* told its readers in 1918 that the oil wells they had counted on to permit continued rapid expansion in the U.S. fleet of motor cars would soon run dry (although the then-upbeat *Geographic* seemed pretty sure that something called "shale oil" would fill the bill instead).[1] That was not the first such warning, nor would it be the last; the case is stronger now than it was then that the era of "easy oil" is behind us. That is *one* of the messages of a careful and detailed study published in mid-2007, entitled *Hard Truths*.[2]

The study had been requested by the U.S. Secretary of Energy from the National Petroleum Council (NPC), a high-powered advisory committee of long standing. The NPC was asked to address the issue and implications of "peak oil"—a logically inevitable point in time at which global oil production will top off and decline. A report on such a question by an industry-dominated group deserves careful inspection for possible bias, but the NPC took unusual care to ensure that it was credibly objective.

Because today's integrated energy markets are so complex, the scope of the study was broadened to include not only oil and natural gas but *all* energy sources. It considered geopolitics and environmental constraints. More than 350 persons took part, drawn not only from industry but also from various agencies of government, finance, academia, think tanks, consulting groups, and a spectrum of non-governmental organizations—including some with strong orientation toward energy conservation and environmental protection. The data for analysis came from both official and some usually inaccessible private sources. Much of it had to be compiled at a secure site by persons sworn to secrecy about the origins of individual inputs, thus protecting proprietary information.

The NPC product did not attempt to predict a firm future matrix of energy sources; but it provided abundant material for further study. In addition to the 256-page report itself, NPC released 38 supporting and related technical papers, which are available on the Internet at www.npc.org. Among the key findings were these:

- Coal, oil, and natural gas will all remain indispensable to meeting projected energy demand growth.
- A combination of risks to oil production from *traditional* sources will make it very hard to rely on them alone.
- Policies aimed at curbing carbon dioxide emissions in the interest of forestalling global climate change will alter the energy mix, raise costs, and require reductions in current rates of growth for energy demand.
- So far as the United States is concerned, the idea of "energy independence" is not realistic for the foreseeable future.

We have begun to shift from what we generally call conventional sources of oil (and natural gas) to new ones. Canada is the largest supplier of petroleum to the United States, but output from traditional Canadian resources in the Western Sedimentary Basin has been dropping for years. If it were not for production (by totally different processes) of more than a million barrels a day of refinable substitutes from its gunky "oil sands," Canada itself would be a net importer of petroleum. Manufactured substitutes for automotive fuels, such as ethyl alcohol (ethanol) and "biodiesel," are also beginning to penetrate the U.S. and world markets. Of course, there might be reasons apart from worries about availability to wish that we could phase out all fossil fuels and embark on a brave new world in which renewable sources of energy form the basis of our economy. It has become a cliché for advocates of strong, vigorous action to avert the potential dangers from climate change to note that "the Stone Age didn't end because we ran out of rocks!" But our discussion of environmental factors will come principally in Chapter 5.

If we are going to concentrate first on whether we will have enough energy going forward, we must look at both supply and demand for the sources we have been using all along. A gap between supply and demand (literally, at any price) is the definition of a true shortage.

Moving people and freight around in the United States—whether by road, rail, or air—depends almost totally on oil. On the other hand, the mainstays of our residential and commercial sectors are natural gas and electricity (the latter being an intermediate rather than a primary source, as defined earlier). At the same time, roughly one-third of our country's electric generating capacity is in plants that burn coal as the primary heat source. Coal plants (mostly "baseload units" that operate 24–7 almost year-round) account for an even higher share of our annual electricity output—about half. Almost all the rest of our electricity comes either from nuclear power plants or gas-fired generating systems. In 2006, hydropower dams supplied a mere 7 percent of domestically produced U.S. electricity.

Domestic production of petroleum and natural gas during 2007 fell more than 33 quads short of the amount of those two energy sources the United States consumed. That disparity represented one-third of our entire national energy diet, and we had to import it. Petroleum (including both crude oil and refined products, such as gasoline) came from 30 different countries, including 10 that are members of the Organization of Petroleum Exporting Countries (OPEC). Some foreign oil purchases were very small, such as our modest imports from China and Australia; but three out of five barrels came from our top five oil suppliers during that year—Canada, Mexico, Saudi Arabia, Venezuela, and Nigeria, in that order. Eighty-five percent of our imported natural gas entered by pipeline from neighboring Canada, and the rest arrived in refrigerated tankers from several different supplying countries in the form of liquefied natural gas (LNG).[3]

FIGURE 2.1
Primary Energy Inputs to U.S. Electricity (2006)

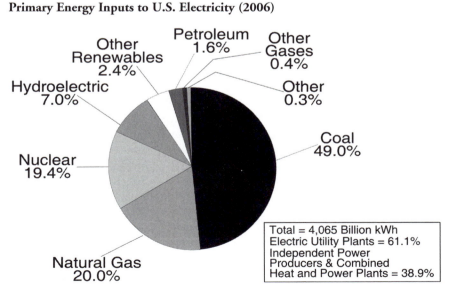

Source: Energy Information Administration, *Electric Power Annual 2006.*

A careful projection in 2008 of future supply and demand by the semi-autonomous Energy Information Administration (EIA) of the U.S. Department of Energy[4] indicates that the gap between production and consumption of both oil and natural gas in this country will remain problematic for decades to come. But, as is customarily the case with routine EIA projections, the analysis assumes that the legal and regulatory policies in effect when the projections were made will continue forever. The EIA recognizes that this is an unrealistic assumption, but such projections are made as planning tools rather than prophecies. They give other analysts (in and out of government) an objective base from which to extrapolate—by adding their own assumptions about changes in policy or circumstances that *might* take place. For example, before Congress in 2007 finally got around again—for the first time in three decades—to tightening mileage standards for cars sold in the United States, there was no lack of projections from various quarters of how much gasoline and diesel fuel could be saved by boosting fuel-efficiency regulations to so many miles per gallon by such-and-such a date. One problem is that such calculations may be perfectly correct mathematically and still be misleading. A legislator, a lobbyist, or a private citizen seeking a fair and useful evaluation must ask more questions. The most important is: "At what rate will new models replace the existing fleet?" That, of course, may hang on other legislation—such as future purchase subsidies—as well as the price of gasoline.

IMPORTS INVOLVE RISKS

Chapter 1 noted that oil is the most pressing problem of energy supply for the United States today. This is because by 2008 about two-thirds of all the oil we use was coming from sources outside the country, and the volume of imports from politically unstable regions is troubling.

Our major cause for concern is not the likelihood of a literal oil embargo. Any unfriendly country—or even a group of countries—would find it difficult to enforce a petroleum embargo effectively on another. Despite significant differences in the quality of crude oil, it is bought and sold in a global market where a degree of substitution is possible. However, war or terrorism can limit the total *adequacy* of supply—through the disruption of production itself, attacks on shipping, or disruption of pipelines. Furthermore, the basic price of oil is governed by the vagaries of a worldwide oil market that is full of unpredictable short-term risks (providing topics for the next two chapters). Price, in turn, interacts with both supply and demand.

In early 2008, a combination of events forced EIA to do a turnabout from an early version of the "reference case" it had prepared for its *Annual Energy Outlook 2008* and had even released tentatively on its website. World oil prices were climbing breathlessly at the very same time the United States appeared to be entering a recession, public perceptions of climate change issues were being aroused, and the first assessments were being made of the potential effects of the Energy Independence and Security Act of 2007 (EISA2007),[5] which had just been enacted. Based on all this, the National Energy Modeling System (NEMS) raised its "reference case" estimate of future domestic oil production and chopped its projections of U.S. liquid fuels consumption in 2030 by 9 percent. That meant—if nothing else changed—that U.S. dependence on net imports of oil was projected to drop from 60 percent in 2006 to 51 percent in 2022 before climbing back up to 54 percent in 2030.[6]

Things *will* change between now and 2030. It is even possible, although unlikely, that another coincidence of quite different circumstances could send projections of future U.S. oil-import dependence up again. Regardless of whether the number is 50 percent, 60 percent, or 70 percent, however, there is ample reason to stay abreast of net import trends and what affects them. At such levels, dependency on imports will always have a close potential link to the adequacy of U.S. oil supply.

This country (and North America as a whole) needs to address the future adequacy of natural gas supplies, too. Natural gas is essential to U.S. industry as a source of process heat and self-generated power, besides being a feedstock for plastics and petrochemicals. In addition to being the main source for space heating in the nation's buildings, natural gas vies with nuclear reactor fuel as the second most important source of primary energy in producing electricity for all sectors of the economy. But electricity itself is critical as a source of *end-use* energy overall; anyone who has experienced an electrical blackout—briefly during a local lightning storm, or for days at a time because of the fortunately rare interruptions in delivery from the grid—will insist that electricity *also* deserves special attention in this chapter on supply adequacy. So, after some general treatment of energy supply, we'll take a longer look in turn at oil, natural gas, and electricity (with its various primary sources).

Having "enough" energy to get things done depends not only on supply, but on pressure from the other side of the basic energy equation—demand. Assuming that we are reasonably sure what potential supplies of various energy sources will be available in whatever we consider "the short run," current consumption statistics give us a chance to anticipate (and take steps to offset) any chronic shortages that are likely to develop over the next few weeks, months, or even years. Unfortunately, assumptions about supply can be fragile; so sudden, briefer shortages may still occur at times without warning—especially if the required amounts of the right kinds of energy are not readily accessible from storage.

A succession of hurricanes in the Gulf of Mexico has demonstrated this as they battered drilling rigs, pipelines, and refineries—sometimes reducing production and transportation capacity for natural gas and oil across more than one season. But anyone who is planning to invest in capital equipment—whether it be a home heating unit or 1,000 megawatts of additional generating capacity—must also consider a longer time-horizon. That spills over into "reliability of supply" (see Chapter 4).

WHAT WE NEED DEPENDS ON WHAT WE DO

In assessing adequacy, we start by looking at what affects the amounts of energy we consume as a nation and what factors and events are apt to cause those levels of consumption to rise or fall—either via actions we take or through events we can at least foresee. For instance, the size of a country's population is fundamental to its total demand for energy, although the number of people alone doesn't tell the full story. An "aging" population may mean less activity—in productive capacity, but also in consumption. Assumptions about how these factors will interact need to underlie energy projections, but they are rarely if ever spelled out.

The most fundamental "driver" in energy demand is our gross domestic product (GDP). This represents the total value (in dollars) of everything the nation and its people produce, both in goods and services. It includes a broad range: from food and steel to toys, computer software designs, TV programs, and the efforts of policemen and hot dog vendors.

GDP itself results from various combinations of factors that can be measured (and analyzed or projected) individually. For some purposes, we might choose to look at the classic economist's factors of production: (1) land (including raw materials, which range from ores and animal fibers to energy), (2) labor (the human input), and (3) capital (embracing not only financial resources but productive machinery—from simple tools to supercomputers and manufacturing robots). From another viewpoint, however, the most basic elements of GDP are population and productivity per capita. From that perspective we have to parse population more carefully. We check the size of the active labor force instead of the whole population (including the total number of person-hours worked) and the average productivity per worker. Regardless of our point of view, though, energy is an important factor in all production. Thus (all other things being equal, which is a phrase economists love to use), we expect energy consumption to rise as a function of national output. Statistics prove that this is *almost* invariably true.

As is so often the case, "all other things" aren't static. For the past half-century or more, the United States as a whole has been shifting away from the energy-hungry production of primary materials and manufactured goods toward a service economy that depends more on such wealth-generating activities as banking, leisure endeavors, and sales. One may argue whether this was a fortunate development; Chinese negotiators on national responses to climate change may insist that countries choosing to import such products as steel and cement from them are "responsible" for the energy (and the global warming gases) that are embedded in their manufacture.

Yet that is not the issue. The point here is that this change in the structure of our economy would have diluted the growing energy requirements of our nation (and especially its industrial sector) even if rising fuel prices and the energy crises of the 1970s and thereafter had not stimulated industry to practice more energy efficiency in its understandable quest for profitable operation. It may make Americans feel good to claim "virtuous" energy behavior over three decades (increasing real GDP two and a half times between 1976 and 2006 while primary energy consumption only rose from about 72 to about 100 quads[7]); but we shouldn't give all the credit to energy efficiency. Now, however, with multiple reasons to reduce energy consumption (environmental concerns, cost-cutting required to stay competitive, and worries about ensuring adequate energy supplies), we are seeing more focused efforts to modify the link between GDP and energy consumption so that we can accomplish as much or more in the future without changing our energy input proportionally.

ANALYZING OUR ENERGY BUDGET

This brings us to the important concept of energy intensity. *Energy intensity* is a measure of how much energy is consumed for each unit (in dollar value) of product or in relation to the size of the population. In discussing energy issues, U.S. politicians often imply that we can keep expanding our economy overall while consuming no more (or even less) energy than we do now. That goal might prove feasible, but it deserves comprehensive and well-informed scrutiny—if not skepticism.

There surely *are* ways to continue reducing the nation's overall energy intensity: (1) by reducing the role of energy itself as a factor of production, perhaps by substituting one or more of the other factors in getting things done; (2) by making the energy inputs themselves more productive; and/or (3) simply by eliminating an activity or operation entirely. An example of the first would be riding a bike to work instead of driving (substituting labor for motor fuel). Instances of the second would include the use of mass transit or carpooling. A clear example of the third is to telecommute by performing most of one's work from home (something I've been doing for decades). For those who are interested in reducing energy intensity (and thus allowing a smaller supply of energy to become "adequate"—with resultant benefits), each individual needs to determine what is practical and desirable for each sector of energy consumption. But even a Herculean effort along such lines (in which we still have much room for improvement) won't eliminate the fact that a great deal of energy will always be part of our lives.

The United States is often portrayed as an energy glutton, and it is true that our population of slightly more than 300 million (less than 5 percent of the Earth's inhabitants) consumes more than 20 percent of all global energy. In fact, the share of worldwide energy we "take" was previously even higher—close to 25 percent as recently as the 1990s. But the story doesn't end there. Think about these factors:

- First of all, this country's consumption of energy is in line with its share of the planet's GDP.
- Second, our living standards are high: A typical U.S. household (averaging 3.8 persons in 2005) occupies more than 1,750 square feet of residential space. We operate a personal motor vehicle for almost every man, woman, and child in the country.[8]
- On top of this, there are factors of geography. For instance, the continental United States extends from a semi-tropical climate in Florida and southern Texas to frigid areas of Maine, Michigan, and North Dakota that routinely cope with outdoor temperatures well below 0°F for several months every year. That makes for both higher air conditioning requirements and the necessity to heat lots of living and work space.
- There is also the matter of distances—and the travel involved in delivering goods or just commuting. U.S. residents are scattered over 3.7 million square miles, which means there are only about 80 people per square mile. On average, our people and our cities are far more dispersed than in a country such as Germany, where there are almost 600 persons per square mile. We may need more energy-efficient mass transit, but that alone won't solve all problems in reducing the amounts of transportation energy that the United States can justifiably consider adequate.

Our neighbor to the north, Canada, faces some of the same difficulties we do in curbing an appetite for energy that deserves a serious review. As a result, even though Canadians arguably have been making a greater effort than U.S. residents do in eliminating wasteful energy use, Canada overall was half again as energy intensive as the United States during 2005, when Canadians consumed 28 percent more energy than we did per capita.[9]

OIL: PAST, PRESENT, AND FUTURE

The chances of producing a totally "adequate" amount of oil or natural gas domestically within the next couple of decades are slim to nonexistent. The United States got started earlier than the rest of the world in extracting those fuels; we were once hailed as supplier of "oil for the lamps of China." But most of the oil wells ever completed have been in this country, and even the huge resource of hydrocarbons we started with has largely been tapped out over more than a century and a half since Colonel Edwin L. Drake showed that it was possible to produce "rock oil" by drilling into the Earth instead of just collecting it from the pools that had been found occasionally.

Oil is what we call a fossil fuel. Like natural gas and coal, it had to develop chemically and physically over tens of millions of years before being dug up (the word "fossil" comes from the Latin *fodere*—to dig). It took millennia of natural heat and pressure to act on the decayed remnants of once-living organisms—which, with a different set of natural processes, might have wound up instead as the fossilized bones of prehistoric creatures we see in museums. Now that the United States has been pumping oil from somewhat porous subterranean rock for all these years, however, there is clearly less oil left and it is harder to get at. Drake had to drill only 57 feet near Titusville, Pennsylvania in 1857 before he "struck" oil, but by 2007 U.S. wells averaged 100 times that in depth. Furthermore, the oil that remains is so intimately engaged in the surrounding rock that it often must be coaxed to the surface by sending down steam, carbon dioxide, or even a detergent to encourage it to flow.

The average size of new onshore fields is also much smaller than the ones that were once to be found, and generally they don't remain productive as long. Among all the producing oil wells in this country, more than half are now classified as "stripper wells"—which generally means their output is less than ten barrels per day. Over the years, some truly giant U.S. fields were discovered (in some cases, where geologists at the time were overwhelmingly convinced that no major underground deposits of hydrocarbons existed); but there have been such improvements in knowledge, science, and technology that by now it would be misplaced optimism to expect any large, totally new discovery of "conventional" oil anywhere onshore within the Lower 48 states.

In a given year, more than 40,000 wells may be drilled in this country in the search for hydrocarbons, overwhelmingly aimed at finding and producing natural gas rather than oil. However, the Lower 48 states are considered "mature" prospects, meaning that the easy stuff is probably all gone. Despite careful advanced study of sites, about half of all "exploratory wells" come up dry. More than one in ten wells overall fails to produce economic quantities of any hydrocarbon.[10] Those statistics are pessimistic enough for us to ask, "At what point will we run out of our most popular fuels completely?"

The simple answer is "Never—either worldwide or in the United States." But, for practical purposes, we will essentially have to stop producing (and thus using) oil whenever the cost of extracting it from the Earth exceeds the value we place on it. This brings us to two very important distinctions that apply to both oil and gas: (1) between "resources" and "reserves," and (2) between conventional and unconventional sources of such fuels. Like many terms in the field of energy, these definitions are actually estimates that change over time (sometimes rapidly); yet they are indispensable to understanding where we stand *vis-à-vis* "adequacy of supply" at a given moment.

SAYING WHAT WE MEAN

The term *resources* identifies the total bulk volume in the ground of something such as oil or gas that the best known techniques can estimate to exist. Calculation of resources now involves satellite imagery, sophisticated geology, various aspects of seismology, and so on; but it still boils down to very highly educated guessing. *Technically recoverable resources* are those amounts within the basic resource that are deemed to be recoverable using current technology, regardless of whether this would be justifiable economically. The term *reserves* is used to designate an even smaller subset of resources based on economics. *Proved reserves* are a more precise measurement of the amount of those resources that could be produced via existing technology and enter the market, based on *current market prices*. Clearly, this still involves judgment; either price changes or the introduction of new technology can affect the level of reserves suddenly. What may be additionally confusing is that reserves are sometimes broken down further into "proved reserves," "possible reserves," and even "speculative reserves." For most purposes it is safest to stick with the "proved reserves" category.

The United States was credited by EIA's *Annual Energy Review 2007* with about 178 billion barrels of conventional, technically recoverable oil resources and another 30 billion barrels of natural gas liquids that might be expected to appear in association with production from the natural gas resource base. Conventional natural gas resources were pegged at a bit more than 1,200 trillion cubic feet, with more than 300 tcf likely to be found as coalbed methane and in "tight" formations requiring special production methods. But the EIA listed its own estimate of total U.S. proved reserves as only about 21 billion barrels of oil, 211 tcf of natural gas, and 8.5 billion barrels of natural gas liquids, respectively. Table 1.3 in Chapter 1 warned readers against confusing "resources" and "reserves"; this comparison demonstrates the reason. It is true that these are both somewhat slippery terms, but the lesson is to look for the most up-to-date listings of either and be wary of any but reliable sources. It also helps to read the footnotes of any energy table to make sure that unusual definitions and other restrictions are not being employed.

Official U.S. estimates of reserves and resources are perhaps the most trustworthy in the world, but individual countries quite often overreport their mineral holdings for ulterior motives. They may wish to boost their international prestige, or—in the case of the Organization of Petroleum Exporting Countries—OPEC members may just be trying to bolster their arguments that the organization should allot them higher export quotas. To bring some order into the picture, most people in the industry tend to rely only on the resource estimates for other countries from such sources as the International Energy Agency or the U.S. Geological Survey. They also use the reserve figures published by a highly respected U.S. commercial periodical, *Oil and Gas Journal*. Criteria for estimating proved reserves are fairly strict in North America, largely because the U.S. Security and Exchange Commission insists on using a company's holdings at the close of business on December 31 of each year to gauge what amounts will be carried on each firm's books as assets. This can be misleading too, of course, if oil or gas prices change radically just before the end of a year. But there have to be ground rules of some sort.

Sometimes we read that this country has only a certain number of years of oil or gas left. Such statements are almost invariably misleading; they misuse another term common to the energy industry—the *reserve to production ratio*, or R:P. A person using this term is most likely talking about proved reserves as of today and current annual production; the numbers themselves (even if limited to "conventional" hydrocarbons) may be misinterpreted as implying exactly the opposite of what they show in some cases. For many, many years the R:P ratio in the United States has hovered at about 11 to 1. This does not mean that we will reach the bottom of a figurative barrel in a decade or so; even a nonexpert might figure that out for him- or herself from the fact that the ratio has remained surprisingly steady. More reserves are certainly being added, even while some of the known reserves are being depleted. A very high ratio *could* mean that a country is swimming in oil and will be for a long time, but this might also show that it is technically inept in production. Quite a different possibility is that a country desperate for cash pushes too hard to drain its reserves quickly (lowering its R:P ratio in the short term to an unsustainable level), instead of tempering current production to extract an optimum, larger volume of oil over a longer period. This is just one more example of why "magic numbers" such as R:P ratios can be deceptive unless the details behind them are explored.

PRICES AND TECHNOLOGY VERSUS DEPLETION

Proved reserves, as noted, depend not only on discovering new fields but on having the technology to extract the oil or gas from new and existing fields at a cost that will justify the effort, considering the market price. This explains how the net level of U.S. reserves has long remained fairly constant. It seems strange, but it is indisputable: Higher prices automatically increase the portion of resources that can be counted as reserves. Of course the prospect of continuing high prices can also be an incentive for fresh investment and a spur to new technology.

Through EIA statistics we can track the ups and downs of the U.S. refiners' average acquisition cost of oil (domestic and imported) over the three-decades-plus since 1973, when it was $4.15. It soared to $28.07 by 1980, but then fell back to $17.23 in 1995 and $12.52 as recently as 1998. By 2000 it was back up to $28.26, only to plunge back to $22.95 for 2001 when a downturn in the economy reduced U.S. and world oil demand for oil. Since then it has climbed sharply. It topped $50 in 2005, $60 in 2006, $80 in 2007, and $100 in 2008.[11] Along the way, although few people observed this (and news media never noted), the level of proved reserves also bounced up and down. What we can read into this is that higher world oil prices encourage domestic producers to scratch harder to raise their output from existing fields and usually invest more in exploration (to the extent that it can go on in a region such as the U.S. Lower 48, which already looks like a pin cushion on some geologic maps from all the drilling that has taken place).

High prices, along with public worries about the complex security issues created by high import levels, have forced frequent debate over moratoria that prevent drilling in various areas that have been considered environmentally sensitive. New technology has also been a huge factor in forestalling slippage in proved reserves. Technology is arguably more important than oil price.

Exploration and production companies have learned to map underground deposits with sound waves in three dimensions. High-speed computers even add the fourth dimension of time measurement, since the rate at which liquid or gaseous hydrocarbons can be induced to migrate through barely porous underground strata often determines production success. Modern field crews can drill deeper and faster, control the direction of the drill bits more precisely, and even drill sideways for a mile or more once they have reached an appropriate depth. This has enabled them to return to some fields that were once abandoned, either to extend their perimeters or to drill "in-fill wells" that bring to the surface more of the resources that were always there but legitimately were not considered proved reserves until technical capabilities matched up suitably with the local market price determined by supply and demand.

This brings us to another fuzzy difference—the one between *conventional* and *unconventional* resources and reserves. Drilling offshore in anything but fairly shallow water was once considered unconventional because drilling rigs had to rest on the sea-bottom and their reach downward was limited by structural considerations. Then along came "jack-up rigs," floating platforms, and the like, so that today it is conventional to operate in depths of a mile and a half or more, drilling tens of thousands of additional feet below the seabed if necessary. Offshore operations in the Gulf of Mexico have also been aided by salt-penetrating radar that can explore visually in advance through strata that were impenetrable to earlier remote-sensing systems.

CANADA'S OIL SANDS

The most dramatic example of "unconventional" becoming "conventional" is Canada's oil sands—vast fields of very viscous material (like tar) that have long been considered a hydrocarbon resource but were too difficult to extract economically until recent years. Prior to 2000, Canada was considered to have roughly 4.4 billion barrels of proved oil reserves—only one-fifth of the U.S. figure. Then a combination of circumstances transformed the oil sands: (1) The world price of crude oil rose and looked as if it would stay above at least $30 or $40 in nominal prices indefinitely; (2) new methods of extracting a useful petroleum product from the oil-sand deposits were developed, so that various techniques that operate far below the surface will gradually replace in large measure the old system of digging down from the surface to produce enormous open pits; (3) prompted by the recognition that its conventional oil reserves were dwindling, Canada (and the province of Alberta especially) launched an all-out effort to attract the heavy up-front investments needed to develop the oil sands; and (4) as a result of the close trade relationship between Canada and the United States that had evolved through a bilateral agreement and then a trilateral one that included Mexico, it became clear that long-term investments in Canada's oil sands would be compensated by a ready and reliable long-term market to the south that could be supplied through pipelines (which are cheaper overall than shipments by tanker ships).

Thanks in part to discreet but effective Canadian lobbying, *Oil and Gas Journal* finally admitted that Canada might claim credit for literally *trillions* of barrels in ultimate oil resources, and that about 175 billion barrels were deemed safe to book as proved reserves. The U.S. Energy Information Administration, the International Energy Agency, and other authorities concurred, and virtually overnight Canada became the holder of the second largest proved oil reserves in the world, ranking behind only Saudi Arabia. Subsequently, Venezuela tried to follow suit on the basis of the large amounts of "heavy oil" that geologists are fairly sure reside in its Orinoco Basin; but so far that country's claim has been rejected—with what seems like good reason. Use of the term proved reserves generally assumes that they could be accessible in relatively short order, presupposing sufficient technological capability and capital to carry through. With Venezuela, neither is evident—although China's courting of President Hugo Chavez might enable him to import both, with major geopolitical consequences.

The story of the oil sands is almost being matched by unconventional sources of natural gas. The first breakthrough came with coalbed methane, or CBM.

Underground coal miners have been plagued from the earliest days by the fact that fossil fuels are often found in conjunction with one another; and the occurrence in coal mines of methane (the major constituent of natural gas) is an explosive hazard. Increasing demand for natural gas finally led energy producers to search for a way to turn this problem into a bonanza; now it is possible to drill into relatively shallow coal seams from the surface and draw off the gas. What started as an experimental effort has long since become commercially successful; today coalbed methane accounts for a healthy percentage of all the natural gas produced in the United States.

WHAT COMES NEXT?

There has been even greater interest recently in "shale gas." In the Barnett Shales of Texas, this means drilling down vertically for perhaps a mile and a half before switching to the horizontal and continuing for another mile or so while various techniques are employed to shake loose a pathway for the tightly embedded natural gas. It is a costly process, made feasible economically only by the fact that wellhead gas prices have risen with those for oil—though not as fast.

Unconventional sources of gas have invigorated domestic production. EIA reported in mid-2008 that proved gas reserves in the United States had increased for eight years in a row, and in 10 of the preceding 11 years.

According to the National Petroleum Council, an increasing share of the domestic production of oil will also be from more expensive unconventional sources. For instance, it has long been known that *liquid* hydrocarbons can be produced from within some underground deposits of host rock. But the porosity of the encompassing material is so low that it was thought the only way to get at the fossil fuel locked inside it was to bring solid material to the surface and heat it to free the hydrocarbons in the form of a material called *kerogen*—which still required additional processing to produce a synthetic approximation of crude oil.

This worked fine in theory and in laboratories, although in field operations it also produced large quantities of messy waste. As noted earlier, *National Geographic* touted shale oil in 1918. Six decades later, a frightened U.S. government poured billions of dollars into a hastily organized Synfuels Corporation in the hope that this and other semi-manmade substitutes for petroleum would stave off serious deficits in conventional fossil fuels. But the laws of nature and economics kept getting in the way. Using the best technology available at the time, too much energy-input and too much expense has long seemed to be associated with the production of oil from oil shale to bring a useful refined product to market commercially.

Now things look somewhat different. As in the case of Alberta's oil sands, an economical and environmentally acceptable solution might be available by doing more of the work of processing shale oil underground. The key seems to be in fracturing subterranean shale to shake loose its precious contents, which then can be drawn to the surface in ways that parallel the production of coal-bed methane. So far, however, shale oil is still only in the "very promising" stage. Unsubsidized production on a commercial scale is now time-slotted somewhere in the decade beyond 2010.

HOW ABOUT AN EVEN BIGGER BREAKTHROUGH?

There are yet other possibilities for augmenting domestic supplies of natural gas, but what might be the most attractive ones are even farther off—(1) methane hydrates, and (2) "non-fossil" gas. There are enough uncertainties about each so that neither may ever become a reality, yet each holds so much potential that hopes for a surprise breakthrough continue to be mentioned. The hydrates are yet another form of true fossil fuel—methane formed by the recognized processes of geologic heat and pressure acting on organic material, but united with water in a crystalline form whose energy density is almost incredible. The second possibility is an unproved hypothesis—that enormous quantities of methane somehow exist very deep in the Earth, resulting from some process other than the decomposition of plant and animal material under geologic heat and pressure. I have spoken with highly reputable Earth scientists[12] who scoff at the latter idea; attempts to prove it years ago by drilling into a relatively thin section of the planetary crust in Scandinavia failed. Yet the abundance of hydrogen (and carbon) throughout the universe gives some hope to imaginative souls (including one very successful discoverer of oil and gas I know).

Methane hydrates *are* real, not wishful thinking. Crystals containing up to 164 times as much methane per cubic centimeter as natural gas under normal pressure are recovered with relative ease from Arctic tundra. "Walls" of them have been found offshore in the far north, and their existence in occasional mounds on the floor of the Gulf of Mexico is evidenced by bubbles of gas that escape from them. To date, however, there does not seem to be any good way to locate deposits that might be sufficiently concentrated to justify mining. We do not know yet how they could be collected in a safe and environmentally acceptable fashion that makes economic sense. In this way, they resemble the nodules of nickel and other valuable metals that we know exist in some parts of the oceans' beds but can't yet "harvest."

In mid-2007 an official federal advisory group of researchers reported to Congress that they did not expect hydrates to be economically viable for a decade or more. Yet they argued that, with relatively modest funding, they could determine by 2012 whether methane hydrates (estimated by some to contain 200,000 tcf of natural gas within the United States alone) are worth trying to push more vigorously.[13] We will have to wait and see.

As for natural gas very deep in the Earth, the leading proponent of this hypothesis was Dr. Thomas Gold,[14] a widely respected geologist at Cornell University who died in 2004 after unsuccessful experiments in Scandinavia (in areas where the geologic crust is relatively thin). A more contemporary supporter is Robert Hefner, who follows up on one of Gold's main points—that basic hydrocarbons are fairly common in planetary atmospheres we know about. Hefner argues principally from the "reasonableness" that vast amounts of the simplest hydrocarbon of all (methane, CH_4) may have surrounded our planet as it was forming. He postulates that the relatively small amounts we have discovered by conventional drilling leave vast remnants yet to be located . . . somewhere. Fantasy? Perhaps, although Hefner's success as a "wildcat" discoverer of natural gas is legendary. All this leads to the burning question: Is the raw supply of energy that we can reach and extract (in the United States and around the globe) adequate to meet future needs?

OIL, GAS, AND SOME DISTINCTIONS

Let's take the United States first. There are contrasts between oil and natural gas. For reasons already enumerated, our domestic production of crude oil has dropped steadily for the past couple of decades. In 2007 it was more than 40 percent lower than it had been in the mid-1980s, when shipments from Alaska to the Lower 48 began to fall off. By contrast, U.S. production of dry natural gas has remained reasonably steady since 1995, and it is actually higher today than it was in 1985 or 1990.[15] We have been going after natural gas more vigorously than we ever did before.

For much of its history, natural gas was produced almost exclusively as a by-product of crude oil. There was even a time when finding gas (while looking for oil) was a disappointment to drillers. Neither fuel source is worth much unless it can be delivered to a point of end-use, but natural gas is considerably more difficult to transport than oil. So in many cases "associated gas" was either burned uselessly (a practice called *flaring*) or perhaps reinjected into nearby oil-wells to stimulate recovery of the liquid fuel that was more highly prized. There was also less incentive to search for gas prior to 1978 because the price of natural gas crossing state lines had been capped tightly by federal regulation. There are many examples in U.S. energy history in which price controls showed themselves to be misjudgments, but this was one of the most egregious.

As with oil, natural gas exploration and production generally respond to market pricing. That is, they increase as prices rise—a reaction that may begin when rising prices are first anticipated, because there can easily be a lead-time of many years between the location of a new prospect, development of a field, and actual production (especially offshore, or in remote areas where market-delivery infrastructure may have to be developed at the same time as the product). In the case of natural gas during this period, however, another factor was at work—the development of the gas market itself. The price-cap-induced scarcity of natural gas during the 1970s convinced policymakers then that natural gas was an especially limited fuel source, which ought to be confined to its "best and highest use." They decided that this was residential consumption (in kitchen ranges and home heating units). In fact, legislation was passed to *forbid* the use of natural gas in U.S. industrial applications or to generate electricity. Part of the reason for these policy blunders was a misreading of basic economics, but correcting them was also simply a by-product of changing attitudes toward political philosophy and the role of government.

During President Jimmy Carter's single term (ended by the election of Ronald Reagan in 1980), the emphasis in energy was on central planning. Even though the Natural Gas Policy Act of 1978 recognized the need to stimulate gas production by allowing greater price incentives for exploration, the statute implemented the principle by decreeing a raft of separate price categories that were supposed to compensate for different degrees of difficulty in bringing gas to market. Once the lifting of price controls on gas during the Reagan era demonstrated in practice that government restraints could be eased without producing a "price flyup," it became clear that supply-and-demand factors may hold greater potential than a command-and-control approach. What complicated the situation, however, was a downturn in the economy that helped produce a "gas bubble"—an unanticipated and lingering surplus of the commodity that caused prices to tumble (although never to the artificially low level that had produced national shortages earlier).

Allowing market prices to adjust for themselves may be the best solution in many respects; but it doesn't guarantee stability (or predictability) in the short run, because so many influences are at work. Answering the question of supply adequacy in general comes down to a simple enumeration of resources and reserves, as best we can estimate them.

THE BROADER FUTURE

It would seem that the outlook for natural gas is bright enough to regard it as a *bridging fuel*, especially for the United States. It is more environmentally benign than either oil or coal (the special subject of Chapter 5); and gas supply seems to be more reliable than that of oil (see Chapter 4). Nevertheless, at some point in the future, the relative availability and suitability of *all* fossil fuels could become less attractive if our long-drawn-out move toward "renewable" energy finally succeeds well enough to make an appreciable contribution to our total supply of around 100 quads (or whatever it is by that time).

Meanwhile, a continuing shift toward natural gas is likely. A side benefit will occur because gas production is accompanied by the volatile liquids already alluded to as NGLs. These liquids, including ethane and propane, are used in the petrochemical industry and elsewhere, so NGLs replace crude oil to some extent as a source of refined products. This justifies including them in statistics for total petroleum reserves and production, although they should usually be called out separately.

As important as oil and natural gas are, the United States gets a critical one-third or so of its primary energy from other sources, mainly domestic ones.

A "mixed" energy diet is a good prescription for any country. We insure ourselves potentially against possible future shortfalls in any single energy source if we can rely on a *variety* of energy—such as the full shelf of fossil fuels, nuclear power, hydro, and the whole tray of "new renewables" (solar energy, wind, sophisticated applications of biomass, etc.). Because there is no practical hope for many years to come of this country's becoming independent of at least some imported energy (an assertion to be justified in a later chapter), we are also wise to diversify our foreign purchases, thus becoming more "energy resilient."

Spreading our energy reliance among multiple types and sources doesn't resolve all questions of supply adequacy, however. This approach assumes the premise that energy of different types and origins can be substituted for one another, but that supposition is valid to only a limited extent. A further complication is that substitutability waxes and wanes as technology and times change.

OIL, ELECTRICITY, AND CHANGING TIMES

As noted earlier, oil and electricity constitute this country's two most critical sources of end-use energy. In the early 1970s they were more closely related. Petroleum was vaunted as an environmentally friendly fuel for electricity generating stations. Quite accurately, oil was portrayed then as being cleaner to burn in power plant boilers than coal. At that time, U.S. coal was more exclusively a high-sulfur fuel from east of the Mississippi and equipment to "scrub" sulfur out of stack gases had not been introduced widely, so huge quantities of noxious and damaging acidic vapors were being given off.

The policy switch from coal to oil was not free of controversy, because at that time utility operators argued that scrubbers were too expensive and power-consuming themselves. For years now, however, the installation of scrubbers has become routine to help new coal plants meet tighter emission standards. This tells us something about how environmental regulation (within reason and given sufficient time, long-term investment, and effort) can stimulate technological innovation and market penetration without producing disaster. In the 1970s, many power plants produced steam from water in boilers that were heated by burning a heavy "fraction" of oil (a grade known as Number Six, which also often releases various air-pollutants). Today, that type of oil use has practically disappeared in this country.

Since the 1970s we have come to prize petroleum itself more highly for two specific refined products—motor gasoline and *distillate*, used as a transportation or home-heating fuel. Today, oil in any form is the primary energy source for less than 2 percent of our nation's electricity. It would not even be that important in the electricity mix if high prices and feared scarcity of natural gas did not from time to time make a specific grade of refined oil (called Number Two) economically competitive in the case of "combustion turbines" that can switch back and forth between the two fuels. In turbines of this type, no steam is used at all; the hot vapors produced by burning the oil or natural gas are themselves directed past the turbine blades—spinning them through a magnetic field and thus generating electricity.

The metallurgy to make this possible grew out of its development for jet aviation engines that operate at high temperatures. Prior to its incorporation in ground-based gas-combustion units, the systems in use in electricity generation could not have stood up to constant operation and thus could not be used to supply baseload electricity.

Now that oil has pretty much been "backed out" of the generating sector, proponents of electric automobiles suggest that electricity can and should replace gasoline and diesel fuel in vehicles completely—thus curing the nation of its "oil addiction." They may yet turn out to be authentic prophets, but the case is by no means open and shut. After all, we must still find ways of generating the necessary additional electricity that suits other public and private requirements.

The U.S. electricity sector has been revolutionized since the early 1990s in the way it is organized. Traditionally regulated utilities still dominate the scene, even though "non-utility generators" supply an increasing amount of our electricity. Between 3 and 4 percent of the total is "self-generated" by consumers in the industrial and commercial sectors,[16,17] and "distributed generation" has its place. But residential backyard units (which attract brief attention after bad storms or the occasional grid failure) are statistically insignificant and will probably remain so. For a long time into the future, our citizens will depend predominantly on the enormous generation infrastructure that already exists and can't be converted lightly from one primary energy source to another.

BACK TO MEASUREMENTS AND COMPARISONS

In *time* (the sticky ingredient of energy policy we will contemplate in Chapter 6), the technologies that prevail today in the electricity sector may seem as outmoded as typewriters do now; but let's look at what we have. Figure 2.2 shows diagrammatically where U.S. generators got the primary energy to produce somewhat more than 4 trillion kilowatt hours of electricity for customers of all types during 2007.[18] (It also shows—perhaps even more dramatically than the spaghetti chart, Figure 1.4—how much primary energy is lost during the generation, transmission, and distribution of electricity.) But it may be worthwhile at this point to review and amplify some explanations in respect to energy flow charts like these.

FIGURE 2.2
U.S. Electricity Flow (2007)
(Quadrillion Btu)

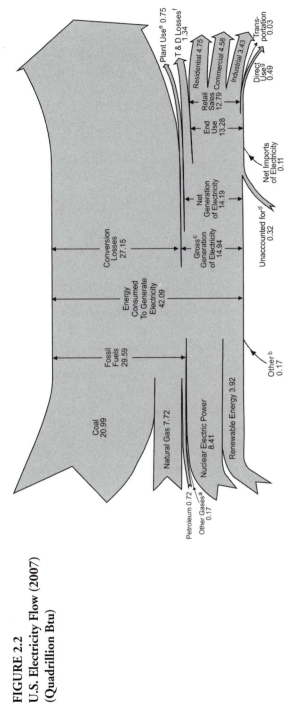

(a) Blast furnace gas propane gas, and other manufactured and waste gases drived from fossil fuels. (b) Batteries, chemicals, hydrogen, pitch, purchased steam sulfur, miscellaneous technologies, and non-renewable waste (municipal solid waste from non-biogenic sources, and tire-derived fuels). (c) Estimated as net generation divided by 0.95. (d) Data collection frame differences and nonsampling error. Derived for the diagram by subtracting the "T & D Losses" estimate from "T & D Losses and Unaccounted for" derived from Table 8.1. (e) Electric energy used in the operation of power plants, estimated as 5 percent of gross generation. (f) Transmission and distribution losses (electricity losses that occur between the point of generation and delivery to the customer) are estimated as 9 percent of gross generation. (g) Use of electricity that is (1) self-generated, (2) produced by either the same entity that consumes the power or an affiliate, and (3) used in direct support of a service or industrial process located within the same facility or group of facilities that house the generating equipment. Direct use is exclusive of station use. Notes: Data are preliminary. See Note, "Electrical System Energy Losses," at the end of Section 2. Values are derived from source data prior to rounding for publication. Totals may not equal sum of components due to independent rounding.

Source: Energy Information Administration, *Annual Energy Review 2007.* Tables 8.1, 8.4a, 8.9, and A6 (column 4).

First, to use "quads" as the common measuring unit for primary energy inputs, the folks who keep such statistics pretend that all generating systems are converting heat into electricity—in pretty much the same way a coal plant would. This works out reasonably well for nuclear plants; they are assigned a "heat rate" that shows their conversion efficiency is lower than a big, modern coal plant because the steam furnished by nuclear reactors generally reaches the turbines at lower temperature and pressure than it would if it were coming from a fossil-fuel-fired boiler. Geothermal power plants are assigned a still less-favorable heat rate, because in their case the steam is at an even lower temperature. But wind turbines and generating systems based on direct solar energy conversion don't involve heat-inputs at all. Their "primary energy inputs" may be set at zero—or at the amounts of electricity they are actually delivering. Depending on one's viewpoint, either of these conventions (or any other that might be adopted in the future) may either inflate or minimize the role in the economy played by the respective energy sources. If the question is critical, further investigation is necessary.

Second, for the sake of simplicity, one element of primary input on a flow chart like this one may just be labeled "renewable energy." For most people, this conjures up visions of wind farms, photovoltaic arrays, and other relatively new (and fast-growing) forms of "green" energy. That is a false image. In fact, this is a common example of Number 11 in Table 1.3, "A Dozen Ways to Confuse People with Energy Statistics."

More than two-thirds of the U.S. generation of electricity from "renewable energy" during 2007 was still the net production[19] from plain old hydroelectricity[20]—which has been around for far more than a century. Roughly 11 percent came from wood and wood-derived fuels; but most of this generation still takes place in the timber and wood-products sector, and there has been essentially no growth in its contribution for decades. In 2005, wind turbines finally surpassed all kinds of "waste fuel" and geothermal energy to assume third place among U.S. renewables in supplying electricity. And by 2007 wind accounted for 9 percent of "renewable generation" and was still increasing its share. Nevertheless, as a reality check we ought to look back at Table 1.3 and review Number 3 in that list of caveats on statistics. Wind's rapid percentage growth from a small base doesn't guarantee appreciable growth overall. Its contribution in 2007 was still less than four-fifths of 1 percent of total U.S. generation. Two types of solar generation[21] have yet to produce more than negligible amounts of electricity nationally—or internationally, for that matter.

A good-sized wind turbine (several hundred feet tall, with its blades cutting a swath of almost equal length from side to side) may have a capacity rating of 1,500 kw (1.5 megawatts). Using a reasonable rule of thumb, this means that over the course of a year a single tower will generate only slightly

FIGURE 2.3
Role of Renewable Energy Consumption in Total U.S. Energy Supply—2006

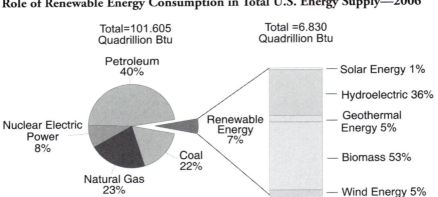

Source: Figure 1 in the Energy Information Administration publication "Renewable Energy Consumption and Electricity—Preliminary 2006 Statistics" (August 2007).

more electricity than a 500 kw diesel generator. To match the effective output of a 500 megawatt coal-fired plant (operating steadily in baseload mode) will take hundreds of such wind turbines—covering many square miles. Even a single 250 megawatt gas-fired turbine requires a huge wind farm to replace it.

When we consider all inputs to our energy menu from renewables (including those that are sources of heating or motor fuels), the outlook for a future of rising energy demand looks like an even more daunting challenge for those tantalizing new sources. That context is depicted graphically in Figure 2.3.

Among "the new renewables," wind shows the greatest promise for growth in the short- to mid-term. Subsidies that have made this possible and other cost considerations will be discussed in Chapter 3, along with the cost factors for energy at large.

NOTES

1. Guy Elliott Mitchell, "Billions of Barrels of Oil Locked Up in Rocks," *National Geographic*, February 1918, pp. 195–205.

2. National Petroleum Council, *Hard Truths: Facing the Hard Truths about Energy (A comprehensive view to 2030 of global oil and natural gas)*, July 2007. Some observers suggest that its fundamental message on "peak oil" is on page 92: "Over the next 25 years, risks above ground—geopolitical, technical, and infrastructure—are more likely to affect oil and natural gas production rates than are limitations of the below-ground endowment."

3. U.S. Department of Energy, Energy Information Administration, *Monthly Energy Review*, Tables 3.3b, 3.3d, 3.3e, 3.3f, 4.1 and 4.3. Although EIA stopped printing its *Monthly Energy Review* in December 2006, the data are still updated

regularly and are available on the Web at http://www.eia.doe.gov/mer. Subsequent references to this data series are identified in this book simply as "*MER*," followed by the appropriate tables or figures. They cite the latest figures available at the time this is written.

4. U.S. Department of Energy, Energy Information Administration, *Annual Energy Outlook 2008, with Projections to 2030* (June 2008).

5. EISA called for higher mileage standards for light-duty vehicles and new energy efficiency measures that will affect everything from light bulbs and household appliances to industrial motors and boilers, while also mandating cutbacks in energy demand within Federal buildings. The legislation also set a timetable for introducing more ethanol into U.S. markets as a motor fuel replacement for gasoline—eventually including "cellulosic ethanol" that can be produced from a great variety of feedstocks, rather than sugar or grain.

6. *AEO 2008*, pp. 2–4. The turnabout in EIA's projections was barely noticed outside the community of energy economists who observe such matters closely. Later in 2008 a self-styled prophet of new energy policy would spend millions to blanket TV with personal commercials proclaiming that U.S. dependence on oil imports had already reached 70 percent and was rising every day. This misrepresentation of facts went generally unchallenged.

7. EIA and U.S. Department of Commerce, Bureau of Economic Analysis, National Economic Accounts.

8. U.S. Census Bureau, U.S. Department of Commerce, *Statistical Abstract of the United States: 2007*, Washington, DC (2006).

9. As is the case with a number of other energy comparisons made in this book, the data were drawn from more than one source on EIA's website or more than one EIA publication. In this instance, Canadians may quibble *somewhat* because EIA ascribes a primary-energy-input value to hydroelectricity, a source on which Canada depends heavily.

10. *MER*, Tables 5.2 and 5.1.

11. *MER*, Table 9.1.

12. Dr. Anthony D. Haymet and Dr. W. Kendall Melville, outstanding chemical and physical experts who are respectively the director and deputy director of the Scripps Institution of Oceanography and who are familiar with the early drilling efforts of the late Dr. Gold as well as more recent deep-drilling experiments (personal communication, November 2007).

13. Federal Methane Hydrate Advisory Committee, *Report to Congress: An Assessment of the Methane Hydrate Research Program and an Assessment of the 5-Year Research Plan of the Department of Energy* (June 2007).

14. See Thomas Gold, *The Deep Hot Biosphere* (New York: Springer-Verlag, 1999), as well as numerous scientific papers by the same author. Dr. Gold, no stranger to controversy, was an early proponent of novel ideas about plate tectonics and pulsars, scorned at first but later accorded respect. His own resulting impatience with "the herd" is reflected in an article he wrote for *Journal of Scientific Exploration* in 1989, entitled "New Ideas in Science."

15. *MER*, Tables 3.2a and 4.2.

16. *MER*, Tables 7.2a and 7.2c.

17. *MER*, Table 7.2a.

18. EIA, *Annual Energy Review 2007*, Diagram 5 (available at http://www.eia.doe .gov/emeu/aer/diagram5.html. The *AER2007* totals show few changes in the pattern revealed by the spaghetti chart for 2006 in Chapter 1 (Figure 1.4). Historical comparisons in *MER* (Table 7.2a) show that the nation's use of electricity increased by 2.3 percent between 2006 and 2007, but there were only slight variations in percentage shares from primary energy sources. Generation fueled by natural gas climbed from 20 percent to 21.5 percent. Largely because of high oil prices, petroleum continued at its lowest point as a generating fuel since the first energy crisis of the early 1970s, accounting for only about 1.5 percent of all U.S. generation.

19. To minimize total cost and ensure continuing reliability of supply, a small amount of the electricity generated by hydro-dams (typically, 2 or 3 percent over the course of a year) is used during periods when demand for power is low and can be satisfied by cheap baseload plants to pump water back to the high reservoir behind the dam. This is called pumped storage and is one of the few ways in which large amounts of electricity can be stored for subsequent use.

20. *MER*, Table 7.2a.

21. Photovoltaic generating cells (sometimes referred to as PVs) employ various materials that convert solar radiation directly into direct-current electricity. Solar-thermal arrays use the sun's heat to raise the temperature of water or some other fluid above its boiling point, so that the resulting steam or other gas can drive a turbine that generates electricity in basically the same fashion as a turbine-generator in a coal-fired or nuclear power plant. Of course the sun's rays can also be used directly for space- or water-heating, and solar conversion efficiencies can be improved in several ways—for example, by sun-tracking equipment or concentrating lenses and mirrors.

Three

How Much Does It Cost?

- Why does a gallon of gasoline cost 20 cents more or 15 cents less from one week to another at the same filling station? And how can you explain a price change of more than $1 a gallon for gasoline over a matter of months?
- Why do companies build coal-fired generating plants *at all* if turbines using natural gas are cheaper?
- Since wind and the sun's rays don't cost anything, will utility bills plummet as more electricity comes from "free" energy sources like those?
- How could my gas bill have *increased* right after a new high-efficiency furnace was installed?
- Is there anything we can do to make all kinds of energy "affordable" again?

STARTING TO FIND ANSWERS

People ask literally hundreds of questions like these every day, ranging from very specific cases to broad generalities. Answering a list of them in random order could fill the rest of this book, but that wouldn't discourage variations of them from popping up. It is more useful to go into some principles of energy costs that you should be able to apply for yourself. That way you can decide if it's worthwhile to prepare for some cost situations that are likely to pose problems or even to try to modify their occurrences. These principles take account of technology as well as applied economics, and this chapter will take occasional detours to add bits of background.

Prices of energy would be easier to understand if the real world were as simple as the straight lines on a supply-and-demand graph like the idealized one in the first chapter (Figure 1.1). It is true that each transaction in energy takes place at the price a buyer is willing to pay at the moment for a given amount of the commodity and a supplier is willing to sell it. But that doesn't begin to explain what goes into the supply curve and the demand curve. Their derivations are complicated, and the lines are never perfectly straight, except in the very short run.

For instance, if technically producible oil might be on the verge of running out completely—or even if no "spare" production capacity was readily available to meet unanticipated additional demand—the supply curve for gasoline (S-S) might bend upward sharply. As suggested in somewhat exaggerated fashion by Figure 3.1, rapid increases in price could not bring more supply to the market quickly. At the same time, the demand curve shown in this hypothetical example (D-D) might represent crudely how U.S. motorists would react to such a sudden and unusual price rise. Recall that there were many complaints at the pumps from 2004 or 2005 onward, but it was only when gasoline exceeded $4 a gallon in 2008 that Americans began to cut back appreciably on driving. It's possible that this diagram depicts in part what actually took place.

Any portion of either a supply curve or a demand curve where the interactions among supply, demand, and price show *quick* response in any direction is "elastic" in economists' jargon. "Inelastic" response is minimal. Figure 3.1 is only slightly more realistic than Figure 1.1. Its purpose is just to show graphically how elasticity of either supply or demand (or both) might change

FIGURE 3.1
"Real World" Supply and Demand Curves
Show Complex Behavior, Hard to Predict

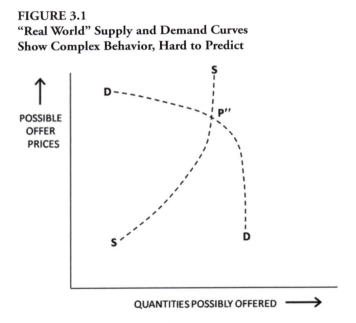

The curves are hypothetical until their intersection indicates a transaction at some price.

as a result of market fundamentals or external events. In this example a number of circumstances might have made the U.S. supply of gasoline almost completely *in*elastic in its short-term response to price while the demand by motorists that had traditionally been quite inelastic suddenly reacted *elastically* to high prices.

When we speak of "steeply sloping" curves and "short-term" versus "long-term" response, it may seem as if energy economists should be able to predict the future of prices with fair certainty. Not quite! The most reasonable-looking and authoritative S and D curves are always those that are drawn retrospectively. When even a careful commentator talks today about "supply elasticity" or "inelastic demand" he or she is projecting largely on the basis of history and informed analysis. Although that is the best we have to go on, such methods cannot account for all quirks of human and national behavior.

Some principles of supply and demand apply to all sorts of energy while others pertain only to particular energy sources or applications, but let's start with some more specific ones. Oil and electricity have already been identified as involving the most obvious immediate problems for the United States. Let's begin then with oil by citing some simplified illustrations, contrast its price behavior with that of natural gas, touch briefly on electricity pricing, and wind up this chapter with some generalized observations about what guides energy investment and some policy options in addressing the goal of affordability.

U.S. motorists drive more during months of pleasant weather than they do in winter, so the demand for gasoline tends to go up in spring and summer; gasoline prices follow. A comparable observation for fuel oil is that U.S. homes obviously use more of it in February than they do in August. However, both gasoline and home heating oil[1] can be drawn from a single barrel of crude oil. Crude is a mixture of compounds that are drawn off in various percentages or fractions, depending on the refining steps involved. (See Figure 3.2.) Different processes can yield gasoline and heating oil in quite different ratios from identical barrels. As the summer driving season approaches, refineries modify their equipment and procedures to turn out more gasoline than heating oil per barrel. In the fall they switch back to favoring the product needed for home furnaces.

Adjusting supplies to try to match changing demand in the nation as a whole helps keep prices from fluctuating quite as much as they might otherwise. But sometimes there's a slip-up, especially when regional differences are considered. The routine maintenance on refinery facilities that is required periodically may also be scheduled during the switchovers. While any given refinery is out of operation, suppliers that ordinarily rely on that source must then draw products from storage, but temporary shortages can easily develop if anything fails to go according to plan. Maybe a problem that could not be anticipated is uncovered during maintenance, or storage in the area turns out to be inadequate because of unusual weather.

FIGURE 3.2
Schematic of an Oil Refinery's Operation

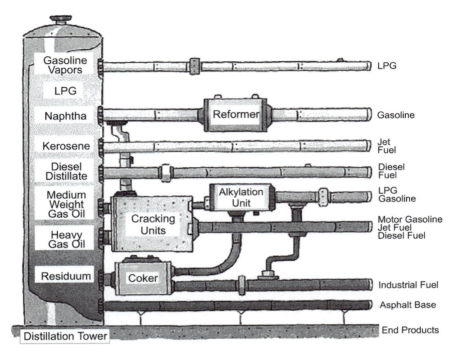

This simplified drawing shows many of a refinery's most important processes.
Source: Energy Information Administration.

Seasons and temperatures are just as important to natural gas and electricity as they are to oil. Analysts of U.S. natural gas prices are wise to keep track of actual or projected patterns for "heating-degree days." They are a measure of deviation from an assumed norm of 65°F, and this gives the strongest basic clue to demand for all heating fuel. Those who study electricity demand to evaluate proper reserve margins for generating capacity pay similar close attention to an index of "cooling-degree days." Air-conditioning loads cause power demand to peak, and electricity storage[2] is a far more difficult challenge than storing fuels. But the U.S. Weather Service is not infallible either. Copious factors like these—and others one can imagine—cause regional or national price-bumps at least a few times every year. We should expect them, almost as we might assume a fly-up in the prices of citrus fruit after a serious frost hits Florida.

The way an oil refinery itself operates holds other clues as to cost and price. Hydrocarbon products—including gasoline and heating oil—are made up of relatively shorter or longer molecule chains of hydrogen and carbon atoms. The fuels differ in physical characteristics, such as boiling point, the temperature at which liquids turn into vapor. They also vary in such chemical characteristics as the way in which each combines with oxygen in the process of combustion. A refinery's task is to use heat and catalysts to turn crude oil of various kinds efficiently into predetermined menus of desired products on a seasonal basis. Hydrocarbons occurring in very long chains or clumps within crude oil have to be "cracked" or broken apart. Some lighter fractions, called naphthas, can be reformatted into high-octane components of motor fuel.

In reality, a refinery produces not only gasoline and heating oil but scores of different products.

Figure 3.3 shows a sample range of important refined products that a typical barrel of crude oil might yield. Generally, the lighter ones in the middle and near the top of the column in Figure 3.2 also command the top prices for a given volume. They satisfy important specialized needs, but they are more expensive to produce.

Heat content by itself is by no means an absolute guide to a petroleum product's value. Asphalt—heavy stuff from the very bottom—typically contains

FIGURE 3.3
Range of Products a Barrel of Crude Might Yield (in gallons)

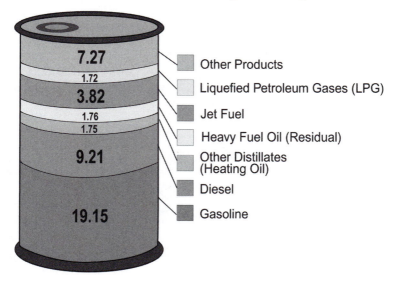

Note: A 42-U.S. gallon barrel of crude oil yields between 44 and 45 gallons of petroleum products. These totals are greater than 42 gallons because some refined products are not as dense as crude oil.

Source: Energy Information Administration.

more than 6.6 million Btu per barrel, but it is such a relatively cheap product we can use it in large quantities to pave roads. Residual heavy fuel oil is used by ships and some old generating equipment, but—despite its high heat content of about 6.3 mmbtu per barrel—it sells for a relatively lower price than other fractions. A barrel of middle-distillate fuel oil might yield no more than 5.8 million Btu and conventional motor gasoline only 5.25, yet in value and price these two come closer to representing the "top of the barrel." This subtlety should caution us that those good old reliable quads of energy—as useful as they may be in gauging energy adequacy overall, as discussed in the preceding chapter—don't tell us enough when we look at other goals, such as affordability and reliability of supply.

IT TAKES ENERGY TO MAKE ENERGY

Processes that yield a larger ratio of the highly desirable light and middle fractions from crude oil necessitate the use of more sophisticated equipment and expensive catalysts. It usually also takes a larger input of energy in the form of heat to split out these products. In fact, this is a *general principle*: A significant amount of energy is frequently consumed in converting the raw materials of almost any energy source into a more convenient form that will actually be used. For that reason, any rise in overall energy prices feeds on itself. This helps explain why synthetic fuels failed to succeed in this country during the late 1970s even though they were a major target of U.S. national energy policy. If the prices of conventional fuels had not been so high, the Synthetic Fuels Corporation (SFC) of that era would probably not even have been proposed, much less established with an initially proposed multi-year budget of around $20 billion. As prices of the necessary energy inputs continued to increase, the cost of producing various chemical alternatives to fossil fuel kept rising too. The SFC wound up chasing its own cost-tail, and after five years it was dismantled as a boondoggle—about the same time oil prices collapsed as a result of other market dynamics.

Does this mean that efforts to introduce synthetic fuels will never succeed, whether they involve processing oil shale or coaxing a substitute motor-fuel such as ethanol from biomass? No. Technology can improve. Other production factors, such as the "cost of money," may change too. This also influences the economic feasibility of projects that are inherently capital-intensive. Furthermore, governmental intervention may tip the balance in favor of or against certain types of energy production. More will be said about this last possibility toward the end of this chapter and again in subsequent chapters. It all comes back to the conscious and unconscious balancing of the goals in the energy mobile of Chapter 1. Affordability may yield to—or trump—other objectives.

The response of prudent investors is to try to discern and evaluate *all* the interacting forces, both short-term and long-term. If customers are especially attentive to pricing, an elastic demand curve will reflect their composite judgment as to how much each form of end-use energy is worth to them. Even when sources have some form of price regulation, as is the case in this country with natural gas and electricity (particularly at the retail level), a partially unconscious balancing of goals influences the way governmental systems handle it. We'll come back to price regulation later on, because it is a common example of how U.S. energy-market operations become distorted.

We started this discussion of gasoline prices with a reference to *storage* in connection with refineries. A storage dilemma haunts suppliers of most forms of energy, just as it does the suppliers of many other wares. Every shopkeeper knows that an adequate inventory of the goods for sale is essential to keep from disappointing both regular and prospective customers. The same applies to wholesalers. Yet commodities on a shelf or in a warehouse bring no direct income, and they become essentially a fixed cost—which ultimately must be reflected in the prices charged to buyers. This has led both producers and marketers in many parts of a modern economy to adopt a "just in time" approach to ordering when possible, thus minimizing the total expense of operation. Dealing in this way with various energy sources is trickier, and delving into details of storage provides an excuse for a slight detour into differences between petroleum and natural gas in this respect.

Everyone has seen above-ground storage tanks for either of these fuels. Each can also be stored beneath the Earth's surface too, either in natural caverns or in huge spaces that have been excavated for the purpose in such formations as salt-beds. The U.S. Strategic Petroleum Reserve is a truly massive illustration of underground storage in a number of sites. It was created in response to fears after two oil crises had occurred in the 1970s that petroleum imports vital to the United States might be cut off. To some extent, natural gas is also stored in the continental network of pipelines that deliver it. This is done by increasing internal pressure. Those pipes are *always* filled with gas, but a large amount of it is needed to keep up pumping operations as fresh supplies continually enter the network and volumes are constantly being drawn off at points of use. The so-called "base gas" required for this function adds up to more than 4 trillion cubic feet throughout the nation. That is equivalent to a couple of months of U.S. natural gas consumption, but this basic amount must be looked on as a fixed asset rather than a potentially salable stored product. There is also another component in the pipelines called "working gas." It may amount to an additional 3 tcf at certain times, but it is drawn down to well below that as needed to supplement the fresh gas being pumped into the system. Working gas *is* part of the inventory counted on to satisfy demand, so its fluctuating level is watched by people trying to predict which way gas prices might be headed in coming months.

A liquid such as crude oil or gasoline is easier and cheaper to transport and store than natural gas, which has to be compressed . . . or even liquefied at very low temperatures. This accounts in part for a basic difference in the unit-price of the energy each contains.

An average barrel of crude oil contains a mixture of potential refined products that would release approximately 5.8 million Btu of heat energy if the crude were burned as is. The "Measuring Energy" feature in Chapter 1 noted that natural gas is customarily priced in terms of its energy content—so many dollars for each one million Btu's (mmBtu). On the face of it then, the price of a barrel of crude should be roughly six times the price of one mmBtu[3] of natural gas. Considering that oil is more convenient to handle than natural gas, we might nudge the differential a bit higher, pegging it at perhaps seven or eight to one. During 2007 and 2008, however, the spread in the United States soared to10:1 and often higher.

Obviously, other factors were at work. One is our ever-important fundamental, supply versus demand. The existence of a true worldwide market dominates oil price formation, but in natural gas a separate market is still largely confined to North America—with its own set of supply and demand players. For the United States, another very large factor in oil-versus-gas pricing is the "risk premium." That is an element of market psychology that has applied directly to oil for the most part. It is related to, but not bound by, the fundamentals of supply and demand. The tangible effects of a risk premium on oil prices will be expanded on shortly.

Despite important distinctions between them, oil and natural gas are often treated in conversation and general energy discussions as if they were almost identical energy sources. Reserve or production statistics for the two are sometimes lumped together under the common heading of "hydrocarbons." Quantities may be expressed in quads, but another set of customary units of measurement for a combination of oil and natural gas is millions of barrels of oil equivalent (mmboe) or millions of barrels per day of oil equivalent (mmbdoe). In any event, volumes of oil and gas can be combined *statistically* by adding together the potential heat content in each. We have just seen, however, that this can be misleading in terms of market value or usefulness in satisfying demand for specific energy applications. The term *hydrocarbons* is frequently convenient shorthand, especially when the exact breakdown is either unknown or not very relevant, but it should be employed carefully, and with the understanding that it may not give us all the information we later decide is needed to evaluate a particular situation.

OIL AND GAS: DIFFERENCES
THAT MAKE A DIFFERENCE

Although global trade in liquefied natural gas is growing, it is far from achieving the size and status of the world oil market. In some regions, significantly including Europe, contracts thus specify for convenience that prices to be paid for gas will be based on contemporaneous oil prices. This is unfortunate, because it distorts the market; and the practice of automatic price linkage between oil and gas may gradually fade away.

When allowed to fluctuate naturally, the prices of oil and natural gas do not track each other as closely as most people assume. This is true even though the two are formed by similar geologic processes and thus may come from the same well. As recently as the middle of the twentieth century, the U.S. distribution network for natural gas was fairly limited, and few U.S. companies bothered to look for gas on their own. Quite often, a driller who struck *only* natural gas in searching for oil would close down such a well in disappointment because there was no way to deliver the gaseous product to a market where it could be sold. If a well yielded *both* oil and gas, the unwanted gas was disposed of by burning it. Today this wasteful and environmentally damaging practice of "flaring" gas is relatively rare, but it continues in some countries that have not developed either domestic gas markets or facilities to export gas economically via pipelines or in the form of liquefied natural gas. Meanwhile, field uses for natural gas have expanded. Gas may provide fuel to generate electricity at a remote location, or provide fuel for pumps and other necessary equipment. In certain situations natural gas is reinjected into wells to increase underground pressure and thus enhance either the volume of oil production or the economic lifetime of a field. Some in the energy business even tout such reinjection of natural gas as a sort of *very* long-term storage, because changing conditions may make it economical to extract the reintroduced natural gas later if its marketability has improved in the meantime.

Some differences between oil and gas have consequences for their respective supply costs and the relative demand for these two energy sources. This helps explain why variations in pricing for the two may result from the different ways in which they are affected by external forces in the marketplace. Those external, price-influencing factors include labor and capital costs, investor attitudes, and consumer habits.

Let's go into a few differences that make a difference.

First, natural gas is made up predominantly of a single chemical compound, methane. Crude oil is complex and nonuniform, with literally hundreds of varieties.

Methane is the simplest of all hydrocarbon molecules. It consists of a single carbon atom to which are joined four atoms of hydrogen. Fractional distillation separates methane from other gases that emerge with it from underground deposits, but the process is simpler than refining the various mixtures of compounds that make up crude oil. The molecules of natural gas do not have to be broken up first.

Furthermore, the sulfur and heavy metals tied to crude either have negligible commercial value or wind up as waste that adds disposal costs, whereas some of the "impurities" stripped from natural gas become valuable by-products to be sold separately. For instance, natural gas as it emerges from the ground can include up to 7 percent helium, and substantial quantities of that commodity are derived from U.S. gas wells. In addition, several important petrochemical products or feedstocks that are found mixed with natural gas as it comes from a well have low boiling points and thus are also in gaseous form because of geothermal heat. These include propane, ethane, pentane, and butane, which together are called natural gas liquids (NGLs) because at ambient temperatures on the surface they condense. These liquids are especially abundant in "associated gas," the output of a well whose primary output is crude oil but which also delivers natural gas in commercial quantities.

NGLs are generally energy sources in themselves. Their production is sometimes combined with that of crude oil in fossil-fuel supply tables, since such NGL components would also be found among the normal yields from an oil refinery. This is one more indication that energy statistics should be scrutinized carefully before drawing conclusions from them. U.S. domestic output of petroleum is often listed as roughly 7 million barrels per day, but about a quarter of that consists of natural gas plant liquids rather than crude oil. NGLs *do* substitute importantly for some fractions of crude that normally go into petrochemicals, but their contribution to such refined products as either gasoline or heating oil is indirect and limited, so this should be understood.

Second, the potential supply-and-demand balances for oil and gas are likely to differ globally in the long run.

Accepting the careful estimates from *Oil & Gas Journal*, the U.S. Energy Information Administration (EIA) reported early in 2007 that the world held roughly equal proved reserves of oil and natural gas, 7,640 versus 6,800 quads.[4] It normally takes longer to assemble the annual international statistics for consumption, so the most up-to-date numbers available at the same time were for 2004. The global consumption figures for 2004 were stated at just under 100 quads for natural gas and a whopping 168 quads for petroleum, including natural gas liquids.

It is only fair to add that the EIA projected simultaneously that worldwide consumption of natural gas would rise at a rate of 1.9 percent per year between now and 2030, while the rate of increase for liquids would be a more gradual 1.4 percent, but that reflects the market's anticipation of which of these two energy sources will be more available, economical, and desirable over that period.[5] Contrasting outlooks regarding each factor will affect willingness to make long-term investments in technologies that are tied to *either* oil or gas exclusively.

Third, oil and gas are interchangeable in only a limited number of applications.

They compete nationally in the industrial and commercial sectors, but oil dominates in U.S. transportation while for many years gas has supplied about three times as much energy as petroleum to residential households, where it is both a cooking and a heating fuel. "Bottled gas," such as compressed propane, competes only where cheaper alternatives are not available, and it accounts for only a few percent of the U.S. residential market.

Industrial use of natural gas slipped between 2003 and 2007, as we seemed to enter an era of generally higher gas prices—brought about in part by the fact that the volume of natural gas used by the U.S. electric-power sector has risen almost every year since the late 1990s. As the average price paid by industrial consumers rose from $4.02 in 2002 to $5.89 in 2003, $6.53 in 2004, and $8.56 in 2005, some previously heavy users of gas either switched fuels or simply went out of business—a phenomenon referred to in the gas industry as *demand destruction*. That tended to dampen what would otherwise have been a steeper rise in gas prices. Some industries switched back to natural gas thereafter, however, when gas prices lagged behind the increases being posted by oil.

Fourth, almost 70 percent of all the petroleum consumed in this country is used in the transportation sector, where natural gas is a negligible fuel component. Oil use in other sectors shrank in the aftermath of earlier crises and for the most part has held steady over the years. Natural gas use, on the other hand, is divided almost evenly among the residential-commercial, industrial, and electric power sectors, and this exposes it to inter-sectoral demand competition. For example, when a large number of new gas-fueled generating units began to come on line quickly during the 1990s the price of natural gas was bid up because of the sudden demand pull from a new quarter. As a counter to this, however, there was also increasing gas-on-gas competition. The extensive U.S. gas pipeline network and the gradual introduction of more LNG encouraged diverse suppliers to vie for sales, while "electronic billboards" and arbitrage developed a continental market in which competition could exert some downward pressure on prices. The result of all this is that the U.S. natural gas market and the U.S. oil market operate with quite distinct dynamics. There is an underlying tendency for all hydrocarbon product prices to move in the same general direction, but they respond to different rhythms.

QUALITY AFFECTS THE PRICE OF CRUDE

It is easy to see why the composition of crude oil affects its price. Gummy crudes containing a high percentage of heavier ingredients are more costly to turn into an optimal slate of products. The same is true of "sour" crudes, those containing large amounts of sulfur. The combustion of high-sulfur fuels releases sulfur oxides into the atmosphere, and these in turn combine with moisture to form dilute acids that cause public health problems, corrode equipment, ruin painted surfaces and construction materials, and in general degrade the environment. Anti-pollution laws and regulations place upper limits on the parts-per-million of sulfur that diverse commercial fuels are allowed to contain.

Even though each sample of crude is technically unique, petroleum is marketed in a limited number of "benchmark" categories for which ranges of sulfur and viscosity have been agreed upon. Within any of these accepted categories, shipments of crude oil are considered *fungible*. This means that a metric ton of the kind called Brent is considered the equivalent of another metric ton that bears the same name halfway around the world. That facilitates worldwide trade, since prices can be expressed uniformly on central commodity exchanges as well as in individual contracts. Similar trading conventions apply to natural gas, refined products, and electricity, since each of those commodities is much more homogeneous than crude oil.[6]

The standard for measuring the viscosity in crudes is set by a trade organization called the American Petroleum Institute (API). The numerical scale API uses—with units expressed in "degrees"—may seem counterintuitive. Lower numbers indicate *heavier* crudes, which are less attractive. Sulfur content is given in percentages, with low-sulfur grades being termed "sweet" and high-sulfur ones "sour."

The nature of a crude can make a large difference in price. In mid-2008, a light, sweet crude such as the category designated West Texas Intermediate (WTI) was selling in Cushing, Oklahoma, for just pennies less than $140 a barrel, but the Maya crude being imported from Mexico at the very same time was bringing $16.30 less. WTI has an API number of almost 40 and contains less than one-quarter of one percent sulfur. The comparable ratings for Maya were API 22 and 3.4 percent.

On average, the crude oil found and produced today around the world is heavier and higher in sulfur than only a few years ago. That alone would have increased the production costs and prices of refined products, even if there were no question about the availability of enough petroleum to take care of greater consumption brought about by population growth and increased popular insistence on comfort and convenience.

The shift in the availability of light, sweet crude has also widened the price-spread between it and less desirable types. Refineries that were designed originally to handle light, sweet crude cannot use other grades without expensive modification. Even then, the refinery's typical yield from a barrel may include less of the products for which demand is highest. As a result, prices for such things as aviation jet fuel soar. A corresponding oversupply of asphalt and the heavy residual oil used as fuel for ocean-going vessels may cause the prices of those goods to fall, but that offers no consolation to a traveler who must pay a fuel-related surcharge on a plane ticket or the motorist who finds that a $50 bill no longer fills the tank.

HOW MUCH IS $50 WORTH?

There is a clear link between world oil prices and the value of the U.S. dollar in international currency markets. As one rises the other tends to fall, and vice versa. But there isn't a single, simple cause-and-effect relationship. During 2008, the weakness of the dollar probably added $15 or more (net) to what a barrel of oil might have cost otherwise.[7] Since some combination of the situation and events then could be repeated (or reversed), here are a few thoughts about some of the interactions:

1. In general practice around the world, oil prices are listed in U.S. dollars. If the greenback's exchange value drops—so that a dollar will buy fewer Euros, yen, or Turkish lira—its purchasing power in commodities also falls. Exclusive of other considerations, oil prices go up worldwide.
2. If that happens the U.S. trade balance weakens, because this country is a major importer of foreign oil. The entire economy suffers to some extent. In a sense we become poorer, and that causes the rise in oil prices to pinch more. General inflation may threaten.
3. On the other hand, a cheaper dollar encourages other countries to buy whatever the United States is exporting. That helps us, and demand for our exports tends to nudge the dollar upward.
4. However, energy costs—and especially the price of gasoline, diesel, and jet fuel—factor heavily in the costs of production for goods and services we provide to the rest of the world. This raises our export prices, makes us less competitive as a nation, and may even depress the value of the dollar more.
5. Economic downturns reduce our own demand for energy, in part because our GDP is lower but also because Americans become more frugal in their use of energy. Because this country is such a huge net buyer of oil and petroleum products on the world market, this dampens oil prices—although there may be a time lag before this occurs. Meanwhile, the other upward and downward pressures continue.

All this is just one more example of the complicated *balances* associated with energy!

"PAPER BARRELS"

An important aspect of today's energy markets is that individuals or organizations anywhere in the world can buy and sell energy "derivatives" such as futures and options. In many cases the commodities designated in such contracts will never be exchanged by the buyer and seller involved, but the existence of a liquid market for these secondary instruments makes it possible for each side to hedge against future price volatility. For example, a potential supplier of crude oil may sell a future contract for so many barrels and receive payment immediately—thus avoiding the risk that prices may drop. An airline may acquire in advance the rights to certain supplies of jet fuel when needed—perhaps paying a premium for the privilege, but receiving assurance that its price will not rise in the interim.

Energy futures and options are both sold in organized markets around the world, just like stocks. Their prices are reached by open bidding between professional buyers and sellers on behalf of clients. An oil futures contract confers the right to collect—or to deliver—a predetermined amount of a specific type of crude oil at a certain location and a *certain time* in the future. An option provides the opportunity to buy or sell a specified amount at any time between the present and a certain date in the future *at a specified price*. Options sell for a fraction of the putative price of the commodity itself. But they will not be exercised at all unless the option owner decides along the way that price movements have made it advantageous to buy or sell at the originally agreed-upon price.

In addition to hedgers, derivatives markets are obviously attractive to those who purely wish to speculate on whether prices will rise or fall in the future. In this they are not dissimilar to traditional markets in stocks and bonds. Trading in derivatives should be overseen closely to avoid possible manipulation—especially so long as markets are relatively thin; but arguments will long continue over the degree to which such markets should be subject to various specific types of government regulation. A later section of this chapter will explain how speculation on the future can affect current prices.

ANALYZING GASOLINE PRICES FURTHER

Prices for gasoline depend ultimately, but not entirely, on the price of crude. Since crude prices revolve around a worldwide market, the respective contributions from various crudes have bounced up and down in recent times with geopolitical developments *and the way they are interpreted*. Combine this phenomenon with regional variations tied to current conditions of refining and storage, and the answer to the first question posed at the opening of this chapter becomes obvious. Because of limited storage space at a filling station, gasoline is dispensed to most distributors more often than once a week, and those big numbers on signposts reveal from a block away that a station's latest prices are tied to what the wholesaler charged for *the most recent delivery*. It is a LIFO system—last in, first out.

Figure 3.4 shows how much of each dollar spent on a gallon of gasoline could be traced to major cost segments as national average retail prices rose by

FIGURE 3.4
Where Your Gasoline Dollar Went in 2004 and 2007

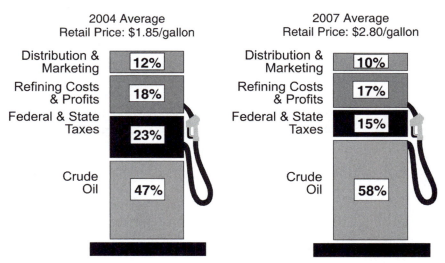

2004 Average
Retail Price: $1.85/gallon

Distribution & Marketing 12%
Refining Costs & Profits 18%
Federal & State Taxes 23%
Crude Oil 47%

2007 Average
Retail Price: $2.80/gallon

Distribution & Marketing 10%
Refining Costs & Profits 17%
Federal & State Taxes 15%
Crude Oil 58%

In mid-2008, crude's share reached 75 percent!
Source: Energy Information Administration.

about one dollar over a three-year period. In 2008 the pace of increase quickened. Like many of the illustrations in this book, this breakdown is only suggestive. Regional and time-varying factors, such as labor and transportation costs, apply at every stage of delivery—from the wellhead to the pump at a service station. Environmental requirements also vary across the country, with specified formulations of gasoline often affecting its price. Finally, there is genuine competition among retailers, not least because even the hint of any conspiracy to fix prices brings the danger of prosecution. Adding all these factors together, it is not surprising that in 2008 Californians often paid at least 50 cents more per gallon than drivers in Texas.

Among the important reasons for *regional* differences in gasoline prices is the way the fuel is taxed. The federal gasoline tax in 2007 was uniform at 18.4 cents per gallon, and Congress showed little interest in increasing that as a means of encouraging conservation. But state excise levies added to this, ranging from an additional 7.5 cents of tax in Georgia to 38.65 cents a gallon in New York.[8] European critics of U.S. energy policy almost invariably point out that they are accustomed to much higher gasoline taxes, observing that this has helped to popularize more fuel-efficient autos there. That is a model worth noting, but it is rarely mentioned that those high taxes in Europe began in many cases as pure revenue measures, or that their origin may trace back to a time when only an affluent minority of Europeans could afford cars at all, so that this was a disguised form of progressive taxation for social purposes.

At the other extreme, many governments around the world fix the total price of motor fuel at low, subsidized levels to maintain popular support. A notable example is Venezuela, where gasoline is almost given away; it cost only 12 cents a gallon in 2008.[9] Iran, a major oil producer and exporter, has inadequate domestic refining capacity and so must import much of its motor fuel at world prices. Yet public protests took place, even in that authoritarian society, when Iranian officials reluctantly raised the price of gasoline to around 40 cents a gallon. China has a stated policy of limiting oil consumption on economic, environmental, and national security grounds since the country has become a major oil importer, so around the time that country was hosting the 2008 Olympics its government cautiously lowered its motor fuel subsidies. Nevertheless, gasoline in China remained a bargain compared with many countries. In all such cases, "affordability" is being put ahead of other considerations in energy policy to varying degrees.

Purposely fiddling with supply and demand through price controls can operate in more than one direction. The idea of *reducing* energy consumption by intentionally *raising* its price is sound conceptually, but is not readily implemented. In 1980, a serious-but-futile independent candidate for the U.S. presidency named John Anderson pledged in his platform to introduce an additional 50-cents-a-gallon gasoline tax, which would have raised the average pump price then by just over 40 percent. We will never know what effect such a measure might have had on U.S. driving habits in the 1980s, but experience intimates that the demand for gasoline among most U.S. drivers *has* been fairly *price-inelastic* below a certain level. This means that consumption trends remained pretty much the same in the short run despite price changes. In 2005 gasoline was selling across the country for less than $2.50 a gallon, while by 2007 the average had topped $3—just about an all-time high in inflation-adjusted terms as well as nominal price. That should have had the same effect as a 50-cent tax increase, yet U.S. sales of the fuel *rose* by about 1.5 percent over that two-year period.

It appeared in 2008 that we had finally found a level in rising prices at which the demand curve would veer sharply enough to make a noticeable difference in total gasoline consumption. U.S. gasoline usage stabilized after the first oil crisis in the early 1970s and went down briefly after the second, but in that case the pump price per gallon was climbing from 38.8 cents in 1973 to 56.7 cents in 1975 and slightly more than $1.19 in 1980. By that time "stagflation" had hit the country and unleaded gasoline was replacing the leaded variety, which also increased refining costs, so those nominal price comparisons are shaky. Based on historic precedents, however, it is now a reasonable hypothesis that the price elasticity for U.S. demand in gasoline adjusts itself *in a step-fashion*—as Figure 3.1 tried to suggest.

Thirty years ago, rising prices were complemented by national awareness that new legislation would mandate an increase in average fuel efficiency for all U.S. passenger cars in the future. There was also a concerted national effort to advertise the positive benefits of carpooling and mass transit, and that higher taxes on vehicle fuel[10] might have been imminent. It might make *some* difference in public reaction these days if motorists came to believe that higher fuel taxes would remain "on the table" indefinitely, for the express purpose of encouraging conservation—either to reduce petroleum imports or to reduce the emission of carbon dioxide (see Chapter 5 on "Environmental Factors").

U.S. gasoline taxes have not thus far been thoughtfully coordinated with other segments of national policy. Although gasoline taxes are paid into a National Highway Trust Fund, there is little linkage between the level of revenue for that fund and the country's actual needs for road-and-bridge construction and maintenance. Even though much of our commercial economy depends on diesel transport and many politicians have often backed the use of diesel for personal vehicles as one way of increasing energy efficiency, the federal tax on "road diesel" has been about one-third higher than that on gasoline. Most importantly, as Figure 3.4 makes clear, the total tax share of pump prices for gasoline inevitably dwindles as the cost of crude oil rises. The average total in gasoline taxes nationwide dropped from 23 percent in 2004 to 15 percent in 2007 and down to 10 percent by mid-2008. This is largely because the federal levy on gasoline is a specific tax (so much for each gallon as the unit of sale), rather than an *ad valorem* tax, which would represent a given percentage of the sales price.

From an economic policy standpoint, a conventional sales tax on gasoline would automatically tend to dampen demand (presumably satisfying certain national interests) as oil prices rise. Don't expect the idea of an *ad valorem* gasoline tax to win many supporters in Congress, however. Part of the reason is that it contradicts the national goal of *affordability* for energy. Equally important is that the committee structure in the U.S. Congress provides that tax decisions are not dominated by the same groupings of legislators who have the greatest power in shaping various aspects of energy policy.

GASOLINE, GLOBALIZATION, AND GEOPOLITICS

All other considerations aside, the largest component of gasoline price by far is still crude oil. In 2004 it accounted for nearly half of the total average pump price, and by 2007 the crude-oil share was 58 percent. Because of globalization, prices for a basically fungible product such as crude are determined by total world supply and total world demand. That brings us back to the offhand definitions of supply and demand implied at the beginning of this chapter.

To repeat and rephrase, prices are set in each of the enormous number of transactions that constitute the "spot market" at any given moment. This is when a potential buyer is willing to part with a certain number of U.S. dollars or their equivalent in exchange for a certain volume of crude that another party is willing to furnish then at that price. Unless the sale is part of a pre-arranged firm contract, a potential buyer who is dissatisfied with the offering from one company or country can seek a match elsewhere. This is why the Arab oil embargo of the 1970s failed to cut off oil supplies to countries such as the United States and The Netherlands, whose support of Israel had annoyed that country's enemies, but succeeded in notching up the world price of oil. Some sales went through third countries to the embargoed parties, while some new oil production in non-OPEC countries that *had* been uncompetitive economically was *now* able to enter the market at a higher price.

Overwhelming shares of the world's proved oil reserves and current production are controlled by national oil companies (NOCs), whose policies may be a mixture of economic planning and political whim. Because they do not have the same obligation to stockholders as private corporations, they don't operate under the same economic guidelines—such as trying to optimize profits and return-on-investment in either the short or the long run. Separate national interests usually prevail, which is why OPEC finds it hard to agree on effective pricing policy. A price of $200 a barrel on the world market might please a *few* members—such as Venezuela and Algeria, although for different reasons. On the other hand, contemplating such a price terrifies Saudi Arabia. Substantial future fluctuations above and below $100 cannot be ruled out. Their magnitude and timing depend ultimately on supply-and-demand, modified by what the United States decides to do. This country is a huge force on *both* sides of the supply-demand balance.

A fuller examination of the effect NOCs have on world oil prices belongs more appropriately to Chapter 4, "Reliability of Supply." In respect to cost, though, one of the watchphrases of energy discussions since at least the 1980s is still "energy security." In its broadest sense, energy security depends on supply that will be both adequate *and* affordable. The most meaningful antonym for energy security, incidentally, is *energy vulnerability*. The latter implies that either a flat cutoff of supplies or rapid ups and downs in the price of necessary supplies can wreak economic havoc with a country. It suffices in this chapter to say that either genuine risk or perceptions of risk probably contributed at least $30 to the price of the first barrel of WTI crude that sold for more than $100 in the United States during January 2008. By the time in 2008 when the price of light sweet crude first approached $150, perceptions of risk might easily have been responsible for $40 on each barrel.

When the magic figure of $100 was reached initially, the official U.S. reaction was to blame abruptly rising worldwide oil demand, as highlighted by an International Energy Agency's projection for 2008 that was half a million to 800,000 barrels per day higher than most market-watchers had been anticipating. OPEC charged instead that the culprits were geopolitics and a shortage of appropriate refining capacity. Some U.S. political leaders held commodity speculators responsible.[11]

All of those commentators were right! But basic supply and demand forces underlay everything, and some added upward pressure on spot prices came from the knowledge that inventories of oil being held in storage by the more industrially developed countries that are members of IEA were slightly below their five-year average. The United States was in somewhat better shape than the European Union for oil in industrial storage, and there was also the enormous U.S. Strategic Petroleum Reserve to fall back on. But oil prices move globally, and the Bush administration insisted repeatedly that it would not draw from the SPR to pull down prices alone. The argument was that national strategic reserves should be used only in case of an actual supply cutoff—as had occurred when Hurricanes Katrina and Rita briefly interrupted deliveries of both crude oil and refined products to customary destinations within the country.

Gauging the risk premium in oil prices is not an exact science, especially before the fact. Its largest element comes from the concentration of oil reserves and production capacity in such politically volatile regions as the Middle East, West Africa, and Venezuela. In today's world, it is easy to conceive of events that could shut down the output of an entire country at a time.

Seaborne deliveries to importing nations are crucial, and there are some natural bottlenecks along some of the most heavily trafficked routes—such as the Straits of Hormuz at the eastern end of the Persian Gulf, the Straits of Malacca between Malaysia and the Indonesian island of Sumatra, and the narrow passages between the Black Sea and the Mediterranean. A politically inspired attack on a supertanker anywhere in the world might rocket prices upward, but the effects of any action within an area where passage is already squeezed down would be multiplied strongly. Imagine what would happen to rates for ship insurance!

SOME FUTURE PRICES MAY ALREADY BE HERE

In another vein, consider the effect of the futures market on the spot market. The price people are willing to pay now for a barrel of oil to be delivered at some point in the future is based on perceptions of what the spot market will be then. Regardless of what market fundamentals are today, the prices for five-year energy futures are influenced by what the composite view is of how conditions will change in the interim. The range of uncertainty dictates the range of risk. Although the volume of trades on energy futures has increased greatly over the years, the market is still relatively thin. That means it doesn't take much to send prices flying one way or the other.

If prices for oil futures are plotted year-by-year on a graph, it is normal for the forward price curve to slope generally downward. This is called *backwardation*, and it is easily understandable. It costs money to store oil for future delivery and, besides, it's natural to discount the value we place on any good in the future from one that's on hand right now to enjoy. In recent years, however, we have seen the less usual situation called *contango*. The price of a barrel of oil that won't become available for some time exceeds one to be delivered immediately. Periods of contango may come and go, but the forward curve bears watching. As markets adjust to the norm and a contango curve flattens out, it appears that high futures prices may translate into high near-term prices. The result is a higher price plateau.

The shift from conventional to unconventional supplies of oil can affect the pricing mechanism in somewhat the same way as geopolitical risk. Unconventional oil tends to be more expensive to produce than conventional, so prices *deserve* to be higher in the future. Refining requirements are changing too, as the crudes being produced get heavier and higher in sulfur. Paul Horsnell, of Barclays Capital, puts the principle of the forward price curve this way: "The general position of the curve is set by changing perceptions about what price is necessary to generate enough investment to balance the market in the longer term."[12] Thus, some observers see a peculiar advantage in the oil market contango. Calling attention ahead of time to an imminent rise in both the cost of producing oil and its future fundamental price is assumed to encourage investment in the near term.

Industry giant ExxonMobil notes that for two decades leading up to 2007, the company put essentially all of its upstream earnings from oil and natural gas into capital investment and exploration in anticipation of future energy needs. That represented an average outlay of close to $10 billion a year between 1988 and 2007. Looking forward from 2008 through 2012, however, it projected more than two and a half times that—an annual average of over $25 billion to be spent on exploration, expanded production and additional refining capacity. ExxonMobil estimated that almost twenty specific new projects it slated for 2008–2010 would collectively add more than 725,000 barrels of oil and oil equivalent to its production.[13]

It is hard to resist the assumption that this correlation indicates a causal relationship, but that is difficult to prove. One reason is that futures prices—even when reflected in spot prices—are based largely on broad perceptions rather than the more comprehensive and detailed analysis that one would expect from a successful company. Another is that investment decisions are influenced by many other factors.

Fundamental prices *could* go *down*, either from reduced demand or from changes in supply-cost considerations and supply availability. Some future methods of recovering a useful product from Alberta's oil sands may cut the costs of production by being less energy intensive. The same might be true for enhanced oil recovery, especially if it can be tied into CO_2 sequestration. There may be new technological breakthroughs we don't foresee at this point; they could be as important as improved drill-bits and horizontal drilling have been. Since such dramatic innovations are less than certain, the tendency is probably for prices to remain higher than historical levels. Volatility is also easy to predict, however. World oil prices are not likely to stabilize without: (1) moves to reduce geopolitical risk, and (2) simultaneous public attention to both supply and demand. Either of these two occurrences will be challenging to achieve, but seeing both take place at once is more than doubly difficult because progress on one front encourages relaxation on the other.

PRICING OTHER FORMS OF ENERGY

Pricing mechanisms for electricity in the United States differ markedly from the way oil prices are formed.

News media generally refer to both electricity and gas as having been "deregulated," and multiple reforms to promote market competition in these two energy sources have taken place since the late 1970s. However, all those changes don't come close to blanket deregulation. What has happened is more accurately described as "regulatory restructuring." Developments toward letting markets determine the prices paid by end-use consumers for electricity and natural gas are neither complete nor irreversible. Those prices are still subject to substantial and sometimes very detailed regulation and oversight at the federal, state, and some local levels.

The regulators with the most significant influence on both gas and electricity prices are the Federal Energy Regulatory Commission (FERC) and the Public Utility Commissions (PUCs) in each state. PUC commissioners are appointed in some jurisdictions but elected in others, and they are generally not tightly bound by precedent. The FERC is a quasi-judicial and essentially autonomous body of seven persons, presidentially appointed for fixed terms. The FERC succeeded a complex of other agencies during broad national energy reforms of the late 1970s. It operates in some ways like a national PUC for wholesale markets in both electricity and natural gas, except that it has gradually established a large body of rules that govern the conduct of interstate and international energy sales and the operation of facilities engaged in interstate or international trade. Both state and federal regulators hold public hearings before issuing decisions.

Specific rate situations vary so much from place to place that averages and generalizations are misleading. Circumstances ought to be examined on a case-by-case basis, which is a challenging undertaking. For example, even a determination as to when electricity transmission into a state becomes subject to PUC rather than exclusive FERC authority is subject to some interpretation.

Market forces play a strong underlying role, but retail rates for both electricity and gas are set by PUCs. That process and its results vary from state to state and can be very political. Different rate schedules exist for residential, commercial, and industrial customers. Utilities typically argue that the rates granted don't jibe with the actual costs of service and that they lag behind real-world developments in becoming effective, but advocates for small consumers insist that at least minimal access to electricity in modern America seems almost like a human right. Public pressure forces some protections for the poorest customers, although such assistance may not be adequate. Year-round payment plans assist budgeting, and many localities forbid either electricity or gas utilities from shutting off service to residential customers for nonpayment of bills during seasons of greatest need. Organized charities, often assisted by suppliers, tend to treat an individual's requirement for energy as equally important as the need for food and shelter.

The system in force today has evolved through a series of legislative and administrative changes, but the details of that history are superfluous in a short volume like this one. Once again, we'll stick to broad principles.

U.S. gas and electricity regulation developed originally in an effort to foster efficient and comprehensive service while avoiding the abuses of monopoly power. The dilemma was this: Unless a company that delivered either electricity or gas directly to retail consumers had exclusive service areas, communities faced a chaotic multiplication of wires and distribution pipelines. At the same time, a single supplier to all consumers would be tempted to discriminate against those who were hard to reach. Also, the monopolistic supplier might insist on charging the very highest prices the market would bear to maximize profits. That seemed intolerable for commodities that are everyday necessities of life. In effect, gas and electricity could be sold in a forced auction for which monopolistic sellers made up all the rules.

The compromise that developed is usually called a "regulatory compact." Companies that supplied gas and/or electricity would be *required* to provide such services to anybody and everybody who requested them within a specified area in return for: (1) protection from competition, and (2) assurance of a "reasonable" rate of return over time on investment, including both capital outlays and operating expenses. That worked smoothly for decades.

THE ONGOING EVOLUTION
OF MARKET REGULATION

The enterprises that supply U.S. electricity are not uniform in the way they have been owned and operated. The largest were traditionally vertically integrated. This means that they owned facilities to generate power, transmit it in large volumes up to considerable distances, and distribute it along networks within their legally assigned service territories. The dominant players tended to be either stock companies owned by investors or federal government entities, such as the Tennessee Valley Authority. Some other utilities were established by municipalities, and still others are cooperatives—owned by the energy consumers themselves and operated by their representatives.

As with most forms of central control, regulatory conditions piled up on top of each other. Public utilities were required to demonstrate in advance the potential net value to the service area of any plan to build new facilities or shut down old ones. The prices each company could charge for electricity had to be approved in advance too, and they were calculated to produce a targeted percentage of return on investment, using as the rate-base the value of facilities already acquired. Fuel-adjustment clauses allowed companies to recover some unforeseen cost increases by passing them through automatically to ratepayers, but rate cases became ever more complicated and long time-lags became routine between market changes and reimbursement to suppliers.

No system of price-regulation satisfies everybody, but this one had serious inherent problems—with both national and local ramifications. They became more obvious as capital outlays and the prices of the primary energy inputs for generation—such as coal, oil, and natural gas—rose. Consumer groups complained that utilities lacked incentive to operate efficiently because they could count on guaranteed returns whether or not they did. Suppliers argued that volatile fuel prices, ballooning construction expenses, uncertainty about new environmental protection costs, and other fresh factors entitled them to a better balance between investment risks and the rewards of profits.

As things worked out, the U.S. regulation of both electricity and natural gas respectively has undergone *evolution* rather than *revolution*, and the long-term results of changes have sometimes surprised their original sponsors.

The Natural Gas Policy Act of 1978 came into effect as almost a caricature of central planning. It decreed dozens of national wellhead price levels for different categories of the fuel, depending on such esoterica as the dates when wells were drilled. Yet it also opened the door to virtually complete decontrol of wholesale gas prices, which followed as soon as the principal occupant of the White House changed.

In another instance, the Energy Policy Act of 1992 set out to subsidize "alternative" producers of electricity. EPAct offered special advantages to small generators, cogenerators who turned out both heat and power simultaneously, and generation using renewables such as sun and wind for primary energy input. But the opening up of the industry led quickly to a whole new category of independent power producers (IPPs) using conventional fuels, and soon the functions of electricity generation, transmission, and local distribution were being handled widely by separate companies rather than vertically integrated ones. Most of the original firms either sold off generation and transmission facilities and continued to focus on local distribution of power at guaranteed rates-of-return or set up subsidiaries at arm's length to *compete* with others in generating electricity that could be sold on a more or less open market. Electronic orders for electricity over long distances became commonplace, and a market even developed in electricity futures.

Basically, the same sort of regulatory "unbundling" took place with natural gas. Since 1992 it has been possible to contract for delivery space on gas pipelines even if the booker of space is neither a gas producer nor a gas distributor.

It was assumed widely that competition within the electricity and natural gas industries respectively would force the service providers of both to focus on efficient operation to compete effectively and thus pare costs, profit margins, and prices all the way down the line to the end users. The underlying theory may have held up in practice, but we may never be able to prove whether or not it did because of two exogenous developments: (1) The costs of primary energy itself soared for different reasons, and (2) some "merchant energy" companies such as Enron took advantage of the system through deceit and manipulation to force up sales prices and collect enormous profits.

Sadly, the lobbyists and legislators who supported what was *called* deregulation had overpromised its benefits. Competition among suppliers should in most cases encourage efficient operation, but extravagant promises were made that regulatory changes by themselves would automatically guarantee lower prices. Those rosy predictions were made despite the fact that independent energy economists were wary of: (1) inexorably rising nationwide demand for electricity in a booming economy, and (2) foreseeably higher future prices for natural gas, which was destined to become for a long while the fastest-growing fuel for new generating plants. The basic supply-and-demand mantra was overlooked.

ELECTRICITY HAS ITS OWN PRICE RECIPES

Just as crude oil is the basic factor in costs and prices of refined products, so the fundamental cost factor in electricity is generation. But national averages in generation costs do not tell us nearly enough to judge how economically competitive primary energy sources are with each other in various locations across the United States. There are multiple reasons for this. Furthermore, the exact combination of explanatory factors that will be most meaningful depends on whether you are a supplier or a consumer. This is because costs can be broken down in various ways.

Let's take fixed costs versus variable costs.

Fixed costs are represented primarily by the capital investment it takes to build a given generating facility and perhaps provide the necessary connecting transmission lines. Those fixed costs are included in the rate base the Public Utility Commission credits to a local distributing utility that owns its generators, although it would be hard to pin down the precise share they represent on the monthly bill of either a wholesale or a retail consumer of electricity. Quasi-judicial proceedings are held periodically by a PUC for fully regulated utilities, and the commission issues a rate schedule for various classes of customers and services that it estimates will produce a specified target return-on-investment going forward, calculated as a percentage of the rate base. This target may be exceeded or missed in practice, however, because there are also variable costs.

Variable costs include administration, operating, and maintenance costs. The major fluctuation in them is most likely to be fuel, and cost-of-fuel effects *will* show up sooner or later in a composite fuel-adjustment charge that is typically called out on bills or at least can be tracked down.

From the consumer's point of view, both fixed and variable costs apply to the entire service area rather than being separated plant by plant. The breakdown between fixed and variable costs is not transparent at all to those being served by a cooperative or a large distributing company that doesn't own its own generating facilities. There, total costs are lumped into a price—the one the distributor paid to buy the electricity from someone else or a price that the end-user agreed to pay via an annual contract from another supplier. Since federal regulatory provisions unbundled generation from distribution, about half the states allow some form of competitive offers from either the local utility or outside companies to sell the electricity. Since the product still usually arrives via the distribution system of the local utility, that company sets a service charge authorized by the PUC and handles billing. Alternatively, large users of electricity may also contract directly with an outside supplier. Some choose to generate some or all of their own electricity in a variety of ways. A growing number of customers, ranging from factories to schools and large residential complexes, may arrange to co-generate electricity while simultaneously churning out heat that can be used directly.

Suppose, however, that you are the chief financial officer of a company responsible for *generating* and/or *selling* electricity. Then, projecting fixed and variable costs before undertaking a new project becomes much more complex.

It is easy enough to say that electricity from coal-fueled plants in the United States costs a certain amount in dollars to produce each kilowatt hour and gas-fired units cost a different amount, but that may have relatively little to do with reaching the most prudent decision (purely on the basis of cost) about whether to build a new coal plant or a bank of gas turbines—assuming that either choice would be capable of generating the amount of power needed and either one could be approved by local authorities.

Much depends on where generation will take place, because transporting either the primary energy input or the electricity output adds expense. Some fossil-fuel plants can be built immediately adjacent to long-term sources of fuel—for example, next to a reliable gas pipeline or in a port that handles bulk shipments of coal. Some large wind farms were developed in California earlier than most places, not only because Californians have long been proponents of clean, renewable energy but because large open areas were accessible with what seemed like suitable wind characteristics in proximity to markets for the electricity they would generate. The ultimate example of bringing source and end-use close together lies in *distributed generation*. Rather than build a limited number of central station power plants to provide service over large areas, increasing amounts of electricity are being produced at the point of use. Rooftop installations of photovoltaic cells are a common example.

DO WE PAY NOW OR LATER?

Just as basic a factor as location is the relative importance of the capital investment needed to build or install generation capacity versus subsequent operating costs, including fuel. In this respect there is an ironic similarity between two broadly different sources of electricity: a coal-burning power plant and a field of wind turbines. Neither supporters nor critics of these two potential competitors might dwell on this parallel, but construction costs in each case are relatively high. They are both generally higher, for example, than those for a combustion turbine of similar capacity fueled with natural gas. The economic payoffs for both coal and wind must come over the long haul. The primary energy input for coal plants has traditionally been less expensive than that for gas on the basis of heat content, while wind comes without a fuel charge at all. The question is: Is it worth digging deeper into one's resources "up front" to enjoy what *might* eventually be an attractive total return?

This is a familiar dilemma in decisions about energy. The same purely economic principles apply to an individual's choice between purchasing a fuel-efficient hybrid auto or buying a more conventional vehicle that guzzles gasoline but otherwise provides comparable comfort, performance and style.

Many considerations besides cost enter into a choice between coal and wind. A variety of them will be taken up in subsequent chapters: reliability, environmental effects, and factors of timing. Practical size in kilowatts and megawatts of capacity (and in kilowatt-hours or megawatt-hours per year of generation output) has already been mentioned as an aspect of "adequacy." Sensible *balance* calls for taking all these into account. Yet even in the "simple" matter of energy costs—which inevitably affects energy prices at some point—more questions need to be asked.

Mathematical techniques for comparing lifetime costs are available in almost any introductory economics text. The problem with applying them to energy is that shorthand cost comparisons in the popular press—and even in some technical publications—rarely offer enough detail about how they were derived to provide a fair evaluation. A more serious analysis has to go deeper:

1. How long will electricity continue to be generated by either type of installation? Coal plants inherently might keep chugging away for more than half a century. Wind farms might last that long too, although data on such longevity have yet to be established.

2. What will be the long-term costs of operation and maintenance?

3. How much electricity will actually be generated and sold during whatever period is chosen for the calculation? Since price differentiation based on electricity demand at the times of sales will continue to be sharpened, the projection of revenues can become very complex.

4. How firm are advance electricity supply contracts or other purchase arrangements? What's their duration?

5. Subsidies or penalties will almost surely be involved, even though they will be almost impossible to predict for the entire lifetime of generating units. Can wind count on governmental support indefinitely? Will coal be subject to environmental taxes in some form?

6. Estimates of future inflation rates fit into the risk assessments for any investment, and energy prices have been more volatile than those in other parts of the economy. Will labor rates rise enough to make much difference?

7. A flock of more or less common accounting questions also arise: What discount rate should be used in either case to measure the net present value of future income? Over what period can an initial capital investment be depreciated for tax purposes?

8. Finally, what else might be done with the construction or purchase funds? What is the "opportunity cost" of either short-term or long-term earnings elsewhere?

The dollars-and-cents economic choice between coal and wind is only one of many being made currently in the energy field. Similar decisions present themselves in respect to biofuels, to the search for and production of unconventional gas and oil, and even to revolutionary proposals for shifting away entirely over time from energy sources that emit gases that could damage the environment. At the personal level they may extend far beyond that selection of either a hybrid car or a less expensive conventional vehicle. They could include backfitting buildings or replacing equipment to provide greater energy efficiency. Along with all the other criteria for energy-related expenditures, we would prefer that they be "cost effective." The trouble comes with trying to define that term.

SOCIETY MAY INSIST ON HIGHER PRICES, BUT WITHOUT SAYING SO

Trying to keep multiple energy objectives in mind simultaneously may lead to frustration at first, because feedbacks among them can take place in almost any direction. When the U.S. government set a course to bring thirty-six billion gallons of ethanol to market here annually by 2022 there was no intention of raising food prices (another part of every family's budget) by diverting substantial amounts of corn into fuel production, yet that is exactly what happened. It is easy enough for a politician to challenge the country to switch its entire generating system to non-carbon-emitting sources within a decade. But, aside from all the other practical impossibilities this would involve, the immediate burden to rate payers from simply scrapping more than half the existing assets of public and private utilities throughout the United States appears nowhere in the happy litany that jobs will be created and stable prices will somehow appear at the end of the road. Those who boost the production of more domestic oil and gas from deep offshore waters and from Arctic frontiers rarely note at the same time that more expensive production and delivery methods must be covered somehow by higher prices.

Regardless of difficulty, however, this country is moving in the direction of incorporating additional costs in energy bills, and the American people may well decide that this is in the overall national interest. "Internalizing externalities" will be discussed more fully in subsequent chapters (specifically in Chapter 5, in connection with environmental protection, and Chapter 8 in more general fashion).

Even energy conservation efforts can yield conflicting price results, despite the fact that reducing energy intensity is probably the most economical and broadly beneficial policy we might pursue. In particular, there is something known as the "efficiency paradox." A concerted rollback in U.S. energy consumption should decrease energy prices by lowering the *entire* demand curve; but, by definition, people are inclined to consume more as soon as energy—or any other commodity—grows more affordable. If inflation-adjusted gasoline prices were cut in half over a few years, it might be hard to keep up resolve on efficiency—which still would carry many benefits. Perhaps it is just as well that we recognize energy supply and demand as many-faceted elements of economy and society.

It is especially easy to confuse causes and effects in regard to any end user's utility bills for either natural gas or electricity. The reason is the way PUCs establish rate schedules, a matter treated further in Chapter 7 on the topic of energy policy and its economic implications. There are many variations, but the bulk of a bill from any regulated utility is usually based on the long-term and many short-term costs to the provider, with the addition of a "target" rate of return on investment (all as overseen by the regulators). Because fuel prices have been volatile for decades, however, a "fuel adjustment charge" is also included. This is supposed to pass through costs over which the gas or electricity supplier are deemed to have little control. Unfortunately, however, each rate schedule has to be approved in advance and may remain in effect well after conditions have changed drastically—even with this attempt at keeping things up to date. Furthermore, when a combination of circumstances caused costs to rise precipitously a few years ago some utility commissions ordered companies to delay for many years bringing new rates into effect. The end-result then was sudden rises in base rates that coincided with unusually high fuel adjustments. Many a poor homeowner who had scrupulously invested in making house, equipment, and habits more efficient and conservation-conscious was rewarded with coincidental rate increases that seemed to wipe out any potential savings.

There is no obvious solution to such problems, and better understanding of energy pricing won't eliminate understandable complaints. Nevertheless, the composition of prices ought to be made as "transparent" as possible. Energy suppliers would do themselves a favor by making their own cost-breakdowns as transparent as possible as well.

The most important principle to take away from this chapter is just that many factors influence cost—and thus price. This doesn't mean that energy suppliers all along the line won't do what they can to maximize their own profits. Nor does it mean that consumers shouldn't be alert to spot price-gouging in the relatively rare instances when it may occur. But competition in the market works quite well overall at both the wholesale and retail levels where it gets a chance, especially in the mid- to long-term.

NOTES

1. Home heating oil is similar to diesel motor fuel, and they can be used interchangeably. In the United States, however, diesel fuel is taxed to provide revenue for highway maintenance. This tax is waived for such applications as boats, farm tractors, and utility vehicles that are not intended for use on the open road, and such fuel is subject to less rigid restrictions on sulfur content than what is used in trucks, buses, and autos. The untaxed fuel is dyed red, and misuse of it on streets and highways can bring five-digit fines.

2. "Pumped storage" uses surplus electricity when demand is low to pump water back up into a reservoir. Gravity will bring it back down again later so that it can pass through a turbine once more to generate power as it is needed. This and other energy

storage techniques will be discussed in connection with ensuring reliability of supply (Chapter 4).

3. Recall that one million Btus of natural gas is roughly equivalent to 1000 cubic feet of the fuel. This is a unit of measurement you may see on your utility bill.

4. EIA, *International Energy Outlook 2007*, Chapter 3, Table 3, and Chapter 4, Table 6 (using conversions by the author). Hereafter cited as *IEO 2007*. The O&GJ document referenced in each case is *Worldwide Look at Reserves and Production*.

5. *IEO 2007*, calculated from Tables A6 and A5.

6. Some countries turn natural gas into LNG without removing most of the natural gas liquids. After such LNG is regasified here in the States its combustion characteristics make it unsuitable for use in U.S. cooking and heating equipment because its energy content is so high, and it must be treated to lower its Btu content to meet U.S. pipeline standards. It may be diluted with "dry gas" or an inert gas, or the NGLs may be stripped out and utilized separately. In either case, the extra step or steps affect the net cost of this imported gas slightly.

7. Although this had been my own personal estimate, I subsequently discovered a similar conclusion in a publication by the Federal Reserve Bank of Dallas—Stephen P. A. Brown, Raghav Virmani, and Richard Alm, "Crude Awakening: Behind the Surge in Oil Prices," *Economic Letter: Insights from the Federal Reserve Bank of Dallas,* vol. 3, No. 5, May 2008. According to those authors, "If the U.S. currency had held its 2001 value against the euro, oil would have traded at about $80 in early 2008, about $21 below its actual price."

8. Tax Foundation at http://www.taxfoundation.org. In Georgia, gasoline is also charged a 4 percent sales tax on each purchase, so Alaska's flat 8 cents per gallon may also justly claim being the lowest of the 50 states.

9. Ariana Eunjung Cha, "Oil Shock: China's Cars, Accelerating a Global Demand for Fuel," *Washington Post*, July 28, 2008.

10. Throughout this discussion, gasoline has been treated as if it were the only vehicle fuel being used. This simplification does not affect the ideas expressed. For the record, however, diesel-fueled vehicles on U.S. streets and highways are responsible for about 2.5 million barrels per day of the petroleum we consume. Most U.S. trucks and many buses use diesel, and the fuel's popularity in lighter vehicles has increased—although not nearly as much as in Europe. Ethanol has been pushed as a supplementary U.S. vehicle fuel and its output has increased more rapidly than was earlier projected, but the 6.5 billion gallons of ethanol produced in this country during 2007 was still the volumetric equivalent of less than half a million barrels per day of petroleum. It actually replaced less than that, because its energy content is lower than either gasoline or diesel fuel.

11. In June 2008 the Commodity Futures Trading Commission (CFTC) formed an interagency task force to examine the influence on oil prices by speculators (that is, non-commercial traders who are not themselves consumers or producers, and who thus apparently regard the paper contracts themselves as the subjects of investment). Its interim report, issued in July 2008, concluded tentatively that most speculative traders typically alter their positions *after* price changes—suggesting that up until then at least they had been followers rather than leaders or drivers.

12. Paul Horsnell, "The Dynamics of Oil and Price Determination," *Oxford Energy Forum*, Issue 71, November 2007.

13. The statistics appeared in September 2008 in a section of the company website entitled "capital investments to meet future energy needs," http://www.exxonmobil .com/Corporate/Images/Corporate/enlarged_global_cap_investment.jpg.

Four

Reliability of Supply

Americans are so complacent about the day-to-day reliability of our energy supply that we tend to forget reliability is an implicit policy goal. When we flick a light switch, in Pittsburgh or Pine Bluffs, we take for granted that the power will come from somewhere to provide illumination. When a U.S. motorist stops at a filling station, the assumption is that the pumps will dispense fuel in response to the proffer of cash or a credit card.

Yet the reliability of our energy supply is not automatic, either in the short term or the long term. We can distinguish it in the energy mobile from overall adequacy and cost. Reliability has more to do with assurance that the system *works*, particularly in respect to delivery of energy from suppliers to consumers whenever it is called for. Almost anything that prevents supply and demand from matching up interferes with reliability. Negative factors that we need especially to watch for range from geography to geopolitics, from maintenance to monopoly.

Third World countries find energy reliability particularly elusive because elements of internal infrastructure such as their electricity networks are often basically deficient. The reliability of natural gas supplies for some European countries has also been troublingly uncertain at times, because so much of that fuel has reached them from a single supplier (Russia) via pipelines that must traverse intermediate countries that can add further problems. In our own country, temporary shortages of gasoline have sometimes cropped up locally because refineries were unable for some reason to keep up with variations in the formulas mandated on a state-by-state basis—a purely regulatory problem that is unlikely to be resolved without firm federal preemption. And most North American adults can remember when failure to keep trees trimmed along an electric powerline right-of-way in Ohio initiated an extraordinary cascade of problems in August 2003 that blacked out large areas of both the U.S. upper tier and Canada for days.

The United States should be aware that our own enviable network of pipe-lines, power lines, and arrangements for receiving whatever imports we count on deserves attention. Internationally, the imperative of reliability is one of the reasons for keeping our sources and supply routes for oil diversified. Domesti-cally, a key to our success in ensuring a high degree of reliability for all forms of energy has been the combination of generally sensible regulation and a reasonable degree of cooperation.

End-users of energy normally have little direct control over reliability of supply, except to complain when they lose it. Yet consumers may share some blame themselves, simply because they are not accustomed to considering relationships within the energy system and accepting some balance among goals to get consensus.

Building in reliability involves costs, and not always just dollar costs. Oc-casionally, reliability may be best served by making some compromises with comfort, convenience, and an absolutely pristine environment. This is not a popular idea. It is equally difficult to admit that there are degrees of reliability, and that the people for whom a given project or policy improves reliability may not be the same as those asked to give up something to carry it through. Reaching agreement may necessitate what economists call "side payments." Politicians call it horse trading. An example that fits either term is the increase in jobs and tax revenue that *sometimes* finally overcomes the NIMBY ("Not in My Back Yard") syndrome when it comes to the siting of new energy facilities and infrastructure.

Finger-pointing isn't the answer. To decide what choices are relevant in mak-ing the system work, we need to understand more about how various energy supply systems operate. This chapter's ambitious assignment is to start the reader on the path to such understanding.

DIFFERENT SUPPLY CHAINS, DIFFERENT CHECKLISTS

U.S. supplies of petroleum, natural gas, and electricity operate within three quite different markets. In discussing reliability, these energy sources should be considered in three different contexts of delivery and distribution:

1. It cannot be mentioned too often that the oil market is global, although this coun-try is so large that potential *domestic* blockages rival the *international* threats to reliable delivery. Both domestic and international factors should be kept in mind.

2. The overwhelming majority of the natural gas consumed in the United States originates in North America. This will continue to be true, even as all three coun-tries on the continent increase their respective imports of liquefied natural gas.

3. Technically, the U.S. electrical network is interconnected from coast to coast, but it does not have a true national grid for electricity—although it comes closer than

other large countries. There is an Eastern Interconnection, a Western Interconnection, and a semi-isolated "reliability region" that covers most of Texas. In addition, back-and-forth trading in electricity goes on between the United States and Canada. That international volume is small as a percentage of either nation's total usage, but it is quite important for maintaining reliability, as well as for keeping costs down and reducing adverse environmental impacts to some extent.

CONDUITS TO WORLDWIDE HYDROCARBON SUPPLIES

Table 4.1 lists the major national sources of U.S. petroleum imports during the first nine months of 2007, distinguishing between supplies of crude oil and refined petroleum products. Two-thirds of the liquefied natural gas (LNG) imported during the same period came from Trinidad and Tobago, a tiny country off the coast of Venezuela, with the rest imported from Nigeria, Algeria, and Qatar (in that order). LNG made up one-sixth of all U.S. imports of natural gas, but this LNG provided only a little more than 3 percent of the *total* U.S. gas supply.

Geography dictates that natural gas pipelines connect the United States with only our two closest neighbors, Canada and Mexico. Canada has customarily sold us eight to ten times as much of that fuel as we buy from it, and for many years has supplied about one-sixth of all the gas we consume. An increasing number of gas pipelines along our southern border are being designed to let fuel flow in either direction, and Mexico has provided minuscule

TABLE 4.1
Top 12 Sources of U.S. Petroleum Imports

Country	Total Imports	Crude Oil	Refined Products
Canada	2434	1865	569
Mexico	1565	1431	134
Saudi Arabia*	1462	1428	34
Venezuela*	1354	1123	131
Nigeria*	1085	1038	47
Algeria*	732	509	223
Angola*	544	530	14
Iraq*	494	494	None
Russia	414	125	289
US Virgin Islands	333	None	333
United Kingdom	289	103	186
Ecuador*	205	200	5

Thousand Barrels per day, average for first 9 months of 2007.

*Denotes membership in OPEC.

amounts to the U.S. market; but since the 1980s it has been a net importer of natural gas *from us*.

How "reliable" are the various foreign sources of hydrocarbon fuels?

Canada and Mexico, our largest fuel suppliers in recent years, are extremely reliable. In fact, Canada and the United States are mutually bound by Chapter 6 of NAFTA to do their utmost not to disrupt the bilateral energy trade, even if restrictions have to be imposed for any reason on their respective domestic consumption. Critics of the treaty fuss a lot over this "proportionality clause," but it is unlikely to ever be tested. It serves primarily as a good faith pledge that contractual arrangements will be respected. Some new receiving facilities for LNG in both neighboring countries—but relatively close to the U.S. border—have been planned with the intention of reexporting part of the gas imported by Mexico and Canada to the United States, and this was a factor in justifying the heavy capital investments involved. Hydrocarbon production from conventional sources in both Canada and Mexico has been declining, but this raises questions of continental energy *adequacy* rather than reliability. North America's friendly "energy interdependence" is in good shape, and it promises to continue that way.

The situation with other international suppliers is not as rosy, and it is more susceptible to adverse change. Petroleum production in Venezuela dropped and that country became precarious as a supplier after authoritarian President Hugo Chavez politicized its previously efficient national oil company and began to rant about withdrawing from the U.S. energy market. We have also been concerned for decades about the possibility of some sweeping political transformation in Saudi Arabia that could cut off our ability to tap the welcome productivity of Earth's largest oil reservoir there. As far back as the late 1970s, I recall Deputy Secretary of Energy Jack O'Leary worrying aloud about what he called "the actuarial projections for *any* feudal monarchy in today's world."

Such intermittent or ongoing concerns affect the "risk premium" in oil prices mentioned in Chapter 3. Since oil is a generally fungible global commodity, however, the question for this chapter is not just how securely we can rely on our current suppliers to keep up deliveries to us. It is the degree to which a sufficient number of barrels will reach the world oil market *as a whole* to satisfy apparent demand. This depends not only on the existence of resources and reserves—the issue of adequacy again—but on capabilities and attitudes of all those countries that can export oil.

HOW DOES OPEC FUNCTION?

The economic *raison d'être* for the Organization of Petroleum Exporting Countries (see Table 4.2 for a list of OPEC's members) is to optimize monetary

TABLE 4.2
Members of OPEC

Algeria	Iraq	Saudi Arabia
Angola	Kuwait	United Arab Emirates
Ecuador*	Libya	Venezuela
Indonesia†	Nigeria	
Iran	Qatar	

*Ecuador quit OPEC in 1992 but rejoined in 2007.
†Indonesia has been a net petroleum *importer* since 2004 and withdrew from formal membership as of January 1, 2009.

returns to its members by adjusting the level of its combined exports to affect oil prices around the world. OPEC's total oil production at the beginning of 2008 represented about 40 percent of global output.[1] For the time being, OPEC's exports represent almost the same percentage of all the oil that enters international trade. Domestic consumption of oil has been fairly low in most of the member countries, although this is finally changing as GDP increases within OPEC and internally subsidized prices there do little to encourage conservation.

OPEC's share of oil supply does not constitute a monopoly, but it *does* provide enormous market power—that is, a perceptible ability to influence prices within the entire market. The organization does not try to control production by individual members, but it does assign quotas for exports. The overall OPEC export target and the country-by-country quotas are adjusted periodically by consensus, although waivers are sometimes given.[2] Also, some members cheat on their quotas consistently. To gain added revenue, they export more than they are "allowed to."

In general, OPEC members with relatively limited reserves and resources are interested in maximizing short-term returns, so they tend to be price hawks. They instinctively resist any increase in *official* overall exports. At the same time they may fear that high prices will not continue indefinitely. They are tempted to monetize their hydrocarbon holdings quickly—that is, turn them into cash—by exceeding their quotas. Because of such vagaries alone, OPEC as a whole cannot be considered a reliable source for the world market—even if constant dangers from political instability did not also threaten some members.

OPEC cannot fine-tune world prices. Especially in the short run, it has been more successful at raising prices than curbing them. This has been especially true in recent years, when demand has risen sharply on the crest of rapid economic expansion by population giants such as China and India while conventional oil production was tapering off. With most producers already operating at full throttle, the demand squeeze has left most countries—in and out of OPEC—lacking in *any* spare production capacity to call on quickly. Around the end of 2007, excess capacity was estimated at not much more than 2 million barrels per day—while more than 85 million barrels of crude per day were being consumed worldwide. Virtually all of that spare capacity was in Saudi Arabia, although a few analysts believe that the Saudis' estimates of their own capabilities were exaggerated.[3]

GEOPOLITICS CAN TRUMP ECONOMICS

Saudi Arabia is a unique player within OPEC, and not only because it holds one-fifth of the world's acknowledged reserves. For all its wealth and nearly absolute domestic control, the Saudi monarchy recognizes its own vulnerability. There is surely some point at which high prices could persuade importers of oil to restrict their appetites for the commodity; but if this resulted in a pronounced downturn in demand, Saudi Arabia could be left with a suddenly fast-depreciating asset. Even more frightening to the Saudis is the prospect of an incursion from jealous neighbors, a possibility that Saddam Hussein came close to realizing with his brief occupation of Kuwait. Iran remains a threat because of Persian-Arab antipathies that go back centuries in a region where historic enmities probably never disappear completely.

Craving stability, Saudi Arabia has repeatedly acted as the "swing producer" within OPEC. It has reduced its own production and exports of oil at times to temper oil gluts that were forcing prices too low to satisfy some other members. On the other hand, it has stepped up production on occasions when that could forestall threats to the economic health of major long-term customers—particularly the United States. The Saudis feel they need the protective umbrella of U.S. military force. They wish this country to keep on functioning as an engine of global economic growth. Saudi leaders feel it is vital for their country to maintain a solid position within the U.S. market as one of its top direct suppliers, and they have been willing to swallow the extra transport costs of bringing oil to our shores instead of seeking a higher net payback by exporting to some other customers.[4]

Friendliness or hostility on the part of countries that supply oil to the United States sometimes figure into public debates here about national energy policy, although the arguments do not always rest on economics and logic. Longstanding U.S. economic sanctions against Libya and Iran were undoubtedly aimed at limiting the military capabilities of those members of the original "Axis of Evil," but they would have had to stifle their oil exports to be effective. This in itself would have been contrary to U.S. energy interests, as expressed frequently by our exhortations to OPEC to *step up* exports whenever world prices seemed to be getting too high for our comfort. In fact, both countries succeeded in finding oil customers who ignored the U.S. legislation. Iran will be able to continue going around this fruitlessly selective quasi-embargo, just as we found ways of making the Arab oil embargo futile—except to increase prices marginally. Even if we choose an "us versus them" strategy in world energy trade, it is good to keep in mind that the countries that suffer most from high oil prices are those who *must* import energy—including some valued military allies as well as poor Third World nations that are simply caught in a squeeze.

From the standpoint of investment efficiency as well as reliability, the optimal situation for the United States would be one of *stable* world oil prices. That broadens the definition of "energy security" to include both suppliers and net consumers. The price-volatility displayed in Figure 4.1 shows that this has been hard to achieve for extended periods. No magic solution for achieving it in the future is yet in sight, although serious talks between the Organisation for Economic Cooperation and Development (OECD) and OPEC might be a start—especially if China and India realized that it was in their self-interests to join in.

FIGURE 4.1
Ups and Downs of Nominal World Oil Prices, 1983–2008

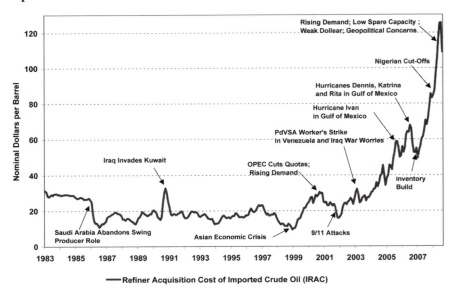

Source: Energy Information Administration.

NON-OPEC COUNTRIES

Roughly 60 percent of the world's oil originates each year *outside* OPEC. However, the list of petroleum-*producing* nations would be somewhat different today if it were not for a few forcing factors: (1) the "energy crises" of the 1970s, (2) intermittently but inexorably rising prices since then, and (3) the booming world economy that pumped up energy usage over time. Doubts about the reliability of oil supply have spurred exploration in some countries and parts of countries that otherwise would still be untouched, and that trend will continue. Technologies that once would have been too expensive to consider developing now see through layers of salt beneath the sea floor to find what have become commercially exploitable resources. They penetrate miles of water and ocean-bed to reach them. Unhesitatingly, they track deposits horizontally as well as vertically to maximize the hydrocarbons extracted from a given well.

Angola, Brazil, Colombia, Norway, and the United Kingdom expanded production notably in response to the initial OPEC challenge. In 1973, OPEC countries had been responsible for a slight majority of the world's output of crude, and for the next few years it was nip-and-tuck between OPEC and the rest. Then, between 1980 and 1985, non-OPEC production rose steadily, while OPEC accepted a lower share of the global market by lowering its own exports in an effort to keep prices within an acceptable range on some higher plateau. After the oil-price drop of the mid-1980s, however, it appeared that the rich natural endowment of the OPEC countries on average would ultimately enable the organization to make all but the lowest-cost producers in the rest of the world noncompetitive in purely economic comparisons. To the extent that OPEC could limit its own export total, the marginal cost of oil for the world market would be set in the mid- to long run by suppliers who sold the final barrels needed to meet demand—and thus at a generally higher price level. That situation is likely to continue, even if the major oil-consuming countries manage to reduce the growth rate for their imports through a variety of actions. That is how supply and demand works.

The responses of non-OPEC countries involved some difficulties. Even the unanticipated wealth from minerals development has at times produced side problems. The classic instance was The Netherlands, where discoveries of natural gas unbalanced the economy and inflation soaked up abundant inflows of money. Some sectors of society suffered while others enjoyed windfalls. Economists quickly christened that phenomenon "Dutch disease." Today the area around Fort McMurray in Alberta, Canada, is feeling similar effects from the success of oil-sand resources.

Canada was slower than some other countries to develop gas and oil exports because of a focus for years on energy self-sufficiency alone, but once its successful exchanges with the United States proved the value of free trade, steady progress took place in developing production in areas that had been ignored or only partially tapped. Offshore drilling ventures multiplied off both its east and west coasts. Large-scale production from Alberta's oil sands transformed that source into the locus of proved reserves that are exceeded only by those in Saudi Arabia, rocketing Canada by 2006 into seventh place in the world for current output. Because Canada is also the seventh largest oil consumer, however, it still ranked only fifteenth in oil exports—behind Russia, Norway, Mexico, and nearly a dozen OPEC countries (see Table 1.1). Canada's oil export capacity is expected to increase as oil sands production climbs within a few years to twice what it is now or more, assuming that lingering environmental problems can be solved (see Chapter 5).

Mexico was slower than Canada in developing oil exports toward the end of the twentieth century, and at this point its largest fields in the Gulf of Mexico are trailing off rapidly. Mexico's constitution has forbidden the use of private risk capital in either looking for or producing oil or natural gas. Unlike Brazil and Norway, Mexico's state oil company (Pemex) has not been allowed by the government to invest adequately in either fresh exploration or down-stream petroleum activities, such as refining and chemical production. Instead, Pemex has been used as a "cash cow"—providing nearly 40 percent of all federal revenues. As of 2006 Mexico was still the sixth largest oil producer in the world, but maintaining that position will depend on energy liberalization reforms that President Felipe Calderón hoped to press in 2008 and 2009, before reaching the mid-point of the single six-year presidential term the constitution allows. Unless Pemex becomes more efficient and better financed, Mexico itself could become a net importer of crude oil within a few years;[5] the second largest non-OPEC source of U.S. imports would dry up.

WILL OPEC GROW OR SHRINK?

OPEC's own membership is not static. Ecuador withdrew as of December 31, 1992. Exactly two years later, so did Gabon. Some Brazilians, whose country in 2007 and 2008 reported enormous new finds of hydrocarbons in deep offshore fields that should make it a significant exporter by 2015, co-quettishly implied that Brazil might find association with OPEC useful. That seems implausible, and such suggestions are grounded more in geopolitics and ideology than economic analysis.

Both geopolitics and ideology offer partial explanations of why we do not expect Canada or Mexico—our two top suppliers of oil—to join OPEC either. Nevertheless, whatever the factors are in determining how much petroleum enters world commerce in the years ahead—or how much of a "call" on that supply is made by growing Asian economies—the *reliability* of supply to the United States will be at stake.

RELIABILITY AND DOMESTIC DISTRIBUTION

The second largest producer of petroleum outside OPEC is the United States itself, ranking only behind Russia. The infrastructure of pipelines, railroad tank-cars, and trucking our nation has developed to move oil and refined products around in response to market demand is comprehensive and well maintained. Yet problems of reliable delivery exist domestically, and they are apt to get worse before they lessen.

The weakest link is in our refineries. Aside from the fact that they require multibillion-dollar investments to build, refineries are not generally considered desirable neighbors. They occupy large tracts of land, and only a career chemical engineer might consider one aesthetically pleasing. Proximity to them can depress residential and some commercial property values. Refineries pose *some* threat of fire and explosions, although statistically the perception of danger to the general population might be discounted. Like all critical links in the energy chain, they could be targets for terrorists—although experience worldwide suggests that concentrations of people seem to be a greater attraction. Finally, as with any large industrial installation, a proposed refinery is justifiably challenged to prove that it will not pollute adjacent land, atmosphere, or water supplies. The accompanying public environmental hearings often magnify initial opposition, regardless of how many expert witnesses testify favorably for the applicant. The result is that no major "greenfield" refinery—that is, one slated for a brand-new site rather than as an enlargement or replacement of an existing facility—has appeared in the United States since the mid-1970s.

It's true that many small, older refineries have been abandoned, and occasionally someone will suggest that U.S. refiners purposely restrict output to limit supply—*à la* OPEC. On its face, a charge of that sort bears investigation, but the argument is specious. Total refining capacity has continued to expand on consolidated sites to match growing demand. Economies of scale and requirements for environmental protection systems that could not be backfitted in many cases have apparently only reduced the *number* of U.S. refineries. In some cases, this might have lengthened distribution lines. Fewer supply centers for refined products also make the consequences more serious if a single installation has to shut down for any reason.

We are better off without obsolete or uneconomical installations. The problem is that overall now we lack spare refining capacity to call on if any unusual circumstances arise. Furthermore, refineries are not positioned optimally around the country. Historically, petroleum refineries have been concentrated geographically—either near sources of crude oil, in proximity to major end-use markets, or both. They are clumped together along our coasts and waterways, including the Great Lakes. Failure to build on new, more dispersed sites has exposed an uncomfortably large segment of refining capacity to potential interruptions from uncontrollable natural events such as hurricanes and flooding along the Gulf of Mexico.

INTERCHANGEABILITY OF PRODUCTS

Chapter 3 mentioned—in connection with cost increases—that changes have taken place in the typical composition of crude oil supplies available today. Far more crude is now very viscous and high in sulfur. Combined with limited spare refining capacity, this shift in feedstock quality also affects the reliability of supply for finished petroleum products. Fewer options exist when one has to direct flows selectively to and from refineries that are properly equipped to handle the heavy, sour stuff.

Another problem has been the multiplication of local regulations on specific formulas that must be followed in motor fuel to be sold within different jurisdictions. The intentions of such rules are good—usually to minimize the release of combustion compounds responsible for air pollution. However, complications arise when adjacent areas insist on slightly different recipes to accomplish the same purpose. U.S. filling stations are compelled by disparate laws to handle a total of several dozen different "boutique fuels," depending on the point of retail sale, so gasoline becomes no more or less of a perfectly fungible commodity than crude oil. One refinery cannot quickly adjust if another is "down" for any reason, and normally reliable supply is harder to ensure.

Overall, the increasing difficulties in handling domestic transportation of crude oil and refined petroleum products are comparable to the international predicaments a country invites by failing to consider a diversity of foreign sources for its energy imports.

The Canadian oil sands are a North American energy blessing. They are an enormous resource, situated in a politically stable country that is disposed toward open trade. By some time in the next decade, their 2007 production of more than a million barrels a day could triple. Yet the heterogeneous nature of their product brings new dilemmas that have only begun to be solved. They come from the fact that more and more emphasis will be given to extracting useful petroleum products *in situ*—that is, converting the energy-rich solid mixtures that exist naturally into material that will flow *before* bringing it to the surface. Eventually, resource geologists say that four-fifths of the oil sands can be best accessed in this fashion. This eliminates the environmental headaches caused by excavating prodigious amounts of near-surface oil sands and overburden, then restoring the terrain over a period of years.

Several different *in situ* techniques have been developed, and all will probably continue in use—because none has yet been declared the clear winner. In the ground, the oil-sand resource resembles ordinary sand onto which somebody has dumped the contents of an automobile crankcase, resulting in a gooey solid. The general idea is at some point to use heat and diluents to produce a material capable of fluid motion. Specifically, however, the products of the various *in situ* processes differ considerably. One is simple bitumen, similar to asphalt. It can be diluted with lighter fractions of petroleum hydrocarbons to the point where it can be pumped through a conventional pipeline. Another winds up with a liquid resembling light, sweet crude. Obviously, the latter is easier to deal with, but—thus far at least—the process is harder and more expensive to carry through.

Canadians anxious to make the most of the oil sands have taken different tacks. Nations often prefer to add value to an indigenous raw material before exporting it, thus expanding both employment and total profit. For this reason, the Alberta government has offered special assistance to oil-sand producers who arrange to have the refining process completed within the province. But time is money too, and refineries take years to build, while some refining capacity suitable for processing bitumen already exists in the United States. With this in mind, an enterprising Canadian pipeline company pieced together one new route by reversing the flow in some stretches that already existed, acquiring other links, and installing some crucial connections. Presto! Diluted bitumen itself was quickly headed south, all the way to Texas. Other companies have followed suit with similar ideas. Some Albertan bitumen will be processed in other U.S. sites closer to the Canadian border. The exact locations will have a bearing on reliability of supply as well as adequacy and cost.

WHAT ABOUT ALTERNATIVE FUELS?

One way to address problems of both petroleum adequacy and reliable petroleum supply could be to replace conventional motor fuels entirely with something else. The principal alternatives that have been discussed in the United States for the past 30 years or so include ethanol, methanol, compressed natural gas (CNG),[6] rechargeable batteries, fuel cells of various types, and an assortment of ideas for hybrids. Visions of a "hydrogen economy" also continue to be evoked.

The situation today is reminiscent of the outlook faced by U.S. vehicular transportation slightly more than a century ago—although for totally different reasons.[7] In the early 1900s, Americans had begun to look forward to a nation in which passengers and freight might travel almost anywhere along roads rather than rails. They would use indefatigable "horseless carriages." Autos then variously employed steam, battery power, or diesel engines. Contending with them was yet another transportation contraption that relied on an internal combustion engine fueled by gasoline. That challenger had both pluses and minuses, but conventional wisdom saw one possibly insuperable disadvantage for it. There didn't appear to be enough crude oil in the entire country to refine into sufficient gasoline to satisfy a large car fleet.

We know now how that competition turned out. Large quantities of oil were discovered at Spindletop, in a part of Texas where geologists had been confident that little or none would ever be found in economical quantities. Geological theories were subsequently modified, the adequacy and reliability of gasoline sources were affirmed for the future, and the automotive age began.

Despite the hoopla about one alternative fuel or another, we do *not* know how the current competition among alternative vehicles will turn out. This could well be a see-saw race, but the next few sections of this chapter will explain the sorts of questions that should be raised as it proceeds.

COMPARING THE OPTIONS

Utilizing methanol[8] necessitates the use in vehicles' fuel systems of non-standard materials that this liquid will not corrode. This is merely a question of inconvenience and adjustment over time, rather than a debilitating problem. A more telling objection is that the only practical source of the necessary quantities of methanol today is natural gas—a primary energy source that already has *some* difficulties of its own matching demand for other applications. This caveat also relates to compressed natural gas, which additionally requires large and heavy fuel tanks that have proved feasible for buses and trucks but might never be fabricated economically in an appropriate size and weight for passenger cars. The availability of natural gas might also be a stumbling block for fuel cells that employ it, although the high efficiency and clean operation of fuel cells could tip the balance in their favor.

Hydrogen is yet another fuel that can be used in fuel cells, and fuel cells can in turn operate electric drives for a vehicle's wheels. Perhaps hydrogen alone might even be used more directly in some other system of surface propulsion that would fit U.S. transport requirements. But where would hydrogen fit into the system most practically? Although people talk about hydrogen as if it were a fuel comparable to gasoline, it is more accurately considered and examined as an intermediate source—*between* primary energy and end-use energy, as explained in connection with Figure 1.4.

Storing hydrogen on board a vehicle hasn't been ruled out completely by auto designers, but effective technology to do so is years from commercialization. Liquefied hydrogen must be stored at super-low temperatures, even colder than those that can keep natural gas in a liquid state. Hydrogen tanks that would work efficiently in autos involve more challenges than those for CNG. The same applies to various schemes that have been proposed for systems that would store hydrogen within a vehicle by uniting it with a metallic element in a compound called a hydride. The hydride would likely have to be heated to yield hydrogen in usable form, and that means a heat-source would have to be carried along too.

Hydrogen is the most abundant element in the universe, but it is not found as relatively free in nature on Earth as fossil fuels sometimes are. Hydrogen is highly reactive. It combines readily with oxygen from the atmosphere, and substantial energy is required to separate it from water (H_2O), methane (CH_4), or any other compound. As with methanol, there is thus also the question of how hydrogen fuel could be produced in volume if it is ultimately to be dispensed at filling stations. Whether production of hydrogen takes place by electrolysis or chemical reaction, a hefty input of either heat or electricity is required. Providing that input energy via solar or wind systems seems out of the question, since these relatively diffuse sources of primary energy are ill-equipped to produce the very large amounts needed and should probably be reserved to serving end-use consumers directly. Nuclear reactor plants might be suitably adapted to help in manufacturing hydrogen fuel, but the widespread deployment of enough new-generation nukes to create and sustain a hydrogen economy is surely decades away.

A comparable need to generate and dedicate enough extra electricity as the primary energy input to rechargeable batteries also complicates their widespread use in vehicles. The gigawatt-hours required are staggering if we contemplate using battery-stored electricity for any sizable part of nearly a quarter of a billion U.S. passenger cars, vans, pick-up trucks, and sport utility vehicles, plus roughly 90 million trucks and buses in the existing fleet.

ETHANOL AND RELIABILITY OF SUPPLY

By the process of elimination, it appears that the current favorites as replacements for gasoline and diesel fuels might have to be liquids that are chemically suitable in most ways, but can be produced from feedstock other than crude oil or natural gas. Ethanol and biodiesel are both contenders according to these criteria, but at the time this was written ethanol had caught the special fancy of Congress, many investors, and much of the public—to the point of being anointed by federal legislation.[9] Although multiple misgivings arose quickly and there were moves to roll back the decision, a 2007 statute decrees that 15 billion gallons of this specific fuel be marketed annually in the United States by 2015. A clause in the law also specified that by 2022 the minimum goal of "renewable" fuels in use[10] should rise to 36 billion gallons annually, with about 45 percent of that total being "cellulosic" ethanol rather than ethyl alcohol that has been derived either from ordinary sugar (the feedstock favored in Brazil) or sugars derived from corn (the base used widely in the United States to date).

The objective of the numerous cellulosic programs being pursued is to produce ethanol (C_2H_5OH) from biomaterials that can be acquired quickly and easily without prejudicing normal agricultural programs for food use—and, incidentally, causing prices for corn or sugar to soar accordingly because of increased demand. These non-food chemical-base materials could include the stalks from sugar or corn crops left in the field after harvest. Other sources might be forest wastes or even "energy plantations" of fast-growing trees such as hybrid poplars and easily tended energy crops of switchgrass or sunflowers. Based on lab results and pilot efforts, these could all be converted into ethanol or its building-blocks by enzymatic action rather than needing to rely entirely on heat and primary distillation.

Efforts are ongoing—in the United States, Canada, and around the world—to demonstrate that cellulosic ethanol can be produced efficiently on a massive scale to match oil refining. Predictions vary, but it is as likely that this will *not* occur before 2020 as it is that much more sanguine forecasts prove justified. The safest course will be to examine the numbers and assumptions carefully when someone first announces, "It's here!"

Legislators and lobbyists who successfully pushed the ethanol mandate were disingenuous in constantly using the measurement of billions of gallons per year rather than millions of barrels per day—the quantitative unit traditionally associated with national consumption of oil or refined products. As Chapter 1 took pains to point out, this is a common trick to make numbers sound more impressive. There is also the hitch that a gallon of ethanol packs only two-thirds as much energy as a gallon of gasoline. Some proponents claim that using mixtures of ethanol and gasoline in certain proportions might help overcome this shortcoming in part by optimizing combustion, but the preponderance of evidence is that the introduction of ethanol involves a perceptible performance penalty in miles per gallon.

Nevertheless, the ethanol ante has gradually been raised so high that bringing this much of the fuel to the market on the timetable established *would* have a large effect on the national supply-and-demand situation. Thirty-six billion gallons a year translates into approximately 2.5 million barrels per day. Allowing for qualitative differences, this much ethanol—regardless of its origin—would still be equivalent to something like one-fifth of the motor gasoline being used now by U.S. drivers. It could replace a lot of U.S. imports of crude oil.

BARRIERS TO GETTING THERE

It is far from certain that the 2022 target of 36 billion gallons will be reached, especially in respect to the subgoal for cellulosic ethanol. Let's leave aside for the moment that the environmental and total energy-saving contributions of a wholesale switch to ethanol invite skepticism (see Chapter 5). The two chief steps that must be resolved in respect to *reliability* of supply for ethanol are: (1) collection of feedstock, and (2) delivery and distribution of product.

There are logistical problems in assembling huge volumes of bulky material. They can be solved for a while at first by co-locating relatively small ethanol production facilities with their agricultural suppliers. Indeed, this has been an added selling-point in winning Farm Belt support for corn-based ethanol. The unofficial mantra is: More income for farmers, more jobs of a new type for the nearby community. Multiplying the initial collection task will be more difficult as output rises and efficiencies of scale compel the erection of larger processing facilities, since larger volumes and greater distances are bound to be involved. The end result will be more opportunities for interruption and less-reliable supply.

Delivering the ethanol product itself raises another, totally different issue. Commercial ethanol cannot use the pipelines that exist for crude oil and/or conventional refined petroleum products. Ordinarily, different grades of crude oil and different petroleum products move along the same pipeline, separated by dividers called "pigs" that move through the pipe. But ethanol absorbs moisture readily, and this would soon cause corrosion damage. That restricts ethanol transport to trucks and rail cars. A shortage of suitable rail cars already exists, and highways are already overcrowded. If ethanol production facilities continue to be widely dispersed and situated far from fuel consumption centers, the predicament will be exacerbated and there might be calls for a completely separate pipeline network—a really expensive and time-consuming endeavor.

There is also the "chicken-and-egg" problem, and this one will dog almost any of the new motor-fuel concepts. Drivers will be reluctant to buy new vehicles dedicated to the use of any energy source that is not convenient to acquire. Fuel suppliers are slow to introduce service locations for a new product unless the demand for that product has been guaranteed by a sufficient deployment of vehicles. Which comes first?

Flexible-fuel vehicles are one partial answer. The federal government has already offered incentives for the production and purchase of vehicles that can utilize some ethanol blends. Plug-in electrics are another response, although their actual convenience is still to be tested. The theory behind them is that most driving is done within short distances of home, so that an extended driving range is not a *sine qua non* for owners of battery-reliant cars who will be content to recharge from ordinary electrical outlets where they live or work. The plug-in hybrid is a more sophisticated solution. It conserves battery life by switching to another energy source—perhaps an ordinary gasoline or diesel engine—as appropriate during each trip.

It is easier for us to talk about these concepts than it will be for any of them to penetrate the U.S. market in sufficient numbers to make a profound difference. As we analyze the potential reliability of any, we should examine the infrastructure to support them as well as their inherent practicality. How long will a battery charge take, and how many recharges will it accept before break-ing down? If a totally new vehicle fuel of any sort is introduced, how far will I have to drive to say, "Fill 'er up!"?

California's "Hydrogen Highway Network" program is worth observing, both for its earnest ambition and its collisions with reality. In April 2004 Governor Arnold Schwarzenegger signed an executive order[11] designating 21 interstate highways as part of the network. He called on state agencies, legisla-tors, manufacturers, financing entities, NGOs, educators, and others to "plan and build a network of hydrogen fueling stations along these roadways and in the urban centers that they connect, so that by 2010, every Californian will have access to hydrogen fuel, with a significant and increasing percentage produced from clean and renewable sources."

Today California can boast that it has more fuel cell vehicles and hydrogen stations than any other region of the world, but it will not even come close to meeting the deadline. In mid-2008, with only 25 limited-access stations in place and only 200 fuel-cell vehicles on the state's roads, the California Fuel Cell Partnership"[12] described new 2008–2012 goals as a "rehearsal for com-mercial." The group's executive director cited "most reports" as agreeing that "hundreds of thousands of vehicles" would reach the market in the *2017–2025* timeframe, but added that "These should not be considered hard num-bers." Hydrogen fuel costs "in the early years" were projected at $8–13 per gallon equivalent (untaxed) and $4–6.50 on a mileage basis if FCVs per-formed with higher efficiency. The Partnership's website went on to say that hydrogen stations "will not be profitable and will, therefore, require govern-ment support."[13]

STOPGAPS VERSUS LONG-TERM MEASURES
IN TRANSPORTATION

Technological change does not adhere predictably to schedules. By the time you read this, some breakthrough may have occurred for one or more of the fuel alternatives discussed. A true crisis or a political fiat might have forced the inauguration of an Apollo-type program in one direction or another. In any case the change will not take place overnight, however, and not even within a single decade. That is one of the time dilemmas treated in Chapter 6.

Looking well beyond a few presidential terms, there is no *absolute* barrier to the possibility that by 2050 Americans could be moving about themselves and transporting goods via a *combination* of systems. Gasoline, diesel, alcohol fuels, batteries, hydrogen, fuel cells, and electric-drive could coexist. Mass transit, including magnetic levitation trains and unmanned interurban buses, might help—although only if truly gigantic public investments of capital and subsidies were authorized.

Economists tend to say that the most efficient solution will be to let the market decide. In the long run, our transportation future—a major part of our energy future—will depend on supply-and-demand. But the long-term equilibrium will not really be reached until all the other factors that go into policy and purchase decisions—adequacy, cost, and so on—are considered. Consumers and voters should keep in mind that reliability of supply deserves to be another important constituent in the decisions they reach if the "public good" is also their personal concern.

If and when cellulosic ethanol becomes available generally, many corn farmers who championed the cause of alcohol fuels will likely feel betrayed. Corn-based ethanol will probably no longer be competitive, especially since subsidies for it may have been phased out gradually by then. Corn prices would sink at the same time small corn-ethanol enterprises collapsed. Will anything useful have emerged from the nation's excursion along a blind alley? Perhaps! The flex-fuel autos that had been introduced would be useful for cellulosic ethanol as well. Even the beginnings of a nationwide network of service stations that handle ethanol blends would have advanced us toward solving the chicken-and-egg problem. The experiences of wrestling with the implementation of a totally new infrastructure should have equipped us to better cope with analogous energy challenges that could appear.

Evolving workable energy policy need not be a blame game. If we expect never to take a false step, we will be disappointed . . . or perhaps will never move at all.

ADEQUATE STORAGE CAN HELP RELIABILITY

Underlying any discussion of reliable supply for petroleum, petroleum products, and substitutes for them are our stored reserves.

Commercial storage forces decisions by industry to weigh risk and benefit in building them up and drawing down from them. Those decisions may be influenced less by fears of actually running short than by the anticipations of changes in spot-price and the movements of the futures markets.

Federally controlled reserves are more certain, although they have been utilized so rarely that their value is largely untested and uncertain. The attitude of most U.S. administrations, through that of George W. Bush, has been that crude oil in the Strategic Petroleum Reserve (SPR) should not be released to commercial buyers solely to curb excessive price rises, but only in cases where there has been an actual cutoff in adequate oil supplies. Natural disasters (such as Hurricanes Katrina and Ike) are cited as an example.

Underground caverns of the Strategic Petroleum Reserve, some manmade and some excavated, now hold about 700 million barrels of oil. This is almost their full capacity, and 60 percent of current holdings are "sour" (high-sulfur) crude. Congress has authorized the SPR to increase its capacity to 1 billion barrels, but it has not appropriated funds to make that possible. With prices as high as they were in 2007 and 2008, a number of legislators called for an end to any new purchases for SPR. A government Home Heating Oil Reserve, split between Connecticut and New Jersey, contains approximately two million barrels of that product. This has been intended since 2000 to provide approximately a 10-day emergency supply in case of a physical shortage in the Northeast region.[14]

If the SPR is ever required to meet a real crisis, Americans will realize that the very simple arithmetic used for years to assess its significance has been flawed. Dividing 700 million barrels by our daily imports of just over 10 million barrels is the careless formula used to describe it as a 70-day emergency supply. This is an inadequate calculation for several reasons: (1) The stored oil could not be pumped out at a rate even approaching 10 million barrels per day. We would be lucky if withdrawals started quickly and perhaps one-quarter of that rate could be maintained on a regular basis thereafter. (2) The SPR crude is of uneven quality and in some instances is a mixture of different grades. Locating suitable refining capacity for it as it is drawn out will be something of a nightmare. (3) At the same time, if circumstances were so grave as to prompt a rapid drawdown of the strategic reserves, measures would surely be taken to reduce demand. World oil prices would climb, and rationing might even be enforced—in the United States and perhaps elsewhere. The gap between domestic U.S. production and the nation's continuing consumption would fall to appreciably less than 10 million barrels a day. (4) The SPR is actually complemented by private oil storage. The exact total volume is uncertain because owners keep their numbers confidential for competitive reasons, but it has been estimated at times to equal or exceed the amount in the government reserve.

It is easy to joke about the past practice of having "bought high and sold low" to fill the SPR. It is sobering to consider the awkwardness that its utilization could involve. Still, it is far better to have it than not. Its existence provides an immediate fallback position against any malevolent attempt to cut off U.S. oil supplies, thus reducing the likelihood that such efforts will be pursued. To some tangible yet immeasurable extent, it contributes to the reliability of U.S. oil supply.

A NORTH AMERICAN GAS VISION

The United States overall is an extremely large gas producer itself, which explains why we can also afford to be the world's largest single consumer of this fuel. This country is second only to Russia in gas output. We produced 19.3 trillion cubic feet (tcf) in 2007, compared with Russia's production of slightly more than 23 tcf. But annual U.S. gas consumption in the same year was 23.1 tcf. This was more than that for all of Europe, excluding Russia. The 16.7 tcf of natural gas consumed in Russia is tabulated separately from Europe by the U.S. Energy Information Administration. Russia fits into the region EIA calls Eurasia.

It would be both nearsighted and shortsighted to appraise the reliability of U.S. supplies of natural gas by looking only at our domestic gas production. There are 55 gas pipelines along U.S. borders and 5 receiving facilities for liquefied natural gas, with prospects that LNG ports will double in this country within a few years and be augmented by some in Canada and Mexico on both coasts that plan to serve continental needs.

Through the first nine months of 2008 we were importing just over one-fifth of the natural gas we consumed, but 80 percent of those imports were being delivered by quite reliable pipelines from Canada. On the order of 10 percent of the gas brought in from Canada's west is really in transit, however. It exits farther east to meet the needs of more populous Canadian areas for which that country's domestic production along the Atlantic Coast does not suffice.

Alaska contains large and remote gas reserves that could also potentially be brought south. Promising Alaskan fields remain to be tapped; but, for lack of a continental pipeline, almost all of the gas produced there now is either consumed within the state or reinjected into wells to stimulate additional crude oil production. A little (only about 65 bcf a year) is exported to Japan as LNG. Delay much past 2015 of an Alaskan gas pipeline, as well as a Canadian one from the Mackenzie Delta in Canada's far north, could threaten reliable delivery from sources that will probably be needed by then.

In the late 1970s Mexico was considered a prime potential source of natural gas for the United States, but a dispute over price persuaded the Mexicans to direct their domestic production thereafter almost entirely to domestic use. In this century Mexico has been a net importer of natural gas from the United States, although Mexican gas production reached a record high in 2007 and the country hopes to become a net exporter through exploitation of hydrocarbon deposits in the Gulf—assuming that fiscal and energy investment reforms will permit the national oil company to devote the necessarily large capital and technological resources to that objective.

The delivery infrastructure for natural gas *within* the U.S. Lower 48 far surpasses any other. It comprises 300,000 miles of interstate and intrastate transmission pipelines; it is subject to regular inspections for integrity. There are nearly 400 underground facilities for natural gas storage, and 29 "hubs" or market centers make it possible to redirect supplies as needed to meet changing demand in different directions. Electronic marketing is monitored closely since the excesses of Enron and some other companies heightened regulatory alertness, and the ability to buy and sell gas all over the map enhances the efficiency of pipeline transport while reducing transfer costs and encouraging prices in the North American market to converge with marginal costs.

According to the EIA, "almost every major metropolitan area in the United States is supplied by, or is the final destination of, one or more of the major interstate pipeline companies or their affiliates."[15] Historic availability of natural gas throughout much of the country has developed gas-on-gas competition for consumers within different sectors. U.S. demand for natural gas is more price-elastic than demand for oil. Between 2001 and the end of 2007, the wellhead price of natural gas roughly doubled, while the world price of oil was more than quadrupling. Multiple factors could have been involved, but this suggests that price determination for natural gas here is primarily continental in origin. Also, the supply-and-demand system *works* for North American gas. When prices *did* rise sharply, a certain amount of "demand destruction" took place. U.S. industrial use of gas dropped between 2004 and 2007. Electric utilities that had routinely selected natural gas as the fuel for new generating units started to look more favorably for a while at coal-fired plants—despite apprehensions about stiffening environmental rulings and even the possibility of a carbon tax that would bring a sharp disadvantage to coal.

Much of the success for gas as a reliable energy source in this country should be ascribed to the close relationship among the three partners of the North American Free Trade Agreement, who have established a functioning North American Energy Working Group and more recently incorporated its activities into a broader, trilateral Security and Prosperity Partnership (SPP)—in which energy is perhaps a linchpin.[16] Domestic gas demand is growing in both Canada and Mexico, however, while production may have reached a plateau in all three interconnected countries. North American imports of LNG will increase, although not to the degree that some scare forecasts have projected.

FINALLY, ONE TECHNICAL GAS NOTE AND AN ECONOMIC ONE

It is common practice in liquefying natural gas to do so without going to the trouble of stripping out the natural gas liquids. This increases the energy content of imported LNG once it is regasified, but in the United States that is hardly a favor. It necessitates some extra processing before the imported gas can enter pipelines here.

U.S. heating units and other gas appliances are adjusted to burn "dry gas," with a slightly lower Btu rating. The regasified LNG may have to be diluted, sometimes even with an inert gas. This is a simple technical fix. It is less important than the one worrisome economic factor about upping LNG imports—exposure to international bidding for the product.

European Union nations are far more dependent on imports of gas—including LNG—than the United States is. They expect to grow even more so in the future, especially as natural gas replaces coal in increasing measure to hold down emissions of carbon dioxide—the major global warming gas by volume. Because Europeans artificially link natural gas prices to those for oil they are accustomed to paying higher prices for natural gas than we do, and receiving facilities along the U.S. Gulf coast have already had the unusual experience of being outbid for individual LNG cargoes.

At present, most of our gas receiving facilities are underutilized. This is not particularly troublesome, because the receiving facilities are the least capital-intensive link in an LNG supply chain, and thus it is not essential that they operate at full capacity continuously. Much heavier investments are required in the liquefaction plants and the specialized ocean-going transport vessels. LNG fills intermittent demand peaks. Underutilized receiving facilities can be considered "spare capacity" for bringing in future supply.

As long as LNG is counted on to supply no more than 10 or 15 percent of the total requirements of the United States and North America as a whole, it should not do more than establish a marginal cost for the fuel—which can be handled by an otherwise smoothly functioning supply-and-demand system. This should not detract from the overall reliability of natural gas supply.

ELECTRICITY AND INSTITUTIONALIZED RELIABILITY

Anybody who describes the United States as "a global superpower with a Third World electricity grid" just doesn't get it.[17] This country is the envy of the whole world for the degree to which it succeeds in keeping the lights on, computers operating, and the engines of industry turning. Nevertheless, the system has its challenges and shortcomings—with occasionally serious economic consequences.

Special problems associated with guaranteeing the reliability of electricity supply arise from the nature of the energy form itself. To understand the economic ramifications of being able to furnish electricity to consumers whenever and wherever it is required, we again need some slightly technical explanations.

With few exceptions,[18] electricity cannot be stored. Nor does it quite emulate natural gas, for which extra volumes can be "packed" into any given long-distance pipeline as "working gas" under higher pressure and gradually drained off to meet demand at various delivery points. The voltage of electricity is often described as analogous to pressure, and it is true that more electricity can be transmitted along cables of higher voltage. But there are severe practical limits to the *variations* in voltage that can be tolerated *within* cables of different ratings, such as 500,000 volts (500 kv), 345 kv, and 13 kv . . . or even the wires with which we are personally most familiar—220 volts for heavy-duty household appliances such as kitchen ranges, and 110 for ordinary lighting and most other uses in homes. Anyone who has mistakenly plugged a 110-volt hair dryer into a 220-volt outlet knows that this is not a good idea.[19]

It may help to think of electricity as the organized movement of electrical charges from one place to another.[20] If movement ceases we are no longer dealing with "electricity" as such. Transformers can be used to step up or step down the voltage when electricity switches from one type of flow-pathway to another; but once delivery of electricity begins it must move continuously until it reaches its final destination.

The result is that once electricity is produced, it must be consumed almost instantaneously, and at the same rate as it is produced. Nevertheless, electricity can be transmitted for great distances before finally being converted into one of the other forms of energy that were depicted in Figure 1.2 (heat, light, motion, etc.). It is this characteristic that has led to the creation of an amazing set of transmission grids from coast to coast with active links—extending, in fact, beyond the United States into Canada and some parts of Mexico.

Think back to the basics of supply and demand. Electricity reaches its ultimate consumers through the distribution networks of local utilities. As pointed out earlier, total demand for electricity varies enormously on an hourly basis each day, on weekdays versus weekends, and from one season of the year to another. Because the quantity of electricity supplied must *exactly match* the quantity demanded at every instant, a full repertoire of generating systems includes the variety mentioned in Chapter 1—baseload, peakers, and intermediate units that can vary their output fast enough to adjust fairly rapidly to changes in demand. If each local supplier of electricity had to rely on generation from within the immediate area, however, large chunks of capacity would still lie idle much of the time. It is much more efficient and economical to trade electricity among suppliers, arranging for total production to match total consumption at all times.

Regulatory restructuring has made it practical for electricity suppliers to cooperate across much larger areas, but U.S. transmission networks were not planned earlier with this possibility in mind. Fortunately, some sections of the grid were overbuilt originally anyway, and this has allowed some extra time to adjust to new circumstances when a more robust grid is needed. But delays of additional investment in transmission capacity could threaten reliability.

TYING IT ALL TOGETHER

A control center for any utility that generates electricity itself must be capable of instantly and smoothly changing the line-up of units that feed power into its own grid. In turn, all units must be synchronized with one another.

What does "synchronization" mean? The U.S. standard is 60-cycle alternating current (AC), which means that the electricity pulsing through the wires and cables changes polarity (i.e., reverses direction) almost exactly 60 times each second, even though the overall movement of AC electricity is one-way. The turbines that spin generation components thus must make 3,600 revolutions per minute (3,600 rpm). How much room is there for error? I have heard engineers say that if rotation is off by a quarter-turn in any single unit within the system, everything can crash.

By organizing networks of cooperating utilities, it would seem that the difficulties are multiplied, but sophisticated control systems make this possible and the advantages are huge. Less reserve capacity is required overall. Furthermore, one can always choose between using locally generated electricity or buying it from anywhere else it is available during any given period. That decision normally depends on which option is economically advantageous. Moving incrementally from the least expensive sources to those that are more and more expensive until all demand is satisfied (instantaneously) is termed "economic dispatch." As "renewable portfolio standards" become more common across the country and each company is required to furnish customers with a minimum percentage of whatever is designated "green" or "clean" energy, it may sometimes be necessary to opt for environmental dispatch instead. A complicated form of energy cooperation will become even more so.

Some multi-state interconnections have existed in this country since the early twentieth century. The very active granddaddy of modern regional transmission cooperation and planning is the Pennsylvania-New Jersey-Maryland system (PJM), whose members created the world's first power pool in 1927. As of 2008, after a series of steps that amounted to regulatory evolution and revolution, PJM had become an officially recognized regional transmission organization (RTO). Today it coordinates the bulk movements of electricity reaching into 13 states and the District of Columbia. From its highly secure headquarters at Valley Forge, Pennsylvania, it matches wholesale suppliers and buyers around the clock while dispatching one-sixth of all the electricity used in the United States.

PJM's more than 500 members include both owners of generation and transmission systems, as well as power marketers, distribution companies, and large consumers of electricity. They and the population of more than 50 million individuals in the area depend on PJM to manage the world's largest competitive electronic market for electricity while also ensuring the reliability of an interconnected grid involving close to 1,300 sources of generation using diverse types of fuel.[21]

Each separate distribution entity for electricity may engage in either short-term or long-term offers to buy or sell power and must still plan daily to meet anticipated demand by its own customers. Much of this advance scheduling is handled via "electronic bulletin boards." During the day, an auction system is used implicitly by the regional system operator to keep supply and demand in balance—with time-blocks for exchanges specified by both potential buyers and sellers. Prices paid by all buyers are stipulated by the final increment of supply, so by definition they are always determined by marginal cost.

THINGS *CAN* GO WRONG

Two major calamities have marked the historical development of regional electricity planning and operation.

A Northeast Blackout in 1965 led to the federal Electric Reliability Act of 1967. This spawned an unusually constituted but basically effective self-regulatory group within the industry called the North American Electric Reliability Council (NERC). Operating within regional councils, NERC persuaded member entities—which included both government and private components of the electricity-supply community nationwide—to agree upon minimum planning, operating, and monitoring standards to protect reliability. But compliance was voluntary, except for peer pressure; and meanwhile the organization of the industry itself became much more complex. The functions of generation, transmission, and distribution were separated. Wholesale competition became sharper. Independent power producers, power marketers, distributed generation, and new types of power generation entered the scene. Public confidence in the energy industry overall declined for a variety of reasons.

In 2003—almost four decades after the 1965 blackout—an even more massive one occurred. There were multiple reasons—including poor maintenance, but also operational and communications failures. Parts of the Energy Policy Act of 2005 aimed at preventing recurrences by putting teeth into the reliability-guarantee system. NERC was reorganized and eventually authorized to operate as the North American Reliability Corporation. It uses the same acronym (NERC), which is confusing; but there is a major difference. For the first time, standards and procedures became mandatory. The Federal Energy Regulatory Commission (FERC) was empowered to levy fines of as much as $1 million a day per violation. Memoranda of Understanding (MOUs) between FERC and each of Canada's provinces guaranteed that sanctions could be imposed in either country.[22]

WHAT REMAINS TO BE DONE?

The "new NERC" operates through a redrawn system of regional councils (see Figure 4.2). It is charged statutorily with making periodic assessments of both the reliability and the adequacy of North America's bulk power system,

FIGURE 4.2
NERC Regions

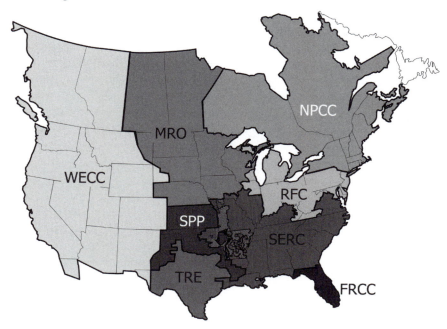

Regional Entities
FRCC: Florida Reliability Coordinating Council, https://www.frcc.com/default.aspx.
MRO: Midwest Reliability Organization, http://www.midwestreliability.org/.
NPCC: Northeast Power Coordinating Council, http://www.npcc.org/.
RFC: Reliability First Corporation, http://www.rfirst.org/.
SERC: Reliability Corporation, http://www.serc1.org/Application/HomePageView.aspx.
SPP: Southwest Power Pool, RE, http://www.spp.org/section.asp?pageID=87.
TRE: Texas Regional Entity, http://www.texasre.org.
WECC: Western Electricity Coordinating Council, http://www.wecc.biz/.
Source: Energy Information Administration.

but its warnings of potential problems tend to be "one-day stories" in the mass media.

Each year, NERC releases assessments of 100+ pages related to the upcoming winter and summer seasons, detailing both progress and items that need more attention. Looking out farther, it provides a ten-year summary of committed and uncommitted capacity resources in the light of anticipated demand. Its 2007–2016 document foresaw possible shortfalls in both the Western/Canadian and the New England regions by 2009, although both the Texas and Southeastern appeared to be in generally good shape until 2016 or beyond.[23]

Reliability depends on the adequacy of both generation and transmission, and additional capacity will be needed. Building additional capacity in either case is costly, however, as was addressed in Chapter 3. It takes time, a matter for Chapter 6. Permissions for siting also raise problems in both cases, since legitimate environmental concerns always need to be addressed (see Chapter 5). In 2008 Duke Energy and American Electric Power (AEP) announced a 50-50 joint venture to build and operate 240 miles of extra-high-voltage (765kv) transmission lines and related facilities in Indiana. It will be needed to improve interconnections serving two NERC regions with electricity from new power plants in central Indiana, including more than 3000 megawatts of wind energy planned for the region. But the projected cost works out to more than $4 million a mile, and the project will not be completed in less than six or seven years—in part because extensive regulatory approvals are necessary and the exact final route cannot be determined until numerous hearings are held on environmental effects and other matters.

A barrier to improving transmission infrastructure that attracts little attention is the reluctance of some players to cooperate because of perceived differences in regional economic interests. There are some U.S. areas where the operating costs of generating electricity have traditionally been low, usually because of the abundance of hydro facilities, nuclear power plants, and/or cheap coal. The suppliers and consumers of electricity in such areas, as well as their representatives in government, have resisted making trade with other regions easier—for fear that distant customers would outbid them for power and force local prices higher (even though there might be some benefit overall from lower *average* prices).

Sometimes there are other factors too. It is no accident that most of Texas is a "reliability region" unto itself. The alternating current in its electric grid is not synchronized with adjoining areas, and there are minimal direct-current (DC) connections that would make exchanges of electricity with the rest of the country feasible. Historically, this situation arose and is allowed to persist because it exempts most electricity policies in Texas from federal regulatory jurisdiction, which is based on interstate commerce. One of the state's unofficial mottos is "Don't mess with Texas," and that is exactly how it has acted in resisting energy regulation from outside its borders.

If alternating current needs to be delivered between adjacent but non-synchronous areas—such as the United States and Mexico, or most of Texas and anywhere else—it has to be converted into the form of "direct current" (DC) and then changed back into AC in synchronization with the receiving system. The equipment to accomplish this is expensive. Direct current is identical electrically to AC except that it always flows in the same direction. It has some advantages; for example DC transmission provides network stability and has lower line losses, although it requires higher voltages. But the United States decided early in the twentieth century to use AC rather than DC for almost all applications. Aside from limited-capacity connections between regions, the principal use of DC is for a few long-distance transmission corridors where conversion only has to take place at the point of origin and the point of major use.[24]

Texas today is in a peculiar position on this issue. Whereas it was once an inevitably low-cost generator, it may within a few years be happy to import power at lower wholesale rates from elsewhere. In an alternate scenario, there has been a push to develop more and more wind generation in Texas—alluding to this as a potential solution to national energy problems. What actually happens depends on developments in technology, costs, and environmental regulation that cannot be predicted; but in any case Texas may some day have to modify its long-standing isolation in respect to electricity. Economic evaluations of alternative courses of action will surely play a role in the change.

In some cases demand for electricity may exist at a considerable distance from potential sources of supply. For the two to be linked, it would be necessary to transmit the power all the way across the service territory of an intervening utility, or even across more than one state. Since FERC issued its "open access" order in 1996, utility owners of transmission lines have been forbidden to discriminate against others who wish to use them to move bulk power; but that didn't end disputes.

Historically, this practice of "wheeling" has brought resistance from those "in between"—who see only inconvenience without benefit. Transmission is complicated by the fact that electricity cannot be directed physically along a prescribed path as the flow of natural gas or petroleum is controlled by valves and pumps. Electricity takes the path of least resistance in traveling from one point to another, so it may "loop" away from a more-or-less straight-line route. The question of who is paid the cost-based transmission fees along a circuitous route and how much they should be is a thorny one. The issue of who is obligated to provide transmission lines to make such exchanges possible is even more complex.

SOME THINGS TO KEEP IN MIND

Overall, the ten-year projection in NERC's 2007 Long-Term Reliability Assessment boiled down to five findings that deserve (along with NERC's conclusions, recommendations, and pledges of action) more public awareness and consideration than they have received:

1. Current commitments for future installation of generation capacity, added to what exists now, would still not be enough to provide adequate reserve margins in meeting demand over more than a few years.

2. The integration of wind and solar generation (because of intermittent operation) and new nuclear plants (because of their large individual size) require special considerations in planning, design and operation of transmission infrastructure with its long lead-times.

3. High reliance on natural gas in some areas must be properly managed to reduce the risk of supply and delivery interruptions.

4. Although the transmission situation has improved, significant additional invest-ment is still required in certain areas to match resource additions with projected demand growth.

5. Because of the nation's age pyramid and early retirements resulting from several factors, the relevant industry workforce may face shortages.

Demand-side management should not be given short shrift either. Fore-stalling growth in overall demand for any form of energy with constrained supply is as effective as creating new sources. Even reducing demand peaks or developing new methods and facilities for storage can contribute to reliability of supply. Continuing to ensure adequate reliability in the U.S. energy pic-ture will be sufficiently difficult so that U.S. complacency about this goal is probably misplaced. Selecting a successful course will require consensus among many constituencies, and this is a challenge to investors, consumers, suppliers, and government officials alike—who need to be better informed of the facts. But this might also be said of the subject of the next chapter— "Environmental Factors."

NOTES

1. Global statistics on oil production are imprecise, in part because natural gas liquids are often but not always combined with crude oil output in reports. Official tabulations almost invariably lag by a couple of years. In addition, some countries either decline to publish production figures or report totals that are obviously not accurate.

2. Iraq is a case in point. There is no OPEC ceiling on its exports, although the slow recovery of its productive capacity from war damage and the continuing threats of internal attacks on infrastructure would render the country an unpredictable sup-ply source anyway.

3. See Matthew Simmons, *Twilight in the Desert: The Coming Saudi Oil Shock and the World Economy* (Hoboken, NJ: Wiley, 2006).

4. The amount of this unacknowledged subsidy by the Saudis to its exports to-ward the United States varies with shipping charges, but over the years it may have averaged only a couple of U.S. dollars or so. With prices of $100 per barrel or more, that may seem relatively insignificant, but when they were under $20 and the Saudis were having genuine budget problems it was clear that consciously accepting such a tradeoff mattered to them.

5. Sidney Weintraub and Rafael Fernández de Castro, "Mexico," in Sidney Wein-traub (ed.), *Energy Cooperation in the Western Hemisphere: Benefits and Impediments* (Washington, DC: The CSIS Press, Center for Strategic and International Studies, 2007), pp. 106–131.

6. *Compressed* natural gas (CNG) is gas stored under moderately high pressure while remaining in the gaseous state. This technique does not require the refrigeration associated with LNG, or *liquefied* natural gas. Another motor fuel that has been used in millions of vehicles around the world for many years consists of various kinds of liquefied *petroleum* gases (LPGs). They are produced both at oil refineries and at natural gas processing plants. Because of their higher boiling points, LPGs such as propane can be kept contained adequately as *liquids* under modest pressure alone, without cooling. This makes them convenient—albeit expensive—as cooking and space-heating fuels, especially when other energy sources are not readily available. Their use in recreational vehicles, trailers, mobile homes, remote communities, and the like will continue to be an important niche market. But propane has less than three-quarters the energy density of gasoline, and the highly volatile LPGs fail to meet other criteria for a suitable automotive fuel in the United States.

7. For a slightly fuller development of this parallel, see Joseph M. Dukert, *A Short Energy History of the United States, and Some Thoughts About the Future*, Edison Electric Institute Decisionmakers Bookshelf, vol. 7 (Washington, DC: Edison Electric Institute, 1980), pp. 49–50.

8. Methanol (CH_3OH) is also known as "wood alcohol." It can be produced chemically from woody fibers or almost *any* form of biomass—or from coal—by combining, assembling, or restructuring the arrangement of atoms within the feedstock molecules. However, no process has yet been marketed to do so at what appears to be a reasonable cost. Manufacturing methanol from methane (CH_4) is easier and cheaper, since this only involves replacing one of the hydrogen atoms in each molecule with an OH radical—which makes it, in chemical parlance, an "alcohol."

9. Public Law 110-140 (December 19, 2007).

10. "Biodiesel" is another broad category mentioned in the legislation. Biodiesel is usually defined as any direct substitute for diesel fuel which is produced from non-petroleum renewable resources that also meets certain emission specifications. The legislative target for biodiesel is much more modest—one billion gallons of all types on the market annually by 2012.

11. Executive Order S-7-04 by the Governor of the State of California, April 20, 2004.

12. The Partnership dates back to the era of Schwarzenegger's predecessor, and has been active since 1999. It includes a blue-ribbon list of member-organizations from government and the private sector.

13. California Fuel Cell Partnership news release, "The California Fuel Cell Partnership Releases Vision for Transition to Fuel Cycle Vehicle Commercialization," August 4, 2008.

14. See U.S. Department of Energy website—http://www.fossil.energy.gov/programs/reserves/index.html.

15. EIA, "About U.S. Natural Gas Pipelines—Transporting Natural Gas," June 2007, p. 2 (available on the EIA website).

16. See Joseph M. Dukert, "North America," Chapter 5 in *Energy Cooperation in the Western Hemisphere:Benefits and Impediments* (Washington, DC: The CSIS Press, Center for Strategic and International Studies, 2007), pp. 132–165.

17. This quote from New Mexico Governor Bill Richardson was widely reported in the wake of the 2003 blackout of the northeastern United States and several Canadian provinces—an event that could and should have been avoided, but should not have prompted such hyperbole either. Richardson might have displayed more knowledge about both the grid and the electric-power situation in Third World countries, since he had served both as Secretary of Energy and U.S. Ambassador to the United Nations—simultaneously for a while. Unfortunately, his catchy phrase has been thoughtlessly repeated many times since then . . . and thus merits a direct rejoinder in this book.

18. Besides "pumped storage" of hydropower, there are of course batteries—or, more properly, electrochemical cells. These are devices designed to release electricity on demand through chemical reactions that may be reversible and thus permit "recharging." Because individual cells are limited in voltage output, clusters (or "batteries") of them are generally used to store practical amounts of electricity, and the term "battery" has become a generic one for any such assembly. Some chemical batteries use exotic combinations of materials. The major limitations in scaling up any of the numerous kinds available include cost, weight, difficulty in recharging from "deep discharge" and through multiple cycles, or in some cases the requirement to operate at very high temperatures. In addition, experiments have continued for decades on schemes to store electricity in flywheels, compressed gases, alternation between freezing and liquefaction, etc. None at the moment seems applicable to electricity supply at the grid level.

19. Some outlets are marked 220-240 or 110-120, indicating that there is some room for variation. Also, when supplies are hard-put temporarily to keep pace with demand—perhaps during a period of high air conditioner use when a downed power line has cut off access to some generation—the local utility may announce a "voltage reduction" of perhaps 5 percent in certain areas, besides asking customers to reduce load if possible. This is usually called a "brownout," although there should be no noticeable dimming of lights or damage to equipment.

20. This raises a question whether international sales of electricity should be regarded as exchanges of commodities or provision of services, since the two might be treated differently in terms of import and export tariffs and rules. Although barely noticed at the time, the implicit recognition in the U.S.-Canadian Free Trade Agreement of 1988 that electricity is entitled to *commodity* treatment was vital to the subsequent development of energy trade throughout North America.

21. For more detail, and to follow the future development of this regional transmission entity, see http://www.pjm.com.

22. For more detail, visit http://www.nerc.com.

23. *North American Electric Reliability Corporation, 2007 Long-Term Reliability Assessment, 2007–2016: The Reliability of the Bulk Power System*, Princeton, NJ (October 2007).

24. The classic example is the Pacific DC Intertie along the West Coast, which can carry 3100 megawatts of power. Since demand peaks occur in different seasons, electricity can flow south in warm weather to accommodate air conditioning loads and north in winter when electricity is used heavily for heating.

Five

Environmental Factors

Environment! We hear, read, or utter the word many times a day, but what does it mean?

The *Oxford American Dictionary* defines environment as "surroundings, especially those affecting people's lives."[1] So it means quite different things to a West Virginia coal miner at work and to a schoolchild in Trenton. As with "energy adequacy," "energy cost," and "reliability of energy supply," the connotation of environment varies from place to place, time to time, and person to person.

The same applies to "environmental impact." However, that term has special economic implications for the energy supply-and-demand balance—and thus for a workable balance in individual, corporate, national, or international energy policies and actions. The National Environmental Policy Act of 1970 (NEPA) orders the preparation and regulatory consideration of an Environmental Impact Statement (EIS) before any major U.S. federal action can be taken that may significantly affect the human environment. Subsequent legislative history and judicial rulings have established that this includes almost any project that falls under the regulatory purview of any federal agency. Most states and many localities have adopted analogous rules that affect actions within their respective jurisdictions. So "environmental impact" is a crucial phrase, subject to differing interpretations and, sometimes, drawn-out litigation.

Compliance with environmental regulations often takes extra time and raises the costs of energy projects. On the other hand, there are positive social values in clean air, clean water, pleasant surroundings, public health, worker safety, and "normal" climatic conditions. Thus, well-conceived environmental protection policies can pay for themselves many times over. A complicating factor is that benefits may be spread over time and may accrue to people who are not directly involved in the regulatory matter at all, while the expenditures to achieve them show up at once. Another problem is that environmental benefits are hard to calculate. They can typically be reckoned in various ways, any of which may be subject to criticism. Depending on perspective, there are usually winners and losers from any market penetration by new energy technology or from the introduction of new energy ground rules with the goal of environmental protection, so what may become long-term improvements start off uphill. In fast-changing times such as the ones we are going through in the early part of the twenty-first century, prudent actors can do little more than look ahead and try to plan. Failure to do so upsets the energy balance.

It is impossible to produce, transform, deliver, or utilize energy at all without affecting *something*. As pioneer environmentalist Barry Commoner explained in the first of his four laws of ecology, "Everything is connected to everything else."[2] It doesn't minimize the wisdom of that observation, or the importance of environmental protection, to add that attitudes toward environmental impacts are not universally identical. They also fluctuate, at times affecting economic considerations dramatically. Consider how attitudes vary from place to place regarding "noise pollution" and "visual pollution." Another example is the prevailing shift in attitudes between 2000 and the present within the Congress and much of the business community toward the need to do something to cope with the risk of anthropogenic (human-induced) climate change.

TIMES CHANGE

The institution of U.S. railroads during the middle third of the nineteenth century was a revolutionary step in transportation and in energy use. It brought widely differing responses over several decades. Baltimore originally allowed the noisy, smoky, smelly locomotives to pass through that city only at certain off-peak hours, at minimal speed, and preceded by someone on foot—alerting pedestrians and horses to their approach. Yet Henry David Thoreau—an icon of quiet living with nature—was lyrical in his praise of the new invention when the Fitchburg Railroad skirted Walden Pond at twenty miles an hour "about a hundred rods south of where I dwell." In 1854, Thoreau took roughly half a chapter of his most famous work to describe the reassurance he derived from the routine transits of an iron horse that could "make the hills echo with his snort like thunder, shaking the earth with his feet, and breathing fire and smoke from his nostrils . . . " The writer even added, "I am refreshed and expanded when the freight train rattles past me, and I smell the stores which go dispensing their odors all the way from Long Wharf to Lake Champlain, reminding me of foreign parts . . . and the extent of the globe."[3]

By contrast, in a more modern setting, champions of renewable energy laud the remarkable multiplication of wind turbines—but perhaps only until a line of generators changes the profile of a nearby hill or threatens to be visible from a seaside resort. Attitudes toward environmental impacts depend on circumstances, and serious efforts to regulate them lead quickly and inevitably to the conclusion that quantification of some impacts is elusive. There are unique circumstances in almost every case study.

As with other chapters, I have tried to make this one as objective as I can. It is safe to project that energy sources as vastly different as wind and coal will continue to be called on in this country, and adverse environmental impacts of each should be minimized to every practical extent. It will be a continual challenge, however, to enunciate strict rules as to where, when, and under what conditions one energy source or another should be employed. This applies whether rules are laid down by public authorities or adopted by energy purveyors and consumers in the interest of their own and the broad community's environmental well-being. The soundest approach—for businesses and customers alike—seems to be to examine potentially useful principles.

To the extent that principles can be agreed on, public policy should be argued in public—but with open minds and the most up-to-date expertise available. Ideally, appropriate research should precede framing of legislation . . . or public mobilization . . . or corporate decisions . . . or even individual actions. Measurement is important whenever possible.

The warnings of Chapter 1 still apply: It is easy to misrepresent what statistics relating to the environment really mean. What's the principle in that? Do your homework!

ENERGY'S ADVERSE EFFECTS

Since the attributes of "the environment" are so difficult to pin down, let's momentarily make an oversimplifying assumption to facilitate analysis. Just for this section, let's put aside the fact that the use of energy commonly helps to *stabilize* or *improve* the environment in numerous ways.

Heating and air conditioning make us more comfortable while safeguarding public health. Contemporary housing, educational institutions, and even the arts wouldn't exist without the expenditure of energy. Motor fuel and electricity makes our lives easier in millions of ways. But let's focus for the moment only on energy's environmental downside. The application of energy *can* have undesirable side effects on our water, air, and land. In the end, we need to analyze those in detail in trying to reach the "right" energy decisions, personal or professional. For a planner of large projects, it is not unusual for such a process to take many months. That time must be built into a realistic schedule for building a new liquefied natural gas receiving facility or an offshore wind farm.

Many adverse impacts can originate in the waste products and other discharges from energy production and use: pollution of groundwater from mining and drilling, unduly raising the ambient temperatures of rivers and lakes by the use of cooling water for turbine exhausts or manufacturing processes, harmful emissions into the atmosphere, and the simple occupation of the Earth's surface in such a way as to disturb its previous "natural" use by human beings and other creatures, large and small. One might even hold the widespread use of energy accountable for certain negative features of urbanization and industrialization, such as nonbiodegradable plastics. After all, those convenient but "won't go away" plastic materials are manufactured from hydrocarbons. Conceptually, there is no limit to what an Environmental Impact Assessment (EIA) must consider.

Most people in the general populace, however, take a narrower view of the energy-environment nexus. The most widespread worries are about the release of certain compounds considered noxious for one reason or another. These involve primarily lead and heavy metals, sulfur, nitrogen, mercury, hydrocarbons themselves, and various particulates. Some other possible sources of particular concern have been:

- *Bulk effects on water*—including interruption of normal flow by dams, excessive consumption by some unconventional oil production, or thermal damage to biota when the cooling water for steam turbines is allowed to exceed temperature limits; and
- *Radiation*—either nuclear (from reactor operation or from other parts of the fuel cycle) or electromagnetic (from overhead power lines).

No two cases of adverse effects from energy on environment are alike in circumstances. No two energy sources of environmental damage are exactly alike. Citing a few examples of release-levels that might be considered acceptable or unacceptable would not provide the generic advice or understanding that this book hopes to provide. The reader can always look up specifics as needed. It will add something useful, however, to suggest how the data discovered or provided should be examined.

First of all, the prospective or actual releases of specific materials into the air or water in most cases will be minuscule amounts—perhaps such-and-so-many parts per million (ppm). This doesn't mean they are insignificant.

Modern environmental concerns linked to massive energy use preceded the energy crises mentioned earlier, which forced the nation to address issues of adequacy, cost, and supply reliability. The historic U.S. Clean Air Act of 1970 was followed during the early 1970s by various prescriptive amendments to much earlier legislation, such as the Federal Water Pollution Control Act of 1948.[4] Limits on atmospheric releases from factories and power plants have been progressively tightened ever since.

Early on, some people opposed rigid limits on point sources, insisting that "the answer to pollution is dilution!" While this is true in a sense, there are limits. The total volume of emissions generally matters less than the resulting concentration of pollutants in sites they might affect. However, "affected sites" could be the lungs of individual coal miners or the entire atmosphere of Earth, and that is where the respective effects need to be measured or estimated in each case. That's a principle!

MEASURING ENVIRONMENTAL EFFECTS

Chapter 1 noted the merits of appreciating the meanings of metric-system prefixes, such as kilo-, mega-, and giga-, in evaluating the significance of large amounts of power. Likewise, familiarity with the prefixes that distinguish some really *tiny* measurement units is helpful in following certain discussions of environmental impacts. Radioactivity, for instance, has been measured traditionally in units called *curies*.[5] The formal definition of curie is "37 billion nuclear transformations in a single second," and that is off-putting. It is also largely immaterial to almost anyone but a nuclear health physicist. It is far more important for anyone who wishes to understand in more than casual terms the environmental implications of what goes into and what comes out of a nuclear power installation to recognize that a millicurie is one-thousandth of a curie, a nanocurie is one-billionth, and a picocurie one-trillionth. Those are more *relevant* units.

There is also an important unit of measurement for the potential biological effects of radiation on human beings—the "rem." Limits on exposure of the public or industrial workers to nuclear radiation under various conditions are generally expressed in millirems, but it is important to note also that actual effects depend on how close one is to the source or how long the exposure lasts. Thus the more significant measurement to look for might be "so many millirem at the property line of a nuclear installation" or "so-and-so-many millirem per year."

Being able to evaluate potential nuclear radiation effects depends on some factors that are common to those pertaining to chemical releases, but others that are not. Above all, it requires some fundamental knowledge of radioactivity and radiation itself, such as the simple concepts in Sidebar 5.1 on the next few pages. If you can read, understand, and remember or refer to what that sidebar contains, you will be far better qualified to analyze the facts in any given situation than nearly everybody else in the general populace, almost all legislators, and all but a very small number of the journalists who routinely write articles about civilian or military nuclear matters. *Getting to* the facts is a separate matter. That may require preparing or studying a multivolume Environmental Impact Statement.

SIDEBAR 5.1
Radioactivity and Radiation

Radioactive materials and the nuclear radiation they emit are potential sources of environmental damage. Yet for many years we have routinely used nuclear power plants to generate electricity, radioactive tracers in medical diagnosis, and radionuclides as power sources for some cardiac pacemakers and deep-space probes. By now, the general public and news outlets should know more about radioactivity and radiation than they do. Once a few definitions are understood, errors or confusion in reporting leap out to a reader. This avoids either exaggerating or minimizing actual and potential environmental threats.

"Radioactivity" refers most properly to the *process* by which the nuclei of certain types of atoms spontaneously decay and thus emit diverse forms of "radiation" at various energy levels. Radioactivity and radiation are not fully interchangeable terms, and being finicky enough to distinguish between them is not an affectation. It marks the beginning of understanding their occurrence, potential usefulness, and potential hazards.

Nuclear radiation is like solar radiation in many ways. In fact, about 10 percent of solar radiation consists of particles very similar to the highly energetic "alpha" and "beta" particles and "gamma" radiation whose emission from disintegrating atoms on Earth enable us to pinpoint radioactivity readily. The ability to detect nuclear radiation easily in minute amounts is a blessing for environmental protection. Nuclear radiation and the radioactivity that produces it can be monitored more exactly than any chemical pollutant. This is important, because in addition to numerous radioactive materials found in Nature we have *added* many—not only from the operation of nuclear reactors, but also for practical energy applications in themselves. These range from medical diagnoses and treatments to quality control in industrial operations.

Thinking of radioactive materials as analogous to the Sun itself clears up one common misunderstanding. Being out on a sunny day tans our skin, but we are unlikely to acquire a tan by standing next to a sunburn victim at night. In most cases, nuclear *radiation* (as distinguished from *radioactive material*) is not transmitted secondarily. The exception involves one type of particle rarely mentioned in articles for the lay reader. Emissions of *neutrons* are usually associated with nuclear fission—the event in which a heavy atom actually splits to release energy; but they can also be found in connection with some other nuclear disintegrations. Their added hazard is that neutrons *can* induce radioactivity in some otherwise nonactive elements. Apart from this, there is no need here to pursue details about various forms of nuclear radiation, except to say that the heaviest particles (alphas) are easiest to stop but may do the most damage through impact because of their greater mass.

Like sunlight and the infrared radiation from the sun that we feel as heat, nuclear radiation of all types tends to move in straight lines. It can be blocked by suitable shielding, just as we can protect our eyes from overly bright light and our faces from the Sun's heat and a bad sunburn by using sunglasses and an umbrella. Earth's atmosphere consists basically of transparent gases, yet it is thick enough and dense enough to keep us from being blinded and roasted. It also helps that our Sun is 93 million miles away. By contrast, we have some naturally occurring radioactive materials inside our own bodies. Others, including some produced artificially, may be as close to us as an energy source in a smoke detector on the kitchen ceiling and yet be of no safety concern.

Radioactive materials may be solids, liquids, or gases, and their physical and chemical characteristics determine how they might be dispersed, absorbed, or even reconcentrated.

Distance from a radioactive source, shielding, the type of radiation emitted by a particular source, and the length of time plants or animals are exposed to nuclear radiation all feed into biological effects. All of these must be known in order to evaluate environmental impacts. Any one of these factors can minimize or maximize the need for concern. Unlike expanding liquids or gases, however, radiation does not build up pressure and threaten to "pop." Its energy is *absorbed* by shielding.

A *radioisotope* is a form of any chemical element that emits radiation, and each radioisotope "decays" in accordance with its unvarying *half-life*. "Radionuclide" is the generic term for any material with a specific half-life.

The significance—if not the meaning—of radioactive half-life is frequently misinterpreted. The term refers to the remarkable natural fact that *exactly half* of the radioactive atoms in a sample of *any* size will emit that atom's characteristic radiation over a precise period of time. Very long half-lives—not uncommonly stretching into hundreds of thousands of years—actually mean that a particular radionuclide will give off its potential radiation more slowly. Radioactive materials of relatively short half-life are favored for medical tests, since they can be ingested or injected into the human body in small amounts and used by external equipment to map organs or pathways. They quickly expend their energy and pass out of the body, producing less damage than would conventional surgery.

As with chemical pollutants, the original concentration and the inherent dilution rate of radioactive materials that somehow enter the general environment are critical items of data that need to be determined as quickly as possible. There may be as little as one-hundredth of an ounce of americium-241 in a smoke detector. This isotope of americium has a half-life of almost 433 years, but it is in a water-insoluble compound. The estimated radiation dose to a resident from a smoke detector is much less than background activity from common rocks, cosmic rays, and other natural sources.

"Spent" fuel removed from a nuclear reactor contains very large amounts of various radioactive materials included in "fission products," besides some uranium that is left over and some plutonium that has been created. The quick decay of shorter-lived radionuclides releases enough heat so that the fuel bundles must be allowed to cool for years at the reactor site before being moved in heavily shielded casks. Materials with "medium" half-lives of about three decades, such as strontium-90, are especially problematic. One rule of thumb is that they should be safeguarded against environmental release for 20 half-lives, roughly 600 years. At the end of that time their radioactivity would be reduced to about one-millionth of what it was to begin with. In the case of one form of plutonium, with a half-life of 24,000 years, such a waiting period would stretch to more than half a million years.

The issue of spent fuel disposal is far from settled, but agreement might be reached to use some form of monitored storage for several centuries, perhaps in geological isolation by deep burial. High-level radioactive waste of any form can be sequestered from human contact, yet technically retrievable for some period. Retrievability is desirable in case human society in the future can devise a completely permanent method of disposal—such as fairly rapid transmutation into harmless nuclides.

When economic decisions are potentially influenced by common perceptions of environmental threats, it pays to examine some basic science. This can help understand genuine problems while avoiding or counteracting easy misperceptions.

A few generalities are indisputable, although they frequently receive too little attention in public discussions. Something to consider in the case of *either* chemical or nuclear-related releases is the physical and chemical form of the material released. Finely divided particles can spread and hang around in the atmosphere. Liquids are less likely to be contained than solids. Gases or vapors may carry even farther than liquids from the point of release, although they gradually become diluted. Physical realities underlie the problem of "acid rain." It is brought about when sulfur-oxide and nitrogen-oxide compounds coming out of smokestacks or vehicle tailpipes produce sulfuric or nitric acid within moving air currents. All this explains why an energy-using or energy-producing installation in one state can face complaints from the government and citizens of another state, hundreds of miles away.

Problems of air quality in cities are often traced to vehicle emissions, although these have been greatly alleviated over the years by the statutory elimination of lead and other contaminants from motor fuels—as well as vehicle inspection laws in state and local jurisdictions. The most obvious example of air pollution related primarily to energy use is smog. Smog is a contraction of the words smoke and fog, and it is an atmospheric mixture that forms under certain weather conditions when the lack of air movement prevents certain *interactive* pollutants from dissipating. A city with high traffic volume and surrounded by mountains, such as Denver, is especially vulnerable to smog because the terrain establishes a natural "punch bowl" that fosters such mixing of the ingredients. The guilty emissions vary, but in the United States the main culprits are commonly nitrogen oxides and unburned fuel particles. Prolonged exposure to smog has occasionally produced deaths, and smog certainly exacerbates the effects of respiratory diseases.

One underlying chemical factor in most environmental pollution problems is solubility, the degree to which any releases dissolve readily in naturally common fluids such as water. Another is the degree to which certain chemical elements either are absorbed preferentially or "reconcentrate" under some conditions. For example, iodine builds up in human thyroids and certain marine organisms. Calcium is a "bone-seeker," and so are its chemical relatives, including strontium and plutonium. In 1998, an expert working group organized by the National Institute of Environmental Health Sciences (NIEHS) of the National Institutes of Health cited *some* studies that showed magnetic fields from power lines might be a cause of childhood leukemia, but the NIEHS group also concluded that these conjectures could neither be supported nor knocked down by the results of animal, cellular, and process studies. There are no federal standards limiting residential or work exposure to the electric and magnetic fields around power lines, and the U.S. Environmental Protection Agency (EPA) cites a general scientific consensus that evidence of a cause-and-effect relationship with such health effects is weak.[6]

THE "GREENHOUSE EFFECT"

Carbon dioxide (CO_2) and certain other gases—including methane, the same natural gas used as a fuel—can produce serious problems if their concentration in parts per-million within our atmospheric blanket becomes high enough in combination to seriously change the planet's "normal" radiation of thermal energy.

Earth's atmosphere itself forms a lens, whose constituents tend to admit or reflect radiation of different types to various degrees. It is somewhat like a filter of colored glass, which may allow only red light or green light to get through—or a mirrored glass surface, which reflects visible light completely to form an image that can reach our eyes. More subtly, the atmosphere somewhat resembles a two-way mirror—one that lets visible light rays pass through from one side, but reflects them in the opposite direction.

In the case of the upper atmosphere, the filtering-versus-reflection effect depends on the wavelength of the radiation involved. Rays from parts of the solar spectrum get through to illuminate and warm the surface, but some of the heat produced is blocked from being *re*-emitted because that same atmospheric layer is semi-opaque to infrared frequencies. This "greenhouse effect" is always present to some extent, but here is another example of the need to maintain a critical balance.

Too much residual heat within the atmosphere could raise ambient temperatures on average over time, in an unpredictable but possibly devastating manner. And there is more to the story. Carbon dioxide, which is by far the most abundant "global warming gas" (GWG) in terms of the volumes released, also mixes with water to form small amounts of a relatively weak acid—carbonic acid (H_2CO_3). CO_2 is constantly being absorbed by the oceans and other bodies of water, and this has "good news, bad news" aspects. The natural process of CO_2 going into solution with surface waters tends to reduce the concentration of carbon dioxide in the atmosphere, but it also raises the normal acidity of the waters—to which fish, whales, plankton, and other organisms have become accustomed. Nature and all of its constituents are quite adaptive, but changes in either temperature or acid-balance can imperil some species and encourage others disproportionately if they occur too rapidly.

BALANCING CONCENTRATIONS

The presence of *some* carbon dioxide in the atmosphere is essential to an environment in which life as we know it can exist. Trapping natural and human-generated heat across the planet's surface maintains temperatures within a tolerable range where humans not only survive but can thrive. Carbon dioxide is also essential to photosynthesis in plants, so—ironically, in a sense—CO_2 keeps Earth "green." It thus helps us feed and clothe ourselves. Sorry to say, however, there *can* be too much of almost any good thing. Another of Barry Commoner's laws of ecology is that "Nature knows best," and his implication was that *any* attempt to improve on nature through technology is bound to upset things. Even conceding that arguable dictum, the question arises as to where the upper balancing point is in respect to atmospheric changes. Most scientists agree that we don't really know, but that we shouldn't wait until we get so close that we drift past it.[7]

Where do atmospheric CO_2 and methane originate? Most carbon dioxide in our atmosphere got there naturally—from sources that range from decaying organic material (such as dead trees) to every human being who breathes. We all inhale oxygen and exhale CO_2 as one of our natural waste products. Methane occasionally leaks from pipelines and is still being flared from remote gas wells, but it also enters the atmosphere naturally in substantial quantities. Some natural gas escapes from underground pockets without human intervention, just as crude oil seeps to the surface by itself in some parts of the Arctic National Wildlife Refuge. Methane also comes from exposed garbage dumps and from flatulent animals. But the biggest variable in the steady net addition of GWGs that has taken place for decades is the production and use of energy by humans.

The atmospheric concentration of CO_2 has risen by more than one-third since the start of the Industrial Revolution and an accompanying spurt in the total use of carbonaceous fuels. Those include all fossil fuels, but also biomass—such as wood and dung, as well as municipal solid waste and synthetic ethanol combusted as fuel. They all produce carbon dioxide when burned. Atmospheric concentrations have gone from about 280 parts per million of CO_2 a couple of centuries ago to 379 in 2005, and the increase between 1995 and 2005 was the largest it has ever been since continuous direct measurements began in 1960. Annual releases for that ten-year period were nearly 2-parts-per-million, as compared with just under 1.5 ppm/year for the entire 45 years.[8]

Each molecule of methane is more potent than a single molecule of CO_2 in building up the heat-trapping blanket, but there is far less methane in the atmosphere. It is measured usually in parts per billion (ppb). The atmospheric concentration of methane has more than doubled since the global beginnings of industrialization, but its growth rates have slowed since the 1990s. One might speculate that this tentative trend toward stabilization is related to the steady elimination of gas flaring and better maintenance of gas pipelines, but the latest report of the Intergovernmental Panel on Climate Change (IPCC) admits that the relative contributions of methane emissions from different sources are not well determined. The IPCC suggests, with what it considers more than 90 percent probability, that the predominant sources are agriculture and fossil fuel use.[9]

Nitrous oxide is yet another of the principal gases involved, but the growth rate in its concentration has been less pronounced—from about 270 ppb in the pre-industrial era to 319 ppb in 2005. More than a third of nitrous oxide emissions are deemed anthropogenic, related primarily to agriculture. A sizable amount also comes from motor vehicles' tailpipes, yet—despite the rapid increase in road traffic over recent years—the overall slower growth rate in nitrous oxide concentration has been roughly constant since 1980.

WHERE DOES THAT LEAVE US?

Libraries, book stores, and the Internet are full of publications that argue in contradictory directions about the extent to which energy has net adverse effects on the environment, regardless of how that term is defined. This book is neither a polemic nor an exhaustive text, so such judgments are purposely being avoided. Instead, here are some observations and principles.

Numbers that express total releases in absolute quantities are often not very informative. The volumes of water being used or discharged are less meaningful than the answers to such questions as whether the water is effectively being consumed or recycled in some fashion for further productive use. If direct thermal effects on water are involved, the critical statistics are not the maximum temperature reached inside an installation but the amount and duration of any temperature rise that is sustained at various distances from discharge—coupled with the measurable effects on the particular animal and plant species associated with the location.

In the same vein, the absolute volumes of solid, liquid, and gaseous releases may seem impressively large or equally impressively small; but the questions that really need to be answered relate to concentration and estimated effect. The number of tons of carbon dioxide released[10] can be staggering, yet in themselves such numbers may tell us very little except as benchmarks in respect to regulating future releases. The more critical statistics are the parts per million of various GWGs in the atmosphere and the rate at which concentrations are growing.

The combined concentrations of "global warming" gases will probably not decrease in our lifetimes. Once emitted, the various gases engage in physical and chemical processes that will eventually remove them from the atmosphere, but the net "residence time" among those mentioned here varies from about a decade to more than a century.

It is sometimes helpful to compare conditions at the surface with the "normal background," but such comparisons may not always determine whether safety and environmental integrity are being threatened. This is especially true when evaluating nuclear radiation effects, since the conservative limits on radiation exposure imposed by the Nuclear Regulatory Commission for many years—which have proved sound—are understandably different in respect to workers, a plant's neighbors, and the general population. The key nuclear radiation unit to consider is the rem—a universally accepted unit of biological effect. Recall that a quad harmonizes the energy content of all sorts of energy sources, so they can be compared or summed up. Similarly, the rem (or, more likely, the millirem—one thousandth of a rem) expresses the equivalent "dose" to human tissue from any one of multiple possible radiation sources, each with its own respective nature that produces distinctive effects.

All these arcane measurements still leave room for honest differences in opinion about environmental consequences. Expert witnesses with Ph.D.s and medical degrees of various types may give conflicting testimony in environmental hearings—just as they do in criminal and civil court cases. Deciding whom to believe is partly a judgment call, although this task is far easier and more rewarding if we understand even a bare minimum about units of measurement and what sorts of follow-up questions to ask.

Purely anecdotal evidence is justifiably suspect, regardless of which side it comes from in a dispute over environmental effects. We should also remember that it's hard to prove a negative. Also that no energy source—or few human activities of any sort—can be regarded honestly as free of *any* adverse environmental impact. When considering all of the interactive elements of the energy mobile in Figure 1.3 from Chapter 1, environmental concerns deserve great attention. *Balance* is tough to find, but it is the most common key to consensus.

Overall, it is important finally to document the existing condition of the environment *before* what you consider a major energy project is undertaken. This may involve extensive formal studies, or it may be as simple as noting that a backyard generator to provide emergency backup in case of a power outage will probably makes lots of noise and may be considered an eyesore by the neighborhood improvement association. The principle here is simple: Think ahead whenever possible.

COMPARING ENERGY SOURCES

Here is a quick rundown on today's most prominent energy sources and some of the environmental consequences to be considered for each:

COAL

Deep mining is hazardous, and surface mining disturbs the landscape. The old problem of particulate emissions—exemplified by the soot that comes from burning coal—has been essentially solved for power plants by electrostatic precipitators. Emissions of various sulfur-and-oxygen compounds (grouped together in the all-embracing term SO_x) or nitrogen compounds (NO_x) can be sharply reduced, variously by controlling combustion temperatures, by the choice of coal, or by the use of "scrubbers" to remove them—although this last process leaves large disposal problems for the gunk that results. Among the fossil fuels, coal produces the largest amounts of carbon dioxide when burned (see Sidebar 5.2). There are a number of different processes that can convert coal into liquid fuels, but their respective environmental impacts must be judged individually.

PETROLEUM

Oil spills can occur during transportation or production, either on land or offshore, and these can endanger sensitive populations of wildlife.[11] As reserves of conventional oil continue to be depleted worldwide, exploration directed at replacing "easy" resources must reach into new areas—geographically and technologically. The footprint of drilling operations in virgin territory requires special planning to minimize adverse effects. Some new sources of crude oil and natural substitutes for it—such as oil sands and oil shales—raise unfamiliar problems of water requirements, land disturbance, and waste disposal.[12] These are all being addressed, but deserve continuing attention.

NATURAL GAS

Environmental protection and safety in drilling and transportation raise challenges paralleling those for oil. The physical characteristics of liquefied natural gas suggest that hazards in delivery are actually minimal and have been exaggerated by opponents of LNG development, perhaps including some who simply favor energy sources that compete with gas. Residential and

SIDEBAR 5.2
Comparing Common Fuels as Sources of CO_2

Among fossil fuels, methane—the principal constituent of *natural gas*—produces the lowest emissions of CO_2 per unit of fuel burned. This is explained by its chemical composition—CH_4. There are four hydrogen atoms for every carbon atom in each molecule. Carbon dioxide forms when the carbon atoms break off from the methane molecules to combine with oxygen. The union of hydrogen and oxygen produces water, H_2O.

Petroleum is a mixture of various carbon-hydrogen compounds, but *all* contain more atoms of carbon than does methane in relation to the number of hydrogen atoms. For example, octane is C_3H_8. Most common petroleum fuels release about one and a half times as much CO_2 as does natural gas. Heavier petroleum fractions, such as bitumen, have high energy content but give off more carbon dioxide when combusted.

Coal is also a mixture, but the burnable portion of it is almost *pure* carbon. Burning coal releases about 1.8 units of CO_2 for every 1 released by an equivalent amount of natural gas.

Biomass fuels such as wood, refuse, ethanol, biodiesel, and so on, may be mixtures or compounds, and all contain carbon in significant amounts. Thus, they all emit substantial amounts of carbon dioxide when used.

One aim of technological research is to "decarbonize" our fuel-mix. Although many difficulties in its broad use remain to be resolved, *hydrogen* can be a fuel in various types of systems that release energy productively. Hydrogen-fueled systems would release no CO_2 at all in operation, only water.

It is a misnomer to characterize any energy source as "clean" or "dirty" exclusively on the basis of how much CO_2 it adds to Earth's atmosphere. Carbon dioxide is colorless, odorless, and nontoxic—unless it replaces the breathable oxygen in an enclosed space. Nevertheless, as explained in the text, excessive releases of it globally are accompanied by environmental misgivings. That in turn has economic consequences.

commercial use of natural gas has always involved occasional accidents, although these have often resulted from carelessness or failure to obey common-sense safety rules—for example, using an open gas oven for space heating.

HYDROELECTRICITY

During much of the twentieth century, hydroelectric installations were considered beneficial to the natural environment. They helped control floods and promoted outdoor recreational opportunities, including wildlife preserves.

However, no new big power dams are likely to be built in the United States in the foreseeable future, and even the relicensing of existing facilities now sparks environmental controversy. Reservoirs built up behind the dams initially flood large areas and change radically the downstream flow, erosion, and silting characteristics. Dams can burst, although such failures are quite rare. Fish ladders facilitate movement past dams, but there are still complaints that life cycles of some species are negatively affected. Although hydropower is obviously a renewable energy resource, it is thus widely denied the tax and other legal perquisites accorded to solar power and wind.

Nuclear Power

Despite the absence of harmful emissions during normal operations and an almost flawless safety record over decades in this country and much of the world, nuclear power is regarded in some quarters as environmentally undesirable. Although such opposition seems to be fading because of the need for large energy sources that do not produce CO_2, there is still public apprehension about possible accidents that have a very low probability of occurring but might affect large areas and large populations if they did. There are also concerns about the potential diversion of nuclear materials to malevolent use by other governments or non-state actors and the fact that no permanent repository has yet been authorized for the storage/disposal of the spent fuel bundles removed from reactors every few years after they have given up heat energy to the maximum practical extent through nuclear fission to generate electricity.

Solar Energy

Photovoltaic cells (PVs) convert solar radiation at certain wavelengths directly into electricity and are perhaps the cleanest of all significant energy sources. Because of low power density, however, the very large arrays of solar cells needed to serve as central-station power sources occupy vast land areas[13] that often cannot satisfy urban energy demands without long transmission lines. Some materials used in PV manufacture are also considered hazardous. Solar-thermal systems use the sun as a heat source, frequently using sun-tracking equipment and focusing-lens arrangements to maximize efficiency. In all cases—even when smaller-scale solar energy equipment is located right at the place where the power is consumed—"sun rights" may become an issue if equipment blocks others from daylight. Generating or heating equipment deriving primary energy from the sun normally must have a direct line of sight to its source and cannot operate when shaded by trees or other structures.

WIND

A single large wind turbine may rise hundreds of feet into the air and use rotating blades that are as wide from tip to tip as the length of a city block. A wind farm may include scores or even hundreds of such machines. Unlike solar installations, wind facilities may permit the land under and around them to continue in such uses as livestock grazing; but they still have a vague resemblance themselves to high-voltage electricity transmission lines, making them the target of aesthetic complaints about visual pollution. Problems of noise and bird kills have largely abated, although there may be specific threats to certain species in some locations.

GEOTHERMAL

Earth's core is very hot—with perhaps half of its inner heat emanating from the natural decay of radioactive elements. Generally in areas where natural hot springs exist, it is possible to drill to a point from which appreciable quantities of steam or hot water will be released—providing useful energy. Geothermal energy is often considered renewable because its source in Nature is gigantic, even though output in a given location might eventually decline. In traditional systems, steam is used directly to drive a turbine-generator and produce electricity. Water at sufficiently high temperature can also be "flashed" in a low-pressure chamber, with the resulting steam being used the same way. In either case an unpleasant odor, similar to rotten eggs, is also emitted, sometimes along with toxic minerals. This problem is solved by using a heat exchanger in a closed system, although this reduces efficiency. Groundwater heat pumps for use by individual buildings are sometimes also referred to as a form of geothermal energy, although this is a misnomer. They generate electricity via the temperature differential between the surface and a *short* distance below the surface—where temperature remains constant year-round at about 50°F. Such heat pumps are generally useful only in regions that have extremes of heat or cold. Their only environmental penalty is that their piping covers a relatively large area underground. In most cases the excavation for installation must take place prior to constructing the house or other building to be served, although piping may be installed vertically at some sites—with the additional cost of deep drilling.

ELECTRICITY IN GENERAL

Rights-of-way and the necessary permissions to build transmission lines are notoriously hard to acquire because of objections to their visual appearance and to the fact that the lines may require removal of trees, passage through sensitive environments, proximity to historic sites, and so on. It is technologically difficult to bury transmission lines because ventilation or cooling is needed to dissipate heat; undergrounding for any great distance is often hibitively expensive—as much as several million dollars per mile. The alleged hazards of electromagnetic radiation from overhead wires have never been conclusively documented, but public perceptions of danger have not been eliminated. This topic is almost invariably addressed at hearings on the acceptability of new transmission lines.

ALTERNATIVE FUELS

Ethanol and several other synthetic substitutes for hydrocarbon products may burn more cleanly, but their various overall impacts on the environment raise many other arguments. Disputes over ethanol as a putative energy source are perhaps the clearest example of how environmental impact studies delve into the complete fuel cycle—from original production of feedstock through delivery, use, and ultimate disposal of waste if necessary. In February 2008, two articles in separate issues of a reputable scientific publication[14] concluded that direct and indirect expansions in agriculture related to biofuels essentially double the greenhouse-gas emissions of the fuel per mile driven as compared with gasoline. Almost immediately after the first article appeared, two federal government researchers associated with biomass-to-energy programs challenged the assumptions and results—only to be contradicted in turn by the principal author in an interview.[15] The debate is almost certainly not over. According to the normally careful British publication *Economist*, another under-considered problem is that five gallons of water are consumed in producing a single gallon of ethanol. Of course, this is only half of the amount of water it took to produce this alternative fuel in the late 1990s, so this particular negative result may be on its way to being solved.[16]

REDUCING ADVERSE ENVIRONMENTAL EFFECTS

In the broadest terms, there are at least five ways to lessen detrimental effects on the environment from the production and use of energy. They apply to individuals, businesses, organizations, and nations:

1. Reduce the absolute amounts of energy and energy resources consumed.
2. Select energy sources when possible whose net effects are more benign, but which can still accomplish whatever positive results are desired.
3. Change the basic processes involved in producing or using the energy to minimize the harmful effects they involve or induce.
4. Capture or clean up pollutants "at the end of the pipe" but before they are released.
5. Try to mitigate any and all residual bad effects, even after they have taken place.

Quite often, these approaches overlap. Also, we shouldn't be surprised if any one of them—especially at first examination—appears to entail a penalty of some sort. It may require additional expenditures. It may cause some delay or other form of inconvenience. By consuming energy itself, it may reduce net energy output. As always, the question arises of *how* to balance costs and benefits in any energy activity, and that is up to the responsible decision makers. A good way to start is simply to list alternatives, using the foregoing five categories of potential response as a checklist.

The first approach—a reduction in energy consumption—covers what was commonly called conservation until someone got the idea that efficiency sounds more appealing. The term *efficiency* does come closer to encompassing the courses people are most willing to adopt, since the tasks they set out to accomplish will still get done. For example, ride-sharing to work by two employees roughly doubles the miles per gallon that one vehicle achieves—at least for that round-trip. It can be a form of cost-sparing efficiency for an employer as well, which is why car-poolers get access to limited parking privileges from some companies.

Efficiency is often the best option in protecting the environment. It avoids pain, and is not as problematic to practice as it might seem.[17] Most local utilities offer free or low-cost energy audits to residential, commercial, and perhaps even industrial customers. Some are quite sophisticated technologically, including such techniques as infrared scanning from the outside to determine how and where the space heat a customer is paying for escapes from a building unnecessarily. Many are purely common sense, such as turning off unnecessary lights. The U.S. Department of Energy[18] and many nongovernmental organizations[19] offer long lists of tips on how to improve energy efficiency in various contexts.

The amount of electricity consumed for illumination in homes, offices, or industrial settings can definitely be cut back in many cases without sacrificing eye-comfort. The manufacture of traditional incandescent bulbs is gradually being phased out, because we have finally come to realize that increasing the temperature of a filament until it is white-hot uses more electricity for heat than for light. The first replacements to gain widespread popularity were assorted versions of fluorescent lighting. Gases and coatings in fluorescents are energized by an electric current, so that they glow brightly enough to provide a comparable number of *lumens* (units of brightness) while remaining an average 75 percent cooler and using perhaps one-third of the electric power needed by incandescents. Typically, an 18- to 25-watt fluorescent is equivalent to a 75-watt incandescent and lasts up to 10 times as long. Once enough public demand for such products developed, manufacturers devised various ways to meet initial objections: higher price, harsh light, delay in switch-on response, unusual shapes that existing fixtures could not accommodate, and so on.

Numerous alternative lighting systems have entered the market, and new ones can be expected by the end of the decade. Purchase price, long-term cost, color, longevity, appearance, and other factors—including style and the familiarity of brands—will be used to seek sales advantages among competing products. Consumer choice will eventually decide which ones survive, but we can be fairly sure that no *one* type of bulb, tube, light-emitting diode, or any other illuminating device will approach the uniform acceptance that helped incandescents enjoy a near-monopoly in lighting for more than a century.

Efficiency efforts can also be outsourced. There are "energy service companies" (ESCOs) whose occupation is to evaluate the energy use of a business enterprise or institution in detail and to advise the client of specific steps that will reduce energy consumption and thus save money. The fees are customarily negotiated on a case-by-case basis and often involve a percentage of the energy cost savings over a specified period. This can be a win-win proposition.

LOOKING AT ENERGY SOURCES IN THEIR ENTIRETY

The second strategy is to give preference and special emphasis to energy sources that are least disruptive to whichever environments concern us most. The reason electricity has become a universal requirement for modern living is not just because of its convenience, but also because it is so clean at the point of end-use—the environment of the kitchen, the office, and the factory. However, a totally environment-conscious decision maker will also consider where the electricity came from. A coal-burning power plant has one set of negative environmental considerations, but a wind farm or solar-thermal array three states away has some, too. In particular, additional transmission lines might be required to reach us with the product of such remote "green" generation.

The massive use of biofuels such as ethanol—far beyond current goals—would change the landscape of America. We might need to dedicate vast areas of land, countless tons of petrochemical fertilizer, and enormous quantities of water to the production of fuel as well as food and fiber. These trade-offs will haunt those who have suggested biofuels as a quick and lasting fix for our national energy predicaments.

Each of these energy sources—and others—will continue to find some valid roles, even if the prime criterion for picking among them consists of environmental considerations. A guiding principle should be that those who consider environmental protection the *most* important guideline should try to analyze the impact of the *full fuel cycle*. That necessitates environmental impact analyses from figuratively or literally planting the seed to safe final disposal of all waste products. Think tanks all across the nation and the world are still trying to agree on the best procedures for such analysis. The task is complicated by the fact that an energy source with clear advantages in respect to one environmental test may score lower in another area. Natural gas does not give off SO_x, NO_x, mercury, or solid particles when it is burned to release energy, but its combustion does release roughly two-thirds as much carbon dioxide as an equivalent amount of gasoline or diesel fuel. Nuclear power plants produce essentially no atmospheric pollutants at all, yet even the minimal possibility that radioactive material could escape from them as part of their full fuel cycle worries many people. Biofuels may affect the environment not only when they are manufactured and used, but also through tilling and fertilizing the land that yields various feedstocks.

There are innumerable ways in which energy production and consumption *processes* have been changed in the interest of environmental protection and public/worker safety, and this constitutes a *third* strategy. More can always be done along these lines, depending on the balance of all considerations. A few examples follow.

Instead of dotting a large area with closely spaced oil or gas rigs, it is now possible to drill vertically in one spot until hydrocarbons are found and then direct drill bits horizontally for some distance and with great precision. The oil sands of Canada, which have become a major source of U.S. petroleum imports, are a different story entirely—but one that is still developing. Most production from the sands still comes through surface mining of tar-like bitumen, which leaves massive excavations to be filled in and restored, while processing bitumen at the surface produces undesirable emissions that have to be controlled. The future lies with extraction of petroleum from the same general area *in situ*, with processing carried out underground by various techniques already being demonstrated, and undoubtedly by others that will be developed. Eventually, the majority of hydrocarbon products from the oil sands will be recovered *in situ*. Although technologically challenging and perhaps more costly and time-consuming, *in situ* approaches will be able to reach more of the known resources while simultaneously exercising additional environmental care.

HUMANS ARE PART OF THE ENVIRONMENT

Some health and safety hazards may always exist in the workplace, but individual occupational and production equipment standards have come a long way and will probably continue to improve—in the energy industry, just as everywhere else. It may seem odd to compare working regulations in coal mines with those for operators in the control room of a nuclear power plant or a totally different set of safety rules for roofers who hoist into place conventional solar cells or strips of photovoltaics disguised as shingles, yet all are integral parts of environmental protection in a universal sense.

Environmental protection must also accompany the *delivery* of energy. It is common practice for electric utilities to remind those who call to report power outages that downed wires should be avoided and that potentially life-threatening emergencies get top priority. Double-hulled tankers protect more and more oil shipments from spillage in case of any accident. Energy cargoes of any kind on land are often either banned from tunnels and certain other routes or required to provide advance notification of planned transit so as to permit any extra precautions that might be advisable.

Perhaps it is not too droll to note that the most prevalent cause of environmental or health concerns related to energy use (namely, in the transport sector) is traffic accidents. More than 10 million occur annually, with approximately 45,000 fatalities reported in most recent years by the National Safety Council.[20] About 40 percent of those deaths are in alcohol-related accidents,[21] but at least they have nothing to do with ethanol motor fuel.

"Cleaning up at the end of the pipe" is industry slang for the fourth strategy. It refers to situations where it is impractical or less efficient to prevent emissions of some sort from being produced. The best course here is to trap harmful components before they would otherwise be released. Electrostatic precipitators in plants that burn pulverized coal have long collected the tiny bits of solid called fly ash in large adjacent structures, called baghouses because of their resemblance in function to the dust-collection portions of industrial vacuum cleaners. Once considered bothersome waste, the uniform flyash from baseload generating plants is now used widely as an ingredient in construction and paving material. This might remind us of yet another of Commoner's four ecological admonitions: Everything has to go somewhere. The clever environmentalist will look for ways any sort of "waste" can be recycled productively. Recycling sometimes—although not always—saves energy as well as expense.

Scrubbers in many power plants trap sulfur compounds. However, the resulting material presents a disposal problem in itself, since there is only a limited market for the pure sulfur that can be extracted from it. Where low-sulfur coal is available, the second strategy can also be used. As emission standards become even more rigid and plants are required to use the "Best Available Control Technology" (BACT), there is pressure to *combine* environment-sparing techniques.

REMAINING PROBLEM AREAS

Perhaps no set of problems relating to the sustainable use of energy worldwide is more important—or more challenging—than what is associated with "carbon capture and sequestration" (CCS).[22] Carbon dioxide is emitted to some extent by every fossil fuel used in every energy consuming sector. Neither a satisfactory means of collecting CO_2 from all major sources nor a foolproof system of preventing its subsequent escape has been demonstrated, and what is really needed is an integrated system for accomplishing both, at a cost that could reasonably be adopted or adapted around the globe. In the short run and in certain areas, carbon dioxide can be used to stimulate the production of oil and natural gas while leaving it trapped underground. This is not an adequate permanent solution. It remains to be seen whether the best long-term answer lies in subterranean disposal, solution in water, or chemical transformation into a disposable solid. One thing that is certain, however, is that we cannot simply stop using energy while waiting for a perfect resolution. Accepting the inevitable imperfections of the energy mobile—including a variety of costs and the exigencies imposed by time—is the most realistic outlook available.

It is technically feasible to use a method corresponding to precipitators and scrubbers to collect carbon dioxide from a plant stack, but it is still uncertain whether it will ever be employed widely because of prohibitive cost. Multiple steps are needed to dispose of or "sequester" the large volumes of carbon dioxide produced. The hot CO_2 gas will have to be separated from water vapor and other gases, cooled, and highly compressed before it can be moved off site. A more likely short-term approach for capturing CO_2 from coal-fueled generating plants, if that practice is initiated generally, may be to change the whole *process*—thus, back to strategy 3. Controlled burning can convert solid coal first into a mixture of gases, from which carbon dioxide can be isolated somewhat more easily. Sulfur compounds can be removed at this stage too, and the burnable gases remaining can be ignited and directed through a two-stage turbine—first at high pressure and temperature and then at lower pressure and temperature. Such a power-producing unit is called an integrated gasifier and combined cycle (IGCC) system. It is highly efficient overall in transforming primary energy into electricity. IGCCs are still in the stages of development and demonstration, but they should become generally available commercially within a few years.

The fifth strategy is to clean up after the fact. Mentioning it concedes that the first four strategies have not always been and will not always be perfect. Perhaps the best example is the model restoration of *some* land sites that have been disturbed by mining, including surface mining of oil sands. Natural contours are reproduced or simulated, vegetation is replaced, and wildlife can even be reintroduced if necessary. But there have been other cases where damage was more or less permanent because mountaintops were literally chopped off and streams among hills were eliminated by indiscriminate dumping. The key to success appears to be advance agreements on the steps that will be taken.

Research and development is continuing to improve cleanup after rare but attention-grabbing oil spills. "Oil-eating bacteria"[23] are still a promising but incomplete solution that can be added to physical methods of controlling the spread of oil film on water and the agonizing, labor-intensive effort to rescue individual sea birds. Fortunately, this aspect of energy's adverse effects on the environment is far more restricted than what Nature itself does every year through fires, storms, and tornadoes. We have fewer means of coping with the latter.

REGULATORY APPROACHES

How might we be kinder to the environment as we produce, transport, and use energy? What would encourage the implementation of the five strategies just touched on? Once again, the chief possibilities can be categorized:

1. Voluntary efforts;
2. The use of positive or negative incentives; and
3. Mandates.

Each of these has its place. One course may blend into the next. The idea of a balanced approach, considering *each* possibility, will not satisfy those who—intellectually or emotionally—are wedded to one or the other. Still, a combination of these three is what we have wound up with in this country over nearly four decades, since the first Earth Day. Whether you are a business or government policymaker, an energy entrepreneur, or "just" an energy consumer, it may be of some value to recognize that all three will continue.

Some find it hard to understand why anyone would fail to adopt efficiency measures that help preserve the environment at relatively little cost, no net cost, or even a profit over time. Yet the majority of modern Americans do just that. Voluntarism alone has failed repeatedly since the 1970s to do more than a small part of the job, and usually only in short-term spurts urged along by some other prods.

High energy prices have periodically reinforced exhortations for environmental protection. Concerns about energy security remind us to eschew wasteful energy habits, which boost demand for energy and in turn force us to move deeper into virgin territory in the search for adequate supplies. As often as not, the dramatic appeals of books, articles, television, and movie documentaries about imminent threats of climate change to civilization as we know it have invited exaggeration. Nevertheless, they have fostered a *voluntary* dedication to Nature that is almost religious, and this seems like a net plus for society.

In the best of all worlds, in which the general public understood energy, environment, technology, and economics better, we could rely less on two methods that augment instinctive voluntarism: (a) stimuli and (b) mandates. But expecting the best of worlds is not realistic. Meanwhile, a number of large companies in the energy industry itself have assigned chunks of their advertising budgets to promoting environmental awareness. That is considered good public relations, and in many cases it is.

The majority of professional economists appear to favor *stimuli* to individual and public action that rely on free-market principles. This translates into offering incentives for actions that are good for the environment and disincentives for those that move in the opposite direction. Federal and state governments have offered tax breaks to purchasers of certain types of vehicles and to homeowners who install solar energy systems. Corn-based ethanol got its initial boost from waivers of gasoline taxes that amounted to a subsidy of about half a dollar a gallon, starting back in the days when gasoline was well under $2. During rush hour, drivers in many states are barred from using certain traffic lanes restricted to "high-occupancy vehicles." Of course, that encouragement to ride-sharing reduces energy use at the same time it cuts back on tailpipe emissions. There are often multiple motivations for societal rules.

Positive and negative incentives may border on mandates. U.S. car-buyers are free to buy any vehicles they choose. On the other hand, Corporate Average Fuel Economy (CAFE) standards *require* U.S. auto manufacturers to offer for sale a mix of vehicles that averages at least a certain minimum mileage specification in miles per gallon. Indirectly, of course, the customers still pay. Building cars, trucks, and sports utility vehicles to meet whatever mileage specs are in place adds to manufacturing costs and sticker prices. If the availability of larger, heavier, more powerful vehicles is limited, the law of supply and demand will push their prices still higher.

TAXES VERSUS CAP-AND-TRADE

Although a deadlocked Congress had not been able by 2008 to enact legislation limiting emissions of carbon dioxide, it appeared that any bill that might pass in the next session would invoke both "soft" mandates and free-choice incentives. Continued dissension was likely, however, about the extent to which carbon limits would be applied; that is, whether only electric generators and some industrial installations might be inhibited or if vehicles and a broader segment of the public would also be affected directly. When it comes, this decision will tell less about the relationship of CO_2 emissions to U.S. energy usage (as discussed and visualized in Chapter 1) than to the forces that really shape U.S. energy policy (as discussed in Chapter 7).

The general scheme of carbon limits that seems to provoke the least resistance within Congress is one called "cap-and-trade." It would set ceilings—and possibly reduction requirements—on emissions of carbon dioxide from designated sectors; but it would allow individual entities such as electric utility companies to meet requirements either on their own or by purchasing credits from someone else for whom equivalent accomplishments were cheaper.

This whole idea is premised on the success of a similar approach taken by the Clean Air Act of 1990 for sulfur dioxide. But it is only the starting base of what must turn into a complex of legislative negotiations and perhaps judicial determinations. To launch the trading, it has been suggested that a certain number of credits should be distributed free, and that perhaps the government should offer credits within a certain time-frame at a guaranteed price. Other players—in and out of government—insist instead that all credits in the initial round be auctioned off. Debate will also take place on the height of the ceiling or the depth of reductions. Some waivers of the requirements will almost surely be granted for special circumstances. The idea of *grandfathering*, or excusing some long-time emitters entirely, will be raised. The definition of what constitutes a credit or an offset for a given number of tons[24] will be argued.

Any cap-and-trade system inherently accepts a principle of "the polluter pays." Some opponents, however, insist that any use of credits means that polluters are being granted licenses to pollute. At any rate, the fundamental laws of economics dictate that for any affected firm that expects to stay in business, most (if not all) of the costs of the credits required will still have to be passed along to end-users of energy. This gives both wholesale and retail consumers a true stake in the debates.

A simpler plan would be to tax carbon emissions, or the carbon content of fuels. Either a cap-and-trade system or some sort of carbon tax would set a price for carbon and a recognizable *value* on emission reductions. This would allow the forces of supply-and-demand to come into play, which should produce an economically efficient result if no other impediments exist. A tax would be a surer incentive for appropriate long-term, large capital investment, because it would provide better grounds for projecting stable costs into the future.[25] But tax is a four-letter word for political officeholders, no matter how one spells it. Taxes will be avoided in Washington at almost any cost.

Taxes are avoided by legislators at the state level too, but states have fewer compunctions about issuing mandates—although they are not always enforced. More than half of the states have adopted *renewable portfolio standards* (RPS) of one sort of another. An RPS orders that a certain fraction of the electricity sold by utilities within a state's borders must come from renewable energy. The generation mix, or portfolio, must include a given minimum percentage of primary energy sources defined on a state-by-state basis as green. Although one objective of such rules could be to limit national imports of scarce energy sources such as oil and natural gas, the public arguments on their behalf are almost entirely directed to the encouragement of clean energy—in other words, to protect the environment and public health.

Electricity demand is still rising, not far behind GDP in its growth rate. Many older generating plants should be retired because they are the most polluting and least efficient. Potential investors ought to be planning for increased net capacity, but the hodgepodge of RPS ground rules adds confusion and uncertainty to all the other factors in deciding the size and type of new facilities to be ordered. There is no uniform definition for renewable energy. Biomass and geothermal projects are sometimes not included. Hydro is generally *ex*cluded, although small-scale undertakings qualify in various states.

There have been many calls for Congress to enact renewable portfolio standards that apply nationwide, but such a step should be taken cautiously. Many state initiatives that have been touted proudly will prove in a few years to have set unrealistic time targets and dollar-cost estimates for the wholesale shifts required. Furthermore, utilities in RPS states have been able so far to rely on paying for electricity that qualifies as green from neighbors or even from other regions—a practice that resembles the trading of environmental credits. That would become increasingly difficult if percentage standards were imposed nationwide. The added demand would press harder on available supply.

So long as half the states do *not* have renewable portfolio standards there can be state exporters and importers of green credits, and this makes double-counting possible. For example, the RPS in Colorado[26] requires a utility "to generate *or cause to be generated* electricity from eligible energy resources in the following minimum amounts" (emphasis added). The majority of renewable energy required can thus be purchased from *outside* the state via book-keeping transactions (especially from states that do not themselves have such mandates and so are happy to trade off surplus "credits"). Credits can even be "borrowed ahead" from future years of generation. The law does not require the physical importation of electricity from a green source. It may not specifically insist that new renewable energy facilities be built ahead of schedule, although in Colorado's case this is probably happening.

Legislation of this type amounts to a Ponzi scheme. It works only unless or until *all* states try to comply with a fixed percentage mandate *simultaneously*. Translating legislation of this type to the national level would have the salutary effect of forcing a clear single definition of eligible renewable generation. But if this is restricted to wind and solar generation, there will likely be insufficient capacity for many years to come to meet the ambitious national percentage requirements that have been bandied about in Congress—beyond the ten- to fifteen-year horizons usually linked to those targets.

There is already evidence that a supply-and-demand crunch for renewable energy is approaching in this era of RPS. In the Washington, DC, area, for instance, one electricity vendor in 2008 was quoting a price of 12.8 cents per kilowatt hour for residential customers who were guaranteed under a two-year contract that 5 percent of their electricity would come from wind generation, but the price was hiked to 13.9 cents per kwh for customers who chose to have *half* their supply designated as being supplied by wind and 15.2 cents for those who asked that *100 percent* of the power they used be offset by wind-generation purchases.[27]

Not all states are alike by any means in their ability to switch to renewable fuel sources for the electricity produced within their borders, so this also raises questions of fairness, regardless of what deadlines and percentage standards might eventually be adopted from coast to coast. Enhancing transmission interconnections considerably offers a solution to this dilemma that promises added benefits, but it would be naive to ignore the fact that this will entail other environmental, cost, and political difficulties.

EXTERNALITIES AND PUBLIC GOODS

All this talk of the various types of costs involved in protecting the environment while producing and using energy may seem discouraging. It ought not be. There is a sound theoretical underpinning for prudent environmental protection, which also applies at times to the other benefits we seek—such as reliability, security, and even affordability.

Public policy seeks certain benefits that are not inevitably or automatically reflected in free-market pricing. Supply and demand in private transactions are balanced when a sufficient number of sellers and buyers agree to exchange a commodity or service for monetary payment at a price that each considers acceptable and appropriate to the benefits received. But this does not take into account *societal* benefits or detriments that may be related to market transactions overall. Those are not included in individual exchanges because, by the definition economists use, the societal benefits of a desirable environment are *public goods*. Their positive or negative values become what are technically termed *externalities*.

Text-books frequently use national defense as the classic example of a public good, because it has the two characteristics requisite in the formal definition: Its benefits extend to all members of the community, and the enjoyment of those benefits by any single member does not diminish their enjoyment by all the others. The same can be said of broad environmental protection and public safety from environmental hazards. It can apply by fairly easy extension to safety in the workplace.

There is no formal market for clean air or clean water, or for public health and well-being as such. Therefore, there is no way for the ordinary interaction of supply and demand to establish prices for them. Energy subsidies, energy taxes, special tax treatment for the suppliers and consumers of various types of energy, and even energy mandates can all be ways to internalize some energy-related environmental externalities by incorporating their imputed value into market prices.

Arguments rage constantly about when and where such internalization is necessary, how much is sufficient, and which mechanisms are fairest. This is not limited to environmental matters. One person's proposal for a "justified subsidy" is another's "giveaway," whether we are speaking of low-interest mortgage rates for energy-efficient smart houses or temporary relief from royalty payments for investors in deepwater drilling for natural gas. Once again, some principles can be offered for the reader's consideration. In this case, they are more subjective than usual—admittedly based on the author's observations and personal judgments:

1. Investment tax credits can be effective in the early stages of a new technology's development, but by the time a process or system reaches the demonstration stage *production tax credits* usually offer a better cost-benefit ratio for society. The latter produces measurable results.

2. Stipulating achievement levels for reducing emissions or for improving efficiency is preferable to specifying the precise technology or methods to be used in reaching environmental goals. Allowing flexibility in means and implicitly spurring competition is more likely to encourage creative efforts.

3. Setting very-long-term goals, such as reducing overall CO_2 emission levels to a certain point by 2050, are admirable but meaningless unless they are accompanied by intermediate goals that permit monitoring and evaluation of progress along the way—including benchmarks for which some of the officials active in setting them will bear responsibility.

4. Some innovations that appear to benefit the environment are less attractive in this respect when *all* consequences are considered. Commoner's final "law of ecology" was: "There is no such thing as a free lunch."

5. The temptation to set feel-good timetables risks disappointment and apathy. On the other hand, nothing new will be achieved without *starting*.

The final principle here leads us to the least-discussed of all elements on the energy mobile—the goal of making acceptable progress toward all the other goals and keeping them in balance while taking the necessary actions in a realistic but timely fashion. That is the subject of the next chapter.

NOTES

1. *Oxford American Dictionary* (New York: Oxford University Press, 1980).

2. Barry Commoner, *The Closing Circle: Nature, Man, and Technology* (New York: Knopf, 1971), pp. 32–46.

3. Henry David Thoreau, *Walden: or, Life in the Woods*, 1854, Chapter 4, "Sounds" (available in many editions).

4. For a quick survey, see Alvin L. Alm, "NEPA: Past, Present, and Future," *EPA Journal*, January/February 1988 (available on the Internet at http:www.epa.gov/history/topics/nepa/01.htm).

5. The International Bureau of Weights and Measures in Paris decided some time ago to replace the curie with a unit called a "Becquerel," which indicates the decay of only a *single* atomic nucleus per second and is thus capable of expressing quantities more precisely. The downside of using the becquerel is that the numbers involved become about 37 billion times as large, and many non-technical references are still in curies.

6. "Electric and Magnetic Fields (EMF) Radiation from Power Lines," retrieved March 10, 2008, from http://www.epa.gov/radtown/power-lines.html.

7. Conflicting views in the climate change debate will be found in Nicholas Stern, *The Economics of Climate Change (The Stern Review)* (Cambridge University Press, 2006), and by Indur M. Goklany, "What to Do about Climate Change," Cato Institute, Policy Analysis No. 609, Washington, DC, February 5, 2008. The validity of "either side" in that debate is really separate from opinions about the Kyoto Protocol, which was poorly designed from the start and offers a severe test in follow-on efforts to achieve its fundamental objectives. Scott Barrett has done a superb job of analyzing Kyoto's conceptual and procedural flaws while offering some advice for the future in *Environment & Statecraft: The Strategy of Environmental Treaty-Making* (New York: Oxford University Press, 2003).

8. IPCC, 2007: Summary for Policymakers. In *Climate Change 2007: The Physical Science Basis. Contribution of Working Group I to the Fourth Assessment Report of the Intergovernmental Panel on Climate Change.* Solomon, S., D. Qin, M. Manning, Z. Chen, M. Marquis, K.B. Averyt, M. Tignor, and H.L. Miller (eds.) (Cambridge and New York: Cambridge University Press, 2007), p. 2.

9. Ibid., p. 3.

10. Statistics of this type can also be misleading in themselves, because sometimes the tonnage is given for carbon alone, rather than for carbon dioxide. It is easy to reconcile such differences in measurement units by a simple calculation when gauging the significance of climate effects data, so we should be wary of attempts to compare "apples and apple pie."

11. The most famous oil spill in history from U.S. drilling offshore came near Santa Barbara, California in 1969, before the Environmental Protection Administration was created. The U.S. Minerals Management Service estimated that a "blowout" there released just over 80,000 barrels. This is sometimes reported as "more than 3 million gallons," which means the same thing, but sounds like more. There is no need to use this trick of statistics to exaggerate its impact, and its vivid coverage by television engendered understandable public opposition that contributes to drilling moratoria that persist. Its relevance today, however, is open to debate because of prevention and control techniques, as well as tighter regulation and monitoring. Analysis by the Energy Division of Santa Barbara County's Planning and Department notes in an analytical paper at its website (http://www.countyofsb.org/energy/information/seepspaper./asp) that a spill of even 100 barrels or less can cause significant damage, depending on circumstances, although it is widely agreed that about 100 barrels of oil seeps up naturally from subterranean deposits in the same area every day. Approximately two miles offshore from Santa Barbara, the "Holly" platform—which began operation before the 1969 spill—continues to produce oil without incident. In 2008, County officials seemed to favor a resumption of *new* drilling after almost four decades.

12. For more detail about Canada's oil sands, see National Energy Board, *Canada's Oil Sands—Opportunities and Challenges to 2015: An Update* (Calgary, June 2006), especially Chapter 6, "Environment and Socio-Economic." For criticism of the pace at which the oil sands are being developed, see publications of The Pembina Institute via its website: www.pembina.org .

13. In February 2008, Arizona Public Service announced that it had contracted for a 280MW solar-thermal installation 70 miles southwest of Phoenix whose equipment would blanket *three square miles* of former farmland. Despite an elaborate heat storage system, the facility will provide less than half the electrical output of a modest new coal plant.

14. Timothy Searchinger et al., "Use of U.S. Croplands for Biofuels Increases Greenhouse Gases Through Emissions from Land-Use Change," *Science*, February 29, 2008, pp. 1238–40; and J. Fargione et al., "Land Clearing and the Biofuel Carbon Debt," *Science* (on line), February 7, 2008.

15. Jenny Mandel, "Biofuels," *Greenwire*, February 18, 2008.

16. Although the *Economist* article appeared in 2008, it was apparently based on a report that had been issued almost two years earlier—Dennis Keeney and Mark Muller, "Water Use by Ethanol Plants: Potential Challenges," Institute for Agriculture and Trade Policy, Minneapolis, October 2006.

17. In December 2007 the Conference Board released a comprehensive report prepared for it by McKinsey & Company entitled *Reducing U.S. Greenhouse Gas Emissions: How Much at What Cost?* Although it is sometimes quoted out of context to make the task of reducing emissions seem simpler than it actually says it is, this is a good document to use as a checklist of options.

18. The Office of Energy Efficiency and Renewable Energy of the U.S. Department of Energy maintains a website at http://www1.eere.energy.gov/consumer/tips/. It provides advice and contact information.

19. Among the best is Alliance to Save Energy—http://www.ase.org. ASE reaches out not only to residential and commercial consumers, but to industrial energy managers and other professionals.

20. U.S. Census Bureau, *Statistical Abstract of the United States: 2007*, Table 1082.

21. Ibid., Table 1088.

22. An excellent survey of the problems is contained in an interdisciplinary study conducted by the Massachusetts Institute of Technology, co-chaired by former Deputy Energy Secretary Ernest J. Moniz and former CIA head John Deutch, and released in 2007. It is entitled *The Future of Coal: Options for a Carbon-Constrained World*. The difficulties in getting total agreement on matters of this complexity, however, are reflected in the partial disclaimer by the members of the study's blue ribbon advisory committee: "Members did not approve or endorse the report and individual members of the advisory committee have different views on one or more of matters addressed."

23. "A Hope for Oil Spill Bioremediation," *Science Daily*, May 17, 2005.

24. Thinking back again to the importance of understanding energy measurements enunciated in Chapter 1 and a specific observation earlier in this chapter, it will be crucial in judging these debates to ascertain whether numbers cited by one

party or another in various contexts refer to tons of carbon dioxide or tons of the carbon component *within* the carbon dioxide.

25. This was the conclusion of the nonpartisan Congressional Budget Office in a study it released in February 2008, *Policy Options for Reducing CO_2 Emissions.*

26. The requirement of House Bill 07-1281, as cited in the 2008 Renewable Energy Standard Compliance Plan of the Public Service Company of Colorado.

27. Private communication from Washington Gas Energy Services, an affiliate of the local gas company in the District of Columbia area. WGES competes with Pepco, the local electric utility, in providing retail customers with generation and transmission services that WGES purchases in bulk. Pepco continues to bill WGES clients for distributing the electricity to individual homes and places of business.

Six

Time, the Often Overlooked Factor

Most discussions about energy ignore or undervalue the influences of time, yet time relationships can make the difference between success and failure for a product, a project, or a policy. Time can affect the adequacy, affordability, reliability, and environmental consequences of energy supply. Demand for energy—and for various types of energy—may be modified in countless ways over time.

The passage of time can be an advantage or a disadvantage for an energy supplier or an energy consumer, although the exact result may be known only in hindsight. Rather than postponing a reaction until the pluses and minuses of time have worked themselves out, a shrewd economic actor should try to make a situational best estimate of what net adjustments are likely to take place over time—and include this routinely as part of a checklist that will help to reach any decisions that need to be made.

The goal of this chapter, as it has been in preceding ones, is to highlight some principles that a small or large energy practitioner on either the supply side or the demand side can apply to particular situations that arise. If we accept the judgment of virtually all professional energy economists, it should prove most efficient to let the private sector and competitive forces implement the bulk of the energy activities that need to occur over the next half century; but *both* government and nongovernment actors need to watch the calendar.

What positive and negative effects does time have? The passage of about a century spelled the difference between the fizzle of the Edison electric vehicle and the possible sizzle of new electric drives. A decade or so of construction delays sapped the vigor of the U.S. nuclear industry as the world's leader, while it took less time than that for China to change from a generally inward-looking energy economy to the pivot point in global energy and environment for the foreseeable future. The past few years have seen the U.S. dollar plunge, investment capital hesitate, and the prices of stocks, bonds, and commodities ride pogo sticks. Most recently, voting on a single piece of legislation (see Sidebar 6.1) flouted almost all earlier predictions of U.S. energy demand by determining how the next generation of Americans will illuminate their homes—with the result in this case that everybody will profit in a variety of ways over the long run.

SIDEBAR 6.1
Why Those Funny-Looking Light Bulbs?

Among many other provisions, the Independence and Security Act of 2007 ordered that after January 1, 2012, certain common sizes and types of incandescent and halogen light bulbs can be manufactured or imported *only* if they meet rigid new energy efficiency standards. While providing equivalent illumination, they will have to use 25 to 30 percent less electricity than those widely available at the time the legislation passed. Some sizes are given a year or two longer to comply, but guarantees will be required by 2020 to cut the energy used by most bulbs in half again. For the time being, the law exempted a number of specialty lamps (including those used in appliances or showcases, 3-way bulbs, bulbs used specifically to provide heat, etc.); but competition was opened for literally billions of sockets across the country once existing supplies run out for successive bulb-categories.

One large manufacturer, General Electric, announced that it was working on a high-efficiency incandescent lamp that might double the old average lumens-per-watt by 2010, prolonging the sales life of this particular technology. An even larger one, Phillips, quickly advertised a new halogen substitute, but also reached agreement with energy-efficiency and environmental-protection advocates to phase out its incandescents by 2016.

Federal buildings were ordered to switch to energy-efficient lighting systems by 2013. General sales of compact fluorescents and other technically competitive substitutes increased, but it still took rebates, coupon promotions, and other inducements to get Americans into the habit of seeking alternatives. Nevertheless, the option to resist change will gradually disappear.

The Alliance to Save Energy estimates that once the market transformation has taken place the savings on electric bills could add up to $18 billion annually. Energy savings would be equivalent to the output of thirty large power plants. Using coal-fired plants as the basis for calculations, close to 160 million tons of carbon dioxide would not enter the atmosphere. The net effect of this "ordered obsolescence" on the economy as a whole would seem to be positive, despite a certain amount of consumer grumbling, which may increase as the magnitude of the switchover gradually becomes clear.

Is there a trick to energy forecasting? Anyone who has thoughtfully pondered the relative merits of buying versus leasing a car, or weighed the down payments and mortgage terms on a house versus continuing to rent, is generally aware of how *some* time factors work. Sufficient information permits the application of similar but broader analysis to energy. The trick lies in knowing what to ask about, how to think about it, and knowing where to seek key data to help the process. Humility also helps, because no one is ever totally successful in predicting all of energy's complexities.

Energy and time cross paths often for everyone. You might ask yourself if you should pay a bit extra for that hybrid car now or wait until plug-in electric models prove themselves a few years hence. The right answer probably depends on the relative values one assigns to affordability, reliability, and environmental protection. Does it make sense for a state public utility commission to approve a new coal-based power plant when it looks as if concerns about climate-change might reduce its economic viability through heavy carbon taxes? The key factor there could be current reserve margins in this particular geographic area, balanced against a reasonable hurdle rate for investment and the expected rate of growth in demand over a minimum operating life of at least 40 years. Or it might be a judgment about supply and price trends for natural gas as an alternate fuel. Most such energy-related decisions are tied as well to how rapidly technological improvements can be banked on for both the supply side and the demand side.

It boils down to this in each individual situation: What are the penalties for assuming that time is on our side, versus the risks of moving ahead in an uncertain atmosphere—which can almost be guaranteed for energy?

A couple of cautionary principles are obvious. (1) Acting promptly speeds the time at which one can begin to enjoy the benefits of an action, but (2) benefits that won't be enjoyed until some time in the future are less valuable than those of equivalent intrinsic value that are already at hand. These lead to a third, corollary principle: After discounting the value of anticipated future rewards to the present, prudent investments aim at achieving *net* benefits overall. Investments should also be weighed against other choices, which include both delay and the full slate of reasonable alternative actions.

Settling things quickly is an implicit goal in energy planning and in reaching energy decisions, but inertia is hard to surmount. The possibilities of adverse results might be lessened by delay in one instance but amplified in another. The volatility of prices within the United States for oil and electricity—the two key energy ingredients—can be gut-wrenching, because even the most carefully considered energy decisions can prove to be wrong. Nevertheless, protracted indecision is rarely rewarded. Time is often an unpredictable or negative economic feature we just have to wrestle with. Sound decision making about energy is tough!

Businesses and astute individuals customarily add contingency factors as they project today's component costs into actions extending into the future. It is not enough to focus only on hypothetical escalations in prices and wages. Lags in schedule can postpone the eventual return on any investment, and delays often affect the expenses of financing itself. This was brought home resoundingly in recent years, during which some significant U.S. energy projects were delayed or even canceled, while interest rates have been bouncing up and down.

The use of money has a tangible dollar cost. Thus, time almost always translates into money, whether the outlays arise from interest on a simple personal loan or credit line to install an energy-efficient heating plant or from the costs of special equity and bond issuances to permit large-scale building and development. From a societal point of view, changes in timing can additionally have environmental impacts. Voluntarily incorporating advanced pollution-control equipment into an energy facility before the date by which it is absolutely required might earn public confidence besides protecting ambience. Capriciously dragging out licensing procedures for a needed transmission line or a well-sited nuclear power plant that emits no atmospheric pollutants is a complete waste of time if it is generally agreed that approval will come eventually.

Some energy choices that confront U.S. society, businesses, and individuals today are the sort for which temporizing demonstrably hasn't worked. Failure to improve the mileage efficiency of our vehicle fleet more rapidly may have damaged the competitive position of Detroit's auto manufacturers as much as it hurt motorists through gasoline prices that are higher now than they might have been if fuel demand had been dampened in this way sooner. Looking back and musing that we "could have . . . would have . . . should have" doesn't change things. It's more productive to look ahead.

An accurate estimate of any *future* benefit we envision—whether it is lower home heating bills over a period of years or better ability to cope with the next potential crisis in some aspect of energy supply—should discount its anticipated value by some logical factor to judge what it is worth to us immediately. A simple approach for any size of investment is also to consider opportunity cost. What else might be done with the capital, and what would the weighted return on that likely be? Such an assessment yields a net present value, or the maximum amount that we can afford—even if we are willing just to break even.

Benefits are not always limited to dollars and cents. Opting for adequate and reliable energy supply at some point in the future involves peace of mind, convenience, and ultimately perhaps comfort for an individual. Environmental protection—whether related to water, land, air, or climate—raises questions of intergenerational equity. What effect might the development of energy-efficient

U.S. living patterns over the next decade have on our global standing as a nation in 2050? These are *economic* questions, which neither legislators nor energy entrepreneurs nor ordinary householders talk about much openly. They *should* mull them over, replacing the generalities in a book such as this with specifics that apply for them and which satisfy their own values as new issues and choices present themselves.

Potential side effects should be analyzed early, since snap judgments may otherwise trigger unintended consequences that linger and cascade. An example has been the increased food prices that should have been no surprise after corn-based ethanol was anointed by federal legislators as *the* prime substitute for gasoline. Such dangers are heightened by the herd instinct that results in successive market stampedes toward the stocks of one energy source after another. At times since the 1970s, the generators of U.S. electricity have been advised for various reasons to switch heavily from coal to oil to nuclear power to coal to natural gas to wind. Some companies literally went bankrupt trying.

Switching quickly has costs. Switching back and forth, unless done by design, is even more costly.

SUPPLY AND DEMAND ARE DYNAMIC, BUT NOT ALWAYS INSTANTLY RESPONSIVE

Hypothetically, some energy dilemmas will self-adjust. Eventually, for instance, we will either have to find ways to live with the problems raised by massive coal usage or else we will need to give up our most abundant energy resource. Considering the multiple conflicting goals that need to be balanced, however, this won't happen completely on its own in any time frame that a majority of our population would consider satisfactory. For that reason alone, it would be unrealistic to pretend that there will be no interventions in the marketplace on the grounds of speeding things up, even though economists will continue to urge that market mechanisms be used wherever feasible to leave competition and initiative as free as possible.

Whatever actions are considered, time factors dictate that the actors should weigh in advance the practicality and net payoff of various actions that might be taken in the short-term, mid-term, and long-term future. Failure to consider *all three* segments of the future yields incomplete planning and makes it difficult to monitor progress. To consider another example, it is a stretch to suggest that research and development programs on cellulosic ethanol will affect filling station prices this year.[1] We can even be pretty sure that motor fuels derived from the enzymatic processing of lumber industry wastes will not be commercialized in less than a decade, under even the most favorable circumstances. Yet it would be irresponsible to dismiss them, because they make sense conceptually and their potential value would be great.

If we content ourselves with only long-term goals we never get started toward them. If we are too short-sighted in planning, time may slip away. The principle here is that an integrated time-series of benchmarks usually works best. This is true even if the original plans and schedules have to be modified along the way up the learning curve.

Supply, demand, and price interact to produce balance, but they are slow to do so if any one of the three is insufficiently "elastic" (i.e., readily responsive to change). A few years ago, energy economists broadly accepted the generality that U.S. demand for energy was rather *in*elastic—especially in the case of motor fuel and electricity. Many Americans look on these almost as necessities of life. Even apart from price, however, energy demand is affected by government regulation, peer pressure, changing technology, and substitution possibilities—as well as economic conditions and simple personal predilection. As a result, historical statistics are hard to interpret definitively in trying to predict the future.

U.S. oil consumption early in 2008 was below where it had been a year earlier, but it is sheer conjecture in the short run to suggest how much of this was due respectively to the high price of gasoline, to perceptions of recession, or to popular acceptance of a new energy efficiency ethic. With more government intervention apparently on the horizon, it will become ever more difficult to foresee how future supply and demand will *really* interact and thus how to modify one's own actions accordingly. Nevertheless, we should try.

Without quibbling over definitions, it won't hurt in evaluating most projects to assume arbitrarily that actions whose tangible results can be gauged within two years are "short-term." "Mid-term" might then refer to any period within 10 years, and anything beyond that can be considered "long-term." We need all three. Other definitions might be used, but these have political significance that is realistic rather than simply symbolic. Two years represents the length of a single term in the U.S. House of Representatives, and Congress controls the federal purse. A decade is slightly more than the administration of a two-term U.S. president. Energy forecasts frequently try to project 20 or 30 years into the future, and this has some value; but interrelated conditions change sufficiently so that planning for results any more than 10 years out requires special caution and thus can be designated "long term."

SECTORAL CHARACTERISTICS, BUT NO SIMPLE FORMULAS

Some observable energy patterns border on being principles. Experience and intuition suggest that there may be modest, short-term blips in the response of residential and personal transportation demand for energy to an economic downturn or fuel price changes, but that more permanent adjustments in energy demand by those sectors take longer. Commercial usage of energy should be more price-elastic than that in the residential sector because of the willingness of businesses to react to perceived cyclical trends. Industry-sector response is perhaps most flexible, because fuel switching and controls on production are more conventional considerations there. This was fairly obvious between 2002 and 2006, when natural gas prices rose sharply and that was followed by industrial demand destruction in regard to that fuel.

Unfortunately, there are no energy elasticity tables that we can refer to currently with any degree of trust. We *do* know that two oil-price crises in the 1970s coincided with successive crimps in what had been an extraordinarily steep climb for oil consumption after World War II. We also know that national use of both oil and electricity then resumed what has seemed like an inexorable rise, but at a slower rate. Since our population was growing and GDP was expanding at an even faster rate, we like to credit ourselves with having become more energy efficient. That claim may be somewhat overstated, because structural changes to the U.S. economy in the meantime have shifted the country toward a service economy and away from energy-gobbling industries such as primary metal production and heavy-duty manufacturing. At the same time, computers and innumerable new electronic devices became as essential to everyday work and recreation as the automobile. Their hunger for electricity was as voracious as an SUV's thirst for gasoline, but in both cases technological fixes can help level things off.

The disturbing reality is that quantitative economic analysis cannot predict with certainty where we will go from here in terms of interactive response by supply, demand, and price. Badgered in a congressional hearing many years ago to skip scenarios of the future and "just give us the facts," the very first director of the Energy Information Administration gave a piercing response that is still true: "There are no facts about the future." This leads to a more controversial principle: Forecasting is not prophecy. Yet forecasting is valid, and perhaps invaluable—so long as it evolves from serious thought and digests whatever trustworthy market research is available.

PRICES MATTER

Everything else being equal, high energy prices curb demand and encourage supply—but only over time. Low prices have the opposite effects, with the same qualifier that reactions take time. By early 2008, the prices of crude oil on the world market and of U.S. gasoline, even adjusted for inflation, were at all-time peaks. Because the construction of new generating plants had slowed and natural gas prices appeared to be headed higher, it seemed inevitable that electricity rates would continue to climb—although, as an earlier chapter noted, this will vary locally because of decentralized price regulation by public utility commissions.

What will follow? Even the authoritative and objective Energy Information Administration cannot be counted on for unequivocal guidance in making future energy purchases and investments, but it can be a big help if its publications are interpreted properly.

The EIA periodically publishes[2] "reference case" projections for supply and demand for all energy sources and across all consumption sectors over the next couple of decades or so. All of its key assumptions are stated quite clearly. By its charter and tradition, the EIA usually does a good job of being "policy neutral" in these projections—even to the extent of irritating the White House and Congress occasionally, regardless of which party happens to be in power.

To preserve neutrality, the EIA begins with what it admits is an unrealistic assumption in its reference case—namely, that whatever governmental policies are in force at the start of the projection will remain unchanged over an extended period. Postulating a specified rate of economic growth, its models for supply-and-demand forecasts of energy and individual energy sources then go on to assume that economically rational choices among competing fuels will be made, based on price alone. This too is unrealistic, because many energy consumers lack complete information and because habits and emotions play incalculable roles. For the sake of simplicity and because the EIA recognizes that trying to project market trends in the very short term is a gamble, it generally shows future prices rising or declining along smooth curves, rather than bobbing up and down as experience shows they often do. World oil prices—always subject to geopolitical machinations—are tied to the agency's current assessments of future supply and demand and its own current evaluation of the international outlook.

All this makes the reference case hypothetical, although media reports almost invariably make it sound flatly predictive. The EIA normally publishes separate projections for high and low world oil prices, and often for faster or slower technological progress than the recent past might suggest. Dozens of alternate scenarios were developed for its 2008 projections. The basis for these various "sensitivity" cases is always described, although perhaps in appendices that the press and general public may ignore completely.

If one recognizes how and why the EIA puts these numbers together, the data are extremely enlightening as a starting point for policymakers, purchasers, or prospective producers. Legitimately, the rest of the work is up to such decision-makers. They must add their own estimates of what deviations from the objective reference-case assumptions are most probable, as well as how these would affect supply, demand, and price.

CUTTING LOSSES CAN BE A VICTORY

More often than not, postponing a well-grounded decision is costly. Yet even taking the best available energy course at the most opportune time does not guarantee short-term gain. Just as the net environmental effects of energy-related actions should be calculated over an entire life-cycle, so should decisions about energy actions in relation to their true cost—as well as adequacy and reliability of supply over some relevant period of time. All this is just as pertinent to the purchase of a durable piece of energy-using equipment such as a refrigerator as it is to investment in a startup enterprise to produce alternative fuels of some sort.

Today there are two extra wild cards in the energy hands being dealt. One is global tightness in energy supply, as treated earlier. The other consists of pressures to restrict emissions of carbon dioxide from the energy cycle. Production of conventional oil is declining, energy demand is booming in developing countries, and we are becoming more alert to the real costs of environmental challenges that range from local pollution to global climate change. The chief economist of the International Energy Agency was candidly correct in summarizing the composite conclusions of IEA's *World Energy Outlook 2007*: "We believe we have enough energy resources worldwide. We have enough money. What we do not have is the time. Time is running out."[3]

This is not an appeal to try to accomplish everything at once, which would be impossible. It *is* a call to action. We should still keep in mind all of the motivating energy goals discussed in earlier chapters: adequacy, cost, supply reliability, and environmental stewardship. But it is more important than ever to keep in mind the way *time* figures into each of these.

RETURN ON INVESTMENT (ROI)

Basic U.S. national energy policy depends at least as much on the chairman of the Federal Reserve Board as it does on the Secretary of Energy. The Fed encourages or discourages investment—on either the supply side or the demand side—by indirectly controlling the total amount of money in circulation in all forms and making it more or less expensive to borrow funds by its influence on interest rates. Trust in the board's actions also builds or nibbles away at public confidence levels, affecting purchases throughout the economy, and those in turn convert into current and prospective energy demand. Finally, the value of U.S. currency in foreign exchange markets has a direct effect on oil prices, because world oil prices are quoted in U.S. dollars.

Concerns about energy itself are never *the* major factor in U.S. monetary policy. Executive and legislative governmental actors who wish to nudge the energy economy in one direction or another will continue to use more narrowly directed tools, such as special tax treatment and conditional subsidies. However, private-sector decisions about energy should be taken with full consciousness of *trends* in national monetary policy, since these produce the base on which rests the structure of energy investments large and small.

Expectations about inflation are a prime energy consideration, especially for short-term and mid-term programs. A future decline in the real value of U.S. currency means that monetary returns from an investment will come in devalued dollars, and this discourages investors. On the other hand, there have been times recently when the Federal discount rates dropped so low that real interest rates became negative for the near future—falling below the inflation rate and thus almost pleading for investment.

"Easy" financing increases the attractiveness of capital-intensive projects in general and those that have longer payback periods in particular. When the time-value of money is relatively high, there is greater incentive to limit the amount of capital at risk and to turn over profits more quickly—even at the chance of reducing overall total return. As this chapter was being written, apprehensions about national and global recession implied that the Federal Reserve would favor the downside in future interest rates for the sake of economic stimulus. Yet statement after statement revealed Fed uneasiness about inflation too, which hinted a willingness at some point to move in the opposite direction. Stay alert!

Questions of the timing of investment in relation to carrying costs and their effects on ROI apply to both the supply side and the demand side. Consider in general how this affects oil and electricity, which have had the leading roles throughout this book—oil as the most critical primary energy source and electricity as the key intermediate form of energy.

There are almost always pros and cons. Resources of "conventional" oil and natural gas may have peaked globally, and in North America they surely have done so. Ultra-deep drilling, offshore drilling, and conversion of the unconventional products of "heavy" oil deposits, bitumen, and kerogen into useful hydrocarbons are all inherently more expensive than traditional oil production. Their development also takes more time. Because these larger investments take longer to amortize, their time-related costs mount. Thus, time becomes a greater risk factor for the investment opportunities of this type that are available. As technology stands today, however, the quantitatively meaningful substitution of synthetic liquids for gasoline and diesel fuel is realistically only a *long*-term strategy as defined above. This argues for prompt and continued heavy investment in oil exploration and development.

OPINIONS DIFFER

Every major oil company has a staff of economists, and one of their tasks is to predict both the price of oil and the price of money. These in-house forecasts are closely protected trade secrets, because they influence strategic corporate decisions that can involve billions of dollars. Thus, one would look for them in vain in the "outlook" documents published annually by such industry leaders as ExxonMobil, Shell, and BP and generally available via company websites. Nevertheless, those are worth examining for their respective slants and insights. As with the EIA's *Annual Energy Outlook*, the company documents may offer more than one "scenario"—depending on different sets of assumptions. A corporate "reference case" may even use or adapt some of the EIA's assumptions, although one should be aware that the published results do not necessarily jibe with a company's own best thinking. That remains a proprietary asset.

At times there appear to be stark differences among companies in the way they approach investment opportunities, despite the fact that they are privy to roughly identical current data and it may be presumed that their economic analytical staffs are comparably competent. In 2007–2008 ExxonMobil promised a legal fight against Hugo Chávez's expropriation of hydrocarbon properties in Venezuela while Chevron and others chose to invest in continued operations there under new, far less favorable rules. ExxonMobil announced that it no longer foresaw an adequate return from a long-proposed Alaskan natural gas pipeline. But Conoco Phillips and BP offered to build one, while even declining subsidies from the state. This is fairly clear evidence that more is involved than what shows up in the balance sheet of a project proposal. Timing is one possible explanation.

The simple fact that new leasing bids, exploration prospects, field development, and investments in supporting infrastructure or anything else promise to be profitable for a company does not guarantee that projects will be undertaken. The availability of capital is not endless, even for the giants of the industry. Alternate opportunities for investment exist globally, and the risk-versus-return prospects must be ranked. With profits in many cases near or at record levels, there are also totally different avenues in which to direct large expenditures. Increasing stock dividends instead of allocating spare capital to investments may strengthen share prices and please shareholders. If broad market weakness has depressed stock prices, it may be a good idea to buy back and retire large blocks of one's own stock.

The national oil companies that control 80 percent of the world's proved oil reserves face different sets of questions in regard to time, and they are not uniform. A few members of OPEC—Saudi Arabia, Kuwait, and the United Arab Emirates—have such large reserves that they can look forward to being global suppliers for decades to come. This makes them leery of allowing prices to rise too high, lest this speed up various programs among customer countries to reduce their dependence on oil. A study in 2008 by Chatham House suggested that some others—including Algeria, Angola, and Nigeria—were so dependent themselves on revenue from oil exports that they would have to develop alternative bases for economic growth within a couple of years or contemplate an inevitable downward spiral once reserves start to decline.[4] An added dilemma is whether to cheat on OPEC production quotas for faster returns or press the organization seriously to limit exports and thus keep prices as high as possible.

The related generic question for owners of depletable resources such as oil and gas is whether to produce and sell them or to hold them in the ground in hopes of achieving more profit eventually. This is a classic problem in economics. The theory that is cited most widely was developed by Harold Hotelling early in the twentieth century. With various caveats and the addition of numerous corollaries since then, its thrust is to suggest that such decisions should be reached by comparing the likely rate of future increase in price over a certain time-period with the rate of return that might be expected from interest in the meantime on the proceeds from producing and selling today—giving the nod to whichever course of action offers greater profit.[5] Since so much depends on foreknowledge of the unknowable and the play between perceptions and reality, however, this is less than a magic formula.

PRICE LEVELS CAN CHANGE

Expectations of general inflation are another factor in decision making, whether by individuals, businesses, or countries. The fear that prices are bound to go up overall may be critical from more than a single aspect in one's determination to replace an older car or truck with one that offers better fuel efficiency. The sticker price this year might be lower than it will be later. The lower operating costs will click in sooner, and they may become even more meaningful if gasoline prices continue to rise. The combination of a slow car market and relatively low loan rates may provide a deal now that couldn't be matched a couple of years hence.

The chief financial officer and other top officials of a big, vertically integrated oil firm have a list of considerations that is much more elaborate than that of a single car buyer, but the two have parallels—and variations. Wages and material costs show little indication of falling in the future, so moving ahead quickly can seem judicious. Most signs point to a world price for crude oil that will keep prospective returns well above the company's hurdle rate in anticipated profits for approving new projects. That gives a "go" signal for capital investment. Still, U.S. officials and even ordinary citizens are talking a lot about the need to kick the nation's "addiction to oil," while—for a variety of reasons—countries throughout the world are seeking ways to limit the growth rate of fossil-fuel demand. Since crude oil is priced and traded worldwide in U.S. dollars, the weakness of our greenback in exchange markets makes motor fuel prices seem even higher—especially in this country, where the cost of crude may account for more than two-thirds of the price for each gallon of gasoline. Prolonged high prices plus more sympathy for conservation could reduce consumption more rapidly than in the past. All that tends to discourage expanded drilling, or any other type of heavy expenditure aimed largely at increasing supply.

From the perspective of national energy policy, a balanced approach on oil supply and demand has many advantages in an era of volatile prices and uncertainty. Although the country cannot look forward in either the short term or the mid term to independence from all hydrocarbon imports, it should discourage the growing gap between total domestic demand and "friendly" supply, and do so sooner rather than later. This acknowledges the relative reliability of imports from Canada and Mexico as well as domestic production. The gap can be narrowed either by jacking up continental supply or by trimming demand, but since either action will take time to make any appreciable difference, it is logical to press both courses simultaneously.

There are numerous ways to reduce petroleum consumption, ranging from energy-efficiency measures in buildings that heat with oil to recycling plastics; but the "biggie" can come in transportation of all varieties. Here it is interesting to contrast the way profit-oriented companies and the mass of individuals have most often reacted.

Squeezed by dwindling net revenues, airlines have juggled schedules and otherwise tried to pack each flight with as many passengers as possible. This is the travel industry's counterpart of ride sharing by commuters. They have also tried to stretch each gallon of costly fuel by limiting weight per paying customer. Luggage limits are being strictly enforced and passengers are charged for bags that used to be free. Magazine racks and other nonessential items are being removed from cabins—the equivalent of clearing heavy and nonessential junk from car-trunks. Above all, fuel efficiency is being pushed closer to the top of the list of preferences for new plane purchases when they take place.

Instead of grumbling about these departures from the emphasis on passenger comfort and convenience we might prefer in air travel, it would be worthwhile if U.S. auto drivers gave even a modest bit of thought to how they might emulate the penny-pinching airline managers in the way they approach car travel. As noted in the preceding chapter, this would spin off environmental benefits for all. Moving about by auto would become more affordable. Energy security would be improved. If such an attitudinal change took place immediately and broadly—based on multiple motivations—time would be on our side.

The other avenue in restraining the projected growth in our national imports of oil *could* be to find ways of stepping up domestic production. This is a far less popular policy recipe. It is easy to portray bigness as badness, and opening up additional drilling areas in Alaska or offshore to Big Oil lacks the advantage that efficiency offers in being environmentally inviting—even though drilling "at home" under tight environmental and safety regulations is preferable to trusting marginal producers in other countries to provide necessary supply as the world market demands it.

The policy instruments available to boost North American oil production merit consideration. These include some sort of relief from royalty payments in government-controlled frontier areas to speed their development. They might involve faster write-offs for certain categories of investments, or even extend to more generous tax credits for specialized research and development. Loan guarantees or low-interest financing are probably off the table, but public-private financing might deserve a look—perhaps even for parts of the Western Gap in the Gulf of Mexico, where rival national claims to mineral rights between the United States and Mexico were resolved by treaty only in 2000 and a moratorium on hydrocarbon production is set to expire in 2010.

Many of the factors in world oil prices are beyond U.S. control, but our very size as both a producer and a consumer of oil gives us leverage that most "price takers" lack. Understanding time elements helps individuals and enterprises formulate plans of action that—with concerted effort—have some hope of stabilizing the supply-and-demand relationships at acceptable levels. Then, everything depends on how anxious the U.S. citizenry and its representatives in government are to confront our domestic shortfall in oil—in the short-term, mid-term, and long run.

ELECTRICITY AND TIME FACTORS

It is fairly straightforward to apply some of the principles enunciated earlier in this chapter to the electricity sector. Gas-fired combustion turbines are essentially off-the-shelf items that can be ordered and installed with far less lead time than coal-fueled plants or generating stations employing nuclear reactors. They are also less capital-intensive and obviously less likely to arouse local resistance or protests organized by some groups that would like to halt the construction of coal and nuclear plants entirely.

The main problem with the natural gas option is uncertainty about future fuel prices. Depending on the source, it is easy to find seemingly authoritative cost-projections that "show" gas-based generation as either better or worse than its competitors in economic feasibility over a 40-year operating span. These assessments depend on assumptions about relative *fuel* costs over time—as well as the degree of certainty regarding the time it will take to complete the steps in design, licensing, procurement, and construction that must precede actual revenue-producing operation for any power plant. A principle for judging such comparisons is to avoid *national* statistics and to hone in on as much detail as possible that is directly relevant to each *local* situation.

Oil can almost be ruled out as a factor for the future in the gradual replacement and expansion of existing U.S. generating capacity. Coal, natural gas, existing hydro installations, and nuclear power will play the leading roles statistically, but a large supporting cast is necessary too. The principal time limitation for solar power and wind generators comes from the same drawback mentioned earlier in respect to providing "adequate" energy. It may take less time to install a wind generator than a turbine-generator that will use coal as its steam source, but the time advantage for wind begins to evaporate if hundreds of wind machines are required to produce an equivalent output of electricity.

A more serious barrier to the fuller development of solar and wind resources is one that Congress could remove easily. Federal support programs of various kinds for these and other renewable forms of energy have existed for decades, but successive legislative provisos have persistently been renewed for only a few years at a time. Since their potential economic competitiveness depends on long-life-cycle calculations, investment on a meaningful scale in generation contribution will poke along until some long-term commitment is made. The broader adoption of renewable portfolio standards for electricity across the United States could be a partial solution, but that raises separate difficulties—as noted in Chapter 5.

EFFICIENCY STARTS TO HELP IMMEDIATELY, ONCE IT STARTS

Time has various roles to play on the demand side of the electricity equation as well. If federal legislation had not set a deadline beyond which conventional incandescent light bulbs could no longer be sold in this country, the ongoing conversion to more efficient forms of illumination would surely have dragged on for several times as long. Efficiency standards for air conditioners, refrigerators, TV sets, electric motors, and other such consumers of electricity are periodically updated, but their effect is still limited to new production only, and the existing stock in use for each is enormous. Furthermore, American habits are such that newly purchased appliances are often not actual replacements. Across this country, old refrigerators and freezers have routinely been moved to basements as kitchens are remodeled and newly efficient models take their places. Electricity consumption actually increases. Convenience is chosen over both cost and environmental concern. Time toward progress stands still.

The best hope for increasing efficiency in residential consumption of electricity at a notable pace probably exists in the slow but inexorable move toward differential pricing and its ultimately indispensable companion, real-time metering. For many electric utilities, demand is highest in summer because of the air-conditioning loads. Such companies have long been allowed to charge more for each kilowatt hour during the season of greater demand. Many have by now also adopted a scale of charges that varies similarly with the time of day. There is generally less call for electricity in homes when family members are more likely at school, at work, or asleep.

There are logical extensions to the practice. If the electric meters themselves can record and report not only the amounts of electricity consumed by a customer household but also the exact times of consumption, the natural law of supply and demand can fairly adjust each portion of the bill. Reordering schedules involves some inconvenience, but if doing the laundry after the sun goes down saves enough money, you can bet that a certain percentage of all customers will make that choice. In fact, some utilities offer a flat reduction in electric bills overall to customers who authorize the company in advance to reduce voltage in their specific electricity service briefly and modestly during periods of particularly high regional demand. This is done with guarantees that appliances will continue to function acceptably and will not be damaged in the process.

Customers are sometimes leery of this approach, and extra incentives must sometimes be offered to allow the installation of the time-of-day meters themselves. Once this is done, however, the efficiency battle is more than half won. Any customer who is *aware* of the differences timing imposes on electricity supply is more likely to cooperate for mutual advantage. The fact that the practice is environment-friendly adds appeal.

What benefit does the seller of electricity derive? Actual demand *peaks* may be brief and constitute only a tiny percentage of year-round deliveries, but they can be very expensive to the supplier. To ensure an adequate reserve margin that avoids system-wide brownouts or blackouts, a utility must either maintain its own peaking units as spare capacity or be prepared to buy electricity on the open market from another supplier—when the unit price may be a hundred times normal or more.

Installing special meters, explaining all this to customers, and developing two-way communication and control systems is not cheap, but some electricity suppliers have begun to decide that the return on investment is justified. Others have been required in some way by state public service commissions to introduce such measures, and there is a move to have demand-reduction expenditures accounted for to some extent in the rate base on which regulated utilities are allowed a putative profit.

Many efficiency efforts would be transformed rapidly if some practical and economical way to store electricity could be developed. Intermittent energy sources such as solar and wind facilities would also get a huge incidental boost from such a technological breakthrough. Unfortunately, electricity storage has been the ever-elusive target of R&D industrywide and nationwide since the 1970s, when a section of the Energy Research and Development Administration—a forerunner to the U.S. Department of Energy—tackled the problem head-on. Today we are still talking about some of the same approaches examined then: flywheels, air compression in underground chambers, sophisticated chemical systems, and so on. Like nuclear fusion, a solution may *always* be "forty years away." Or it could start to emerge next week. It's another question of time.

WHEN WILL IT BE READY?

Once any householder makes the decision to convert to a new, high-efficiency hot water heater, it becomes obvious that the unit won't be installed instantaneously. After determining how to finance the improvement, he or she runs into the problem of vendor selection, choosing the appropriate size and other model characteristics, and finally scheduling the plumber. Local regulations will undoubtedly also require that official safety inspectors check the quality of the work on completion. Considering the complexity of coordinating schedules, this relatively simple process may take weeks from start to finish.

Multiply that by several hundredfold to appreciate the lead times that may be involved in a major energy project. Regulatory approvals for new generating plants, refineries, pipelines and power lines require a prudent planner to build in lead times; and the most common complaint about overall U.S. energy policy that has come from the energy industry for the past quarter-century has been about regulatory barriers. From a national planning perspective, however, licensing hearings and procedural delays in winning the necessary government approvals are not in themselves the only sources of time lag.

Uncertainties about the future will always exist, and they will always impede investment because of the difficulties in quantifying risk, but energy companies operate to such a great extent within matrices of legislation and regulation that apprehensions about prospective *changes* in the ground rules can be the most serious sources of delay. The first federal CAFE standards were introduced in the 1970s, and there have been periodic efforts to increase or broaden their mileage requirements for vehicles ever since. But the first major revision did not follow until 2007—leaving potential investors in mileage improvements to tread water. Once either energy mandates or energy incentives are established in law, it also takes months if not years for the implementing mechanisms to come into force.

The Energy Independence and Security Act of 2007 gave specific and tangible support to the development of ethanol, more efficient lighting, higher-mileage vehicles, and new nuclear power plants; but in each case major results were not scheduled to appear until the second half of the following decade. Thus the time scales for these initiatives were comparable to what might have come from ending various prohibitions on drilling for oil and natural gas—a supply-side reform proposed at the same time but rejected because it could not promise quick benefits.

Major accomplishments always seem to take time, and this may be prolonged further by legislative and administrative foot-dragging. Fed up with the amount of guesswork imposed on investors by governmental failure to clarify its intentions in one respect, many of the nation's top industrial leaders have taken an unprecedented step for a regulation-burdened sector. They have urged the government to impose limits on the emissions of carbon dioxide, but to resolve quickly the details of how this is to be done. The group they formed, the U.S. Climate Action Partnership (USCAP), is backing new regulation rather than fighting the difficulties this would impose on business. A key reason is admittedly self-interest. By accepting the inevitability of such restrictions—and perhaps having some voice in how they are designed—companies are in a better position to develop strategies of compliance.

One of USCAP's founders was the chairman and CEO of General Electric, Jeff Immelt, who is even more aggressive in acknowledging the importance of the time factor to all involved in facing the challenge of possible global climate change. GE had already launched and publicized a corporate program called Ecomagination in 2005, addressing both the supply side and the demand side in an effort to limit harmful emissions. Explaining why he had moved so vigorously at that time, Immelt told the *Wall Street Journal*: "There's no percentage for any CEO in the world to run his or her business thinking that there are not going to be carbon caps some day. Because the day it becomes law, you're five years late. And you either get out ahead of these things or you get stomped by them."[6]

As energy technologies mature and change, a minimum critical path of time develops between the stages of concept, demonstration, public acceptance, market penetration, and really making a difference. Along the way, delays can appear in places that the public rarely thinks about. For instance, it has been so long since a commercial nuclear power plant has been ordered in the United States that the country is no longer capable of manufacturing certain key components, such as large forgings like reactor vessels. They now must be ordered from Japan. Nuclear engineering has also faded as a U.S. course of study, and the necessary pool of specialized labor has all but dried up.

Another source of delay consists of waiting for the appearance of supporting physical infrastructure. Other chapters have noted that it is lacking for other energy sources that need to be expanded: transmission lines for wind and solar facilities in areas remote from demand centers, rail transport for biomass sources to central locations for processing into fuel, dedicated pipelines for alcohol fuels, and—perhaps at some point—a network of pipes that might rival the one we have for natural gas to deliver compressed carbon dioxide from collection points at sources such as factories and power plants to regions where the gas can be pumped safely into geologic formations that will prevent its rerelease.

CLIMATE CHANGE: A NEW KIND OF PROBLEM

We have seen some of the reasons why foresight and active planning are critical in respect to energy. They will be necessary to keep supplies adequate, reliable, and affordable in relation to demand—and without serious interruption to any of these goals. Chapter 5 noted the additional requirements involved in avoiding pollution of land, air, and water. But an immensely larger scale is involved in the issue of avoiding the atmospheric concentrations of certain gases—many related closely to energy production and use—that could disrupt the entire planet's climate. This necessitates thinking in time horizons that have never before been contemplated seriously.

In March 2008, the National Academy of Sciences sponsored the Summit on America's Energy Future in Washington. It brought together the top minds in related fields to discuss the very sorts of problems treated throughout this book. One presentation in particular helped to crystallize time factors in reference to our present circumstances.[7] The impression it left was that it may take five years of intense and well-informed policy and political discussions to begin to see a mid-term and long-term path along which we might sensibly begin to cope with issues on a global basis. That is because those who make investment decisions must look out 25 to 35 years. The approach to new technologies and resources should survey the future over half a century to 80 years. And all of this grows out of the fact that the entire human race is hurtling in the direction of a time horizon for climate-change impacts that extends meaningfully for at least a century or two.

Such time factors are not being taken seriously now by enough people, in large part because the numbers themselves can be bewildering. Let's try simplifying.

The atmospheric percentages of carbon dioxide, methane, chlorofluorocarbons, and certain other compounds build up in the same way finance charges do over time—especially if we keep adding to the "debt" with apparently no prospect of "paying down the principal" in our lifetimes. As Chapter 5 pointed out, these gases are being released in widely varying amounts. Each has its own distinctive residence time in the atmosphere before breaking down or being absorbed in some way. Rather than trying to deal with *all* the offending gases, though, let's just look at carbon dioxide—the most important one.

Scientists tell us that Earth's atmosphere now contains about 800 billion tons of carbon in this form—approximately one-third more than it did when we started burning fuels at a much faster pace as a result of the Industrial Revolution. Since Chapter 5 noted that the current carbon load is equivalent to roughly 380 parts per million, we might keep in mind that we increase concentration by 1 ppm each time we add 2 billion tons of carbon. We are actually pumping about 7 billion tons of fresh CO_2 into the atmosphere annually by burning fossil fuels, but that number has been rising. At the rate global energy demand has been growing, emissions are projected to rise even faster in the future. Thanks to absorption of CO_2 by water that covers most of the planet's surface and by vegetation that covers some of the rest, the *net* increase annually now is roughly 4 billion tons—or about 2 ppm. Half a century from now, according to an amalgam of forecasts, we may well be adding *14* billion tons each year. At this rate, the atmospheric concentrations by then would exceed 500 ppm—the point at which many scientists assume serious damage to public health, the economy, and the environment unless the growth in concentration can be stabilized.

Despite loose talk about "tipping points," we aren't *sure* how much more CO_2 Earth might tolerate before a growth in planetary warming could run away. Nature has a marvelous capacity for self-healing, although we certainly cannot predict how long it might take to kick in, if ever. Evidence of possibly substantial adverse consequences from anthropogenic climate change seems almost indisputable, yet we cannot rule out a lesser likelihood that the global warming seen thus far arises from other causes. Nevertheless, the risk-reward ratio is such that countervailing human actions (including both emission reduction and adaptation) are justified. We should probably assume that they can do some good.

Actions that can be taken by the United States alone promise only puny results in comparison to what seems to be happening. China has already passed this country in emission of "global warming gases," and the Chinese are building one or two new coal-burning power plants every week. The energy infrastructure being developed there will be with us for a long time.

Such problems deserve a broader arena of discussion than this book. What can and should be done here, however, is briefly to suggest their scope. In this task one can do no better than refer to the visualization conceived by Professor Robert Socolow of Princeton—the "wedges of sustainability." Figure 6.1 reproduces the simple illustration Professor Socolow and co-author Stephen Pacala published in 2004,[8] and which has been widely copied and adapted ever since in serious discussions of how to address possible climate change. The top line in the upper graph shows *annual* carbon emissions rising from around 7 billion tons to 14 billion in fifty years, as now projected. In this "business as usual" (BAU) scenario,[9] the trend continues upward beyond that—because natural absorption of CO_2 can't keep pace with the new volumes being added. Concentration wouldn't be stabilized until it had increased even more—into what might be presumed to be a true danger zone. Simple arithmetic shows that a target *ceiling* of 500 ppm requires instead that the annual volume of emissions level off by then at somewhere around the current rate of 7 billion. Such a course is suggested by the smoothed-out lower line in the same graph, labeled "WRE500."[10]

Socolow concedes the hopelessness of stabilizing emissions quickly. Instead of allowing the emissions rate to double over half a century, however, he

FIGURE 6.1
Socolow's Decarbonization Wedges

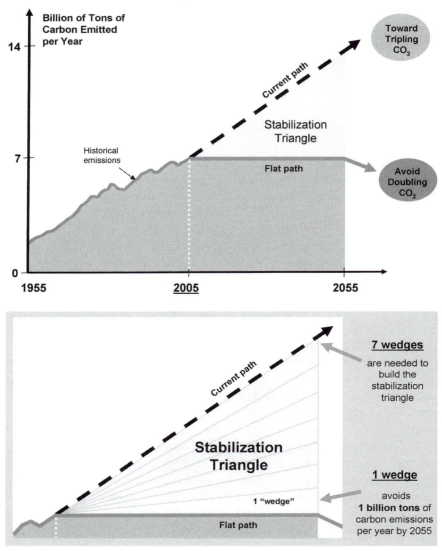

Source: Carbon Mitigation Initiative, Princeton University. Used with permission.

hypothesizes the heroic but perhaps achievable goal of slowing that growth *gradually* so that the emissions rate will be no higher in fifty years than it was at the start of this ambitious effort. That course is idealized in the lower graph.

Recognizing that the gap between an ultimately flat projection of emissions and our present course cannot be handled by a single "silver bullet," the lower graph subdivides the resulting "stabilization triangle" into seven wedges.

The idea was to get people thinking about a composite strategy that might include a number of emission-reducing steps—each tasked with only part of the whole job.

What would it take to reduce the annual projected inputs of carbon dioxide by a total of 7 billion tons over 50 years? Socolow has even made these considerations into a game that is available on line on Princeton's website. In it, he ticks off 15 elements of forward-looking energy strategies and invites students, teachers, and anybody else to select seven "wedges" that together represent "the best" composite approach to forestall a total of 7 billion tons of additional carbon emissions by the end of half a century. None of the strategies would require completely new technologies, such as nuclear fusion, but each would require massive deployment. Some are on the demand side, such as increasing transport or heating efficiency. Some deal with fossil fuel, such as switching from coal to natural gas, or continuing to use coal-fueled generation, but providing plants with means of capturing carbon dioxide during operation and tucking it away safely somewhere. Socolow includes nuclear generation, wind, solar, and biofuels as options. He admits that the strategies overlap and in some cases are contradictory.

Socolow's charming game is not realistic, but it is basically accurate and surely thought-provoking. It gives a vivid idea of how much would be required from *each* of these contemporary technological "solutions" to accomplish the reduction of 1 billion tons annually at the end of 50 years. For example, he says that one fuel-switching wedge would require the displacement of 1,400 coal-electric plants of 1,000 megawatts each by their equivalent in new plants using natural gas. He admits also that this would then mean quadrupling the amount of gas generation capacity that existed worldwide in the year 2000. If natural gas were supplied in the form of LNG, this would involve multiplying current shipments by ten.

Based on current spacing among turbines, the wind-power wedge would cover a total area the size of Germany. The solar wedge would require arrays spread across the equivalent of the state of New Jersey. Improving the efficiency in all existing residential and commercial buildings, as well as all new ones, could also take care of a billion tons—but only if the actual result were to reduce carbon emissions from that enormous source by 25 percent. To do the same by boosting the efficiency of autos would require that they all average 60 miles per gallon.

Remember that *seven* such wedges would be needed to avoid increasing annual emissions from where they are now, despite 50 years of growth in the global economy, population, and improving standards of living. These specific numbers are less important than the concept. It is immaterial that a few years have passed since Socolow's remarkable intuition. Even after 50 years from whenever we do start, the job would be incomplete if these assumptions are anywhere near correct. Whether concentration is at 500 or 600 or 450 parts per million then, it would not remain stable unless emissions continued to decline. Socolow calculated that they would have to drop by another two-thirds during the next half century, with more modest reductions even beyond that.

WILL NEW TECHNOLOGIES
COME TO OUR RESCUE?

An almost forgotten part of the Energy Policy Act of 2005 was the authorization of a Climate Change Technology Program (CCTP), which has functioned as a multi-agency planning and coordination entity. Although the CCTP was tasked to provide strategic direction for what it terms an investment portfolio of climate-change-related technology research, development, demonstration, and deployment of several billion dollars, it has attracted relatively little attention inside or outside government. There was no guarantee that it would be continued under the new administration taking over in January 2009. But its Strategic Plan[11] is worth reviewing by anyone especially concerned with national energy policy—the formulation of which is the subject of the next chapter of this book.

The CCTP, incidentally, takes a *truly* long-range perspective. It sees demonstrations of cellulosic ethanol, post-combustion capture of carbon dioxide from coal plants, hybrid and plug-in hybrid electric vehicles, and cost-competitive photovoltaics as near-term developments; but it takes this to mean "less than 20 years." Its mid-term period is 20 to 40 years beyond that, and that period is expected to include solid-state lighting, proof of the geologic safety of sequestered carbon dioxide, advanced biorefineries, and vehicles using fuel cells and hydrogen fuel. To CCTP, "long-term" designates the period even beyond that. Only then—well past mid-century—does it foresee super conducting transmission, a hydrogen economy, fusion power plants, and "zero-emission agriculture."

Who is "right" in predicting our energy future? Socolow's projections may be overly pessimistic. It would be surprising if by 2020 there were not a number of new technological approaches or methods of penetrating energy markets on both the supply side and the demand side more quickly and effectively than seems possible now. But the idea of a single Apollo-type project to achieve goals that are being bandied about blithely is naive. Promises that our energy and environmental goals can be realized quickly and at essentially zero cost are even worse, because they can lull people into forgetting that balance is necessary . . . and that time is part of the balance.

NOTES

1. It is conceivable that the announcement of a significant scientific breakthrough in the field, coupled with rapid investment pledges by companies willing to carry it

through to commercial scale without subsidies, could reduce crude oil prices by a perceptible amount in anticipation. This simply concedes that initial public perceptions may have little connection with economic reality. The short-term effect would vanish, with the exact timing dependent on many other factors.

2. The U.S. Energy Information Administration's *Annual Energy Outlook* is usually available on EIA's website months before it appears in print. In fact, passage of significant energy legislation late in 2007 forced a recalculation of the tentative 2008 projections already released. Each spring EIA also holds an energy conference in Washington dedicated to an amplification and public discussion of its AEO results, and major parts of the conference presentations are made available electronically on the Web. For non-professionals who are only seeking insights for small-scale energy decisions, EIA's *short*-term outlooks may be sufficient; and they are also available on EIA's website—http://www.eia.doe.gov.

3. Dr. Fatih Birol, presentation at the Center for Strategic and International Studies in Washington, DC, November 16, 2007.

4. John V. Mitchell and Paul Stevens, *Ending Dependence: Hard Choices for Oil-Exporting States*, Chatham House (available at www.chathamhouse.org.uk).

5. A more conventional way to express "Hotelling's Rule" is that resource prices will rise at the same rate as the annual rate of interest. Withholding production in order to pursue relative long-term gain then tends to force prices up, but higher prices suppress demand. See-sawing back and forth maintains a long-term equilibrium. Martin Feldstein pursued the possibility further by suggesting that "We Can Lower Oil Prices Now" if oil importers announce and begin to take steps on either the supply side or the demand side that were seen as reducing future demand for oil (*Wall Street Journal*, July 1, 2008, p. A-17).

6. "Ahead of the Pack: GE's Jeffrey Immelt on why it's business, not personal," interview by Alan Murray and Kimberley A. Strassel, *Wall Street Journal*, March 24, 2008, p. R3.

7. These specific time frames were mentioned at the March 13, 2008 NAS meeting by Ged Davis, co-President for Global Energy Assessment of the International Institute of Applied Systems Analysis, in a presentation entitled "Global Energy and Environment Projections: Next Steps," but the interpretations and applications of them are personal conclusions by the author of this book.

8. S. Pacala and R. Socolow, "Stabilization Wedges: Solving the Climate Problem for the Next 50 Years with Current Technologies," *Science*, August 13, 2004, pp. 968–972.

9. "Business as usual" is an unfortunate term in this case, since it might imply that nothing is being done to slow the rate of gas emissions. Measures to do so already in place or firmly planned were taken into account, but no extraordinary new programs were considered.

10. The designation "WRE" is a bow to Wigley, Richels, and Edmonds, researchers who developed a family of "stabilization curves" on which this one is based mathematically.

11. *U.S. Climate Change Technology Program: Strategic Plan*, U.S. Department of Energy Document DOE/PI 0005, September 2006.

Seven

National Energy Policy
and Its Economic Implications

"National energy policy" is a phrase that is used a lot but is generally misunderstood. In a representative federal democracy such as the United States, its sources are diffuse and its contents are continually being transformed. This explains why U.S. energy policy cannot be given a tidy description. Yet *policy*—for all its fuzziness—is the arena in which economic and legal boundaries are fixed on how we can buy, sell, produce, consume, or invest in energy and energy-related products on a day-to-day and year-to-year basis.

The overall national policy *atmosphere* makes various energy sources cheaper or more expensive, more or less readily available in adequate amounts when needed, and more or less benign for the United States and world environment. It can certainly change energy intensity, which was alluded to earlier as the ratio between the quantities of energy consumed and what is being achieved constructively—usually condensed nationally by economists into the single measure of gross domestic product. Policy is reflected in supply, demand, and price.

Since every citizen and each enterprise in this country has a distinct opinion about the proper balance among the energy goals discussed in earlier chapters, it is valuable to have some grasp of how policy develops, or even what it consists of at any particular time. We'd all like to be able to influence policy in what we consider our favor. In explaining how this might be possible, this chapter will draw on some data and concepts that have been offered in the chapters that precede it.

Many people regard national energy policy as a set of economic driving forces steered by the President, or by the Department of Energy (DOE), or by Congress. That is only partly so. Meanwhile, some conspiracy theorists insist that monied interests and their lobbyists manipulate all the important levers. That also falls far short of the full truth. In a sense, everybody is occupied in shaping U.S. energy policy all the time, since local, national, and international market forces are its central economic determinants. Knowing this is potentially helpful, however, only if we probe a little more deeply to determine who can *modify* those market forces. That type of analysis is the realm of the political economist, and many a successful business executive.

WHAT CONSTITUTES "ENERGY POLICY"?

Over the years, I have had the opportunity three times to draft the actual words of the official document that carries the title of National Energy Policy Plan. I served as chief editor for two others. The legislation that established the U.S. Department of Energy in 1977 says that a policy plan is supposed to be issued every two years by the national administration and sent to Congress, but this mandate has been ignored more often than it has been observed. That is unfortunate, because the document focuses Americans' attitudes on policy options for at least a while. Referring to those periodic issuances from the executive branch as "the national energy policy" is misleading, however. It is more of an administrative wish list. My own definition of what *effectively* constitutes "national energy policy" is much broader:

It is a framework of written and unwritten rules and attitudes, often built up over decades, involving all branches and levels of government (as well as the private sector), affecting all those aspects of economic, social and political life which—although they may not always be linked obviously and exclusively to energy—significantly modify (or try to modify) the ways in which energy resources are produced or consumed.[1]

DOE may not always be the *major* departmental contributor to energy policy formulation and implementation. The State Department can have a powerful input from time to time via our country's relations with oil suppliers in the world market. Oil and gas leasing on federal lands is administered by the Minerals Management Service, which is part of the Department of the Interior. Elements of the Department of Labor affect energy policy by the way they handle work rules, wage statutes, and labor union practices. The Office of Management and Budget (OMB) influences fiscal policy, and the Treasury Department interacts with Congress on federal tax policy; so all three of these set practical limits to the subsidiary policies we associate more directly with energy. There are other departmental and agency influences, whose relative importance varies with the issue at hand.

Funding for federal initiatives is not just ordered by the White House. It must *first* be authorized and *then* appropriated by the Congress in two separate actions. Making either personal or business decisions as soon as new energy programs have been authorized can be a costly presumption.

Even after the necessary bills are signed by the president and become law, courts have the final say. Judicial decisions interpret energy laws, the precise statutory powers of energy regulators, and—if affected parties disagree and bring suit—even how regulations may be implemented.

Thus, all three branches of the federal government participate in making national energy policy. Sometimes they do so without intending or realizing it. National energy policy rarely evolves in a coordinated fashion.

The president—and at times recently, the vice-president—can obviously wield great influence, and this is markedly true when a single party controls both the White House and Congress. Yet even this is not automatic. Federal energy legislation is more likely to reflect the relative strength of regions and economic sectors than a single forceful vision by the chief executive. In many cases regional interests supersede party affiliation. For better or worse, national party platforms and candidates' position papers have short half-lives.

PROMISES, PROMISES

Presidential pledges of "energy independence" for the United States are an impractical, imprecise, and improbable goal, which was initiated by Richard Nixon's 1974 promise to reach it within six years. The pledges by Nixon and some of his successors have never resulted in a coherent program of energy independence to send to Congress, and we should probably be thankful for that. It has been more than two centuries since Adam Smith and David Ricardo explained the advantages of open international trade,[2] but it is still clear that blind "import substitution" can hobble an economy.

The United States imports far more petroleum than it produces domestically. It probably imports more than it should, for its own security, and it certainly imports more than it may need to. Yet some imports always make economic sense in the case of any commodity—including energy—for which a country is ill-fitted to produce all that it normally requires. Total energy independence would not be healthy for the United States, even if it were feasible. Future policy measures can limit the *degree* of U.S. dependence on imports—or at least the damage that can result from wildly fluctuating prices and possible cutoffs in supply. That should be a national aim, in proper balance with other national goals.

Because of OPEC, however, the global oil market is by no means a free one. There is no guarantee that the core of world oil supply will always be available from OPEC on reasonable terms, and this engenders national insecurity for a large-scale oil importer such as the United States. When circumstances produce inordinately high prices, they skew the trade balance of any country with large import volumes that finds rapid adaptation difficult. Reducing our nation's *energy vulnerability* and increasing our *energy resiliency* are necessary objectives. The exaggerated promise of "energy independence" within a few years was reintroduced here only to document the fact that a presidential statement of national energy policy may be totally ineffectual.

It is ironic that Al Gore as a defeated candidate almost certainly had a more sweeping and long-lasting effect on U.S. energy and environmental policy than he might have had as president. His book and movie on global climate change[3] resonated with latent public sentiment, especially because of widespread resentment against President George W. Bush—a good deal of which was unrelated to energy or environment. Gore's personal pronouncements about the Earth's problems tended to hyperbole, and he greatly oversimplified the ease with which energy efficiency measures and renewables could solve them; but photos of polar bears began to appear everywhere after his movie was aired, and Congress began to discuss how carbon emissions might be reduced, rather than whether they needed to be. The popular outlook had changed, and Gore had been the prime individual instigator of change.

There was no way Gore could have pushed through U.S. ratification of the flawed Kyoto Protocol in 2001 if he had been president. An almost unanimous expression of opposition sentiment in the Senate proved that. Two presidential terms later, however, it is possible to envision some follow-up agreement with a more realistic timetable that involves both the United States and the two new energy-consuming titans (China and India). This seems achievable in the period of 2010 and beyond. Thus, Al Gore *earned* his Nobel Prize, by demonstrating that national energy policy can be made outside the fence of the White House, and even outside Washington's much-publicized Beltway.

WHO SHOULD PAY? WHO WILL?

As president, even the most charismatic and visionary figure is reduced to proposing ideas about energy and environment that will remain mere figures of speeches unless they are translated into executive orders, specific instructions to the Cabinet, or proposals for legislative action by the House and Senate. By existing law and even firmer tradition, though, bills before Congress are subjected to scrutiny for their probable budget impacts. The OMB, the Congressional Budget Office (CBO), the Government Accountability Office (GAO), and innumerable think tanks are prompt in pointing out that someone must *pay* to adjust any of the goals of the energy policy mobile upward. Money is a sticking point.

In the private sector, some promising projects founder because of a lack of capital—especially when risks and rewards play out in different time frames. National government projects face similar upfront challenges. Funding is quite often a final stumbling block, whether the aim is as grand as curbing the emissions of global warming gases in a meaningful way or just holding down the pump price of gasoline.

Economic awareness does not shut off the seemingly endless succession of ideas that show more rhetoric than reflection. One proposal by presidential candidates from both political parties during the 2008 primaries was to reduce gasoline prices at the pump by a temporary moratorium on the federal gasoline tax of 18 cents per gallon, with or without replacing the revenues this brings in for ever-needed highway maintenance. Because a newsy election campaign was in progress at the time, it didn't take long for a few economic analysts to speak out and be quoted, with the result that those proposals were criticized soundly in press and broadcast editorials.

Cutting energy prices artificially by price caps or retail tax breaks is quite likely to increase consumption. This tightens the market and could force underlying prices higher. Imposing so-called windfall profit taxes on energy suppliers when prices are high makes investment in production less attractive, again forcing the supply-demand balance in the wrong direction if one is interested mainly in avoiding long-term price escalation. Supply and demand must both be kept in mind always.

The fact remains, however, that energy is such an important part of everyday activities that runaway prices can threaten life and health for those with relatively low incomes. To preserve the balance of market forces while averting widespread personal hardship at times, the "best" solution from a purely economic standpoint would be to augment the incomes of poorer people somehow and allow them as individuals to make informed choices among spending options—including energy use. That is an approach that few politicians are willing to espouse, however, and it is complicated even more by the fact that many Americans regard access to some amount of energy as an automatic entitlement anyway. The arguments about this will continue in much the same vein as those about universal health care.

MIXED SIGNALS ON THE SAME TEAM

Even within the executive branch, agreement among departments and agencies on attitudes toward energy may be more coincidental than controlled. The Department of Energy and the Environmental Protection Agency (EPA) have traditionally had little horizontal communication at the working level, and they have sometimes worked at cross-purposes—even though the interactions of energy and the environment are widespread and profound.

At least one former head of EPA, Christine Todd Whitman, has suggested that this grows out of the fact that she lacked full Cabinet status. This made relatively little difference near the top of the respective bureaucratic pyramids, she said, but at mid-levels the careerists were very conscious of where their bosses seemed to stand in the administration hierarchy.[4] Apart from titles, such a pecking order varies with the administration and the personalities involved.

Whether they are political appointees or careerists, groups of bureaucrats in different agencies also reach their positions via different experiential paths. With different private and political motivations, they tend to work independently. This pattern could change as interlocking problems related to energy become more pressing, and we should hope that it will. Until it does, however, the most successful advocates for any energy policy initiative will usually be those who can simultaneously tailor appeals to multiple power centers—in or out of the federal government. Let's look at an example.

There has been increased interest in the area of energy technology known as "carbon capture and sequestration" (CCS). This might involve any of a variety of approaches and methods to make sure that carbon dioxide resulting from the combustion of fuels—coal, biomass, petroleum products, or natural gas—is not released into the ambient atmosphere at all. Emphasis on CCS development in some form is especially critical to the coal and electricity production sectors, because about half of all U.S. electricity comes from coal-fired plants. The nation has enormous and relatively inexpensive supplies of coal, but coal is the fossil fuel that produces the most CO_2.

Serious national targets of "carbon reduction" in any meaningful time-frame cannot be reached without CCS, because U.S. dependence on more than 300 *gigawatts* of baseload coal capacity for power means that it would not be feasible to back coal out of the U.S. generation mix in much less than half a century—and then only at gigantic capital cost and probably a considerable loss in operating efficiency. Yet commercialization of CCS is years away, even if investment in it is pushed well beyond a "business-as-usual" pace by some type of penalty on carbon dioxide releases. This means that some system of special incentives to speed up its introduction is worth investigating. There are so many calls for government support, however, that pleas for additional R&D grants or public-private partnerships always need champions. Where could we look for them if we should choose to focus on CCS?

One could expect the "FE," or Fossil Energy Office of the Department of Energy, to be a supporter because of both economic and technical interests. Officials of the EPA might lend their voices as well, especially if some well respected nongovernmental organizations (NGOs) with special interest in the environment—such as the National Resources Defense Council (NRDC)—adopted the cause too. Yet NRDC might do so for a somewhat different set of reasons than either the DOE or EPA . . . and in different ways. Nongovernmental organizations of its standing can shift public opinion. Through studies, reports, news releases, testimony at hearings, and frequent interaction with the staffs of public officials, NGOs definitely influence legislators. Some messages to the White House on behalf of CCS, on the other hand, might stress a third set of arguments—supply reliability and national security. The most logical substitute for coal at the moment is natural gas, but imports of that fuel are increasing and are likely to keep on growing because of various barriers to domestic production.

Once specific measures relating to CCS begin to be debated in Congress, regional interests and preferences can be expected to come to the fore more often. Representatives of coal-producing states, such as Wyoming and West Virginia can probably be counted on to go along with federal support, but California might reinforce its long-standing efforts to discourage coal use within its own boundaries by blocking any and all CCS initiatives in the hope of killing the coal industry completely. This may sound callous, if not cynical; but it *is* the way the energy policy game has been played in the United States for a long time. We may as well admit that politics can trump economics. Consensus in any legislative body frequently depends on either the chance or orchestrated conjunction of quite different expressions of self-interest.

OURS IS A FEDERAL SYSTEM

State-by-state officialdom contributes to our composite national energy policy in numerous ways.

States' rights in respect to energy are founded largely in the final section of the Bill of Rights, the Tenth Amendment to the U.S. Constitution. It decrees, "The powers not delegated to the United States by the Constitution, nor prohibited by it to the States, are reserved to the States respectively, or to the people." In large measure, federal energy jurisdiction is based on its express power "To regulate Commerce with foreign Nations, and *among the several States*, [emphasis added] and with the Indian Tribes."[5] The federal government has exclusive control over duties or other restrictions on imports or exports, but it is enjoined constitutionally from playing favorites among its constituents via any "Regulation of Commerce or Revenue to the Ports of one State over those of another."[6]

There are many permutations, but all this boils down to saying that states are pretty much free to encourage, discourage, or regulate energy production and use, so long as the actions involved don't cross state lines or national borders. The actual application of constitutional law emanates ultimately from decisions of the Supreme Court and subsequent acceptance of precedents.

In practice, energy traffic crosses state lines in one fashion or another in most cases—unless care is taken to guarantee that it doesn't. For instance, it has already been explained that most of Texas evades regulation of electricity by the Federal Energy Regulatory Commission (FERC) by maintaining its own Electric Reliability Region—albeit at the cost of limiting power ties that might in some circumstances improve its own reliability of supply.

In the great majority of cases, FERC exercises regulatory power over all bulk, wholesale transactions in electricity and natural gas, including their transportation. "Unbundling" of both industries provides for separate ownership of production, transmission and final distribution functions, so that competition is allowed in each area. Interstate movement of both electricity and natural gas also involves *open access*, which means that those wishing to purchase delivery rights may not be refused the right to do so if such service is available.

Retail rates and conditions of service for both electricity and gas, on the other hand, are controlled by the respective state utility commissions. The degree and manner in which free-market pricing is allowed to take place among competing suppliers varies greatly from state to state. In a metropolitan area such as Washington, D.C., this has led to three separate sets of ground rules—one for the District itself, but different ones for residents in adjoining Maryland and Virginia. Moving from one side of a street to the other can switch customers automatically from one energy supply company to another, and either raise or lower monthly bills.

HOW THIS CAN AFFECT SUPPLY

As observed in Chapter 5, about half of the states have some form of renewable portfolio standard (RPS). Some public utility commissions (PUCs) go even farther in influencing the energy mix to be used for electricity to be used *within their jurisdictions*. Typically, an electric distribution utility must justify to its PUC the prudence of the utility's fuel selections, its contracts to acquire power, and any construction of its own new generation capacity; but the commission dictates the economic assumptions on which the supporting financial calculations must be made. This can lead to economic distortions.

California has long insisted that the price-per-kilowatt-hour of competing generation proposals include an artificial "adder" to compensate for the damage to public health and environment that coal plants may produce. This is a legitimate demonstration of "internalizing externalities," but the practical effect of the large adder is that coal-fueled plants are no longer being built in California because it is impossible to demonstrate their legally interpreted economic competitiveness. As a result, only a few small coal plants are left in California, supplying a bare 1 percent of the state's electricity output.

California's tactic to ban additional nuclear power plants has been equally effective, although existing nuclear reactors still provide 19.5 percent of its generation—roughly matching the national average. State law in California forbids the issuance of necessary permits for any new nuclear plants until and unless a site is available for the permanent disposal of the high level waste (HLW) it generates in the form of spent fuel. Many technical experts, including some who oppose new nuclear plants themselves, believe that it will be safe and most desirable to keep spent fuel for as long as a century at well-monitored but distributed temporary sites. It could thus be retrieved later if the long-delayed permanent geological repository in Nevada is finally approved and completed, *or* if fuel reprocessing and recycling of the still-useful material within the fuel bundles is deemed acceptable, *or* if a technological break-through is achieved to treat HLW further to make isolation of long-lived radionuclides easier. That approach is rejected by California authorities, however, so the state maintains an effective moratorium on new nuclear power plants.

Conversely, some state PUCs and legislatures give economic *preferences* of various kinds to energy sources that they regard as particularly desirable—usually renewable forms and generally those that they judge to fit best into local circumstances. Cases of special treatment range from tax breaks on motor fuels to benefits of various kinds for homeowners and businesses that adopt either energy efficiency measures or some type of local self-generation of electricity. Once again, these are logical exercises of local rights to internalize externalities and consciously override straightforward economics for some purpose. But the sum of their effects must also be reckoned as elements of U.S. energy policy.

WHEN INTERESTS COLLIDE

Most government interference with market forces in energy supply, demand, or pricing is explained as an attempt either "to provide a safety net for the needy" or "to level the playing field." In a system as complicated as the one in the United States, however, this can often lead to instabilities or inequities of different types. For instance, one might argue that subsidies for the installation of energy-sparing equipment and substantial weatherproofing in the interest of energy conservation discriminate only in favor of homeowners as opposed to those who rent residential space. More pointedly, they exclude families whose budgets are so tight that they cannot afford at all to invest capital today with the prospect of recouping it and profiting thereafter. As a different kind of example, multiple federal supports for corn-based ethanol—which could not have competed economically without them—caused grain prices to shoot up. This cascaded into food costs generally, contributing to other inflationary pressures in 2008.

Adjustments can always be made, and thoughtful efforts to do so may achieve reasonable success, but the outcome can often be hodgepodged layers of laws and regulations. The impoverished might be better protected from high energy prices by allowing markets to operate more freely while targeting the poor with redistribution of tax revenues,[7] but such a plan would face strong opposition and could not guarantee effectiveness. Much could be accomplished by instituting nationwide building efficiency standards, but few energy analysts believe that this can take place either. Construction trade unions are one barrier, opposition of landlords and developers are another, and simple differences in climate and lifestyles within this huge and diverse nation are a third factor. All these are factors in the energy policy ambience within which individuals and corporations act.

Introduction of federal renewable portfolio standards as a part of national energy policy has been a rallying cry among the states, but the advantages in simplicity and certainty that this step would appear to offer may again be outweighed by practical considerations. The large disparity from state to state in conventional or unconventional energy consumption per capita or per unit of economic productivity cannot be read as indicating directly which ones are conservation heroes and which are villains. Much depends on climate, distances, urbanization, industrialization, and so on. Nor does the degree to which the respective states have succeeded in relying on renewable energy sources necessarily reflect their desire to do so. Renewable energy resources are simply not evenly distributed among them.

State-to-state variations will make it quite difficult to reach the renewable portfolio goals alluded to glibly by politicians and some advocacy groups—such as "25 × 25." This organization is dedicated to the proposition that renewable energy should supply 25 percent of total U.S. demand by the year 2025, and its website regularly lists officials and subnational governments who endorse this objective. The enormous challenge of such a goal crystallizes when its promoters are asked to project a *realistic* spaghetti chart for 2025, similar to the one in Chapter 1 of this book (Figure 1.4), that showed how renewables might provide such a share of the energy required in the United States by then. I have yet to find an organization or individual that has even tried to do so.

Deriving one-quarter of our total energy budget from renewables in this time frame would necessitate sharp absolute reductions in demand that are hard to envision, as well as unclearly defined technological breakthroughs and incredibly ambitious market penetration for energy sources that have not yet reached commercially competitive status, such as cellulosic ethanol. It would also require a total revolution in the nation's electric generation system.

A LOOK AT SOME NUMBERS

As of 2006, the United States as a whole produced 9.5 percent of its electricity from renewable sources, but three-quarters of this came from hydroelectric dams, where there is little likelihood of any meaningful expansion.[8] More significantly, only seven states could count on *non*-hydro renewables to generate more than 5 percent of their home-grown power; and most of them had taken advantage of special circumstances that are not fully duplicable in other states.

Idaho, Maine, and Vermont depend heavily on wood and wood-derived fuels from the timber industry. Iowa and Minnesota are especially well-suited for wind generation. Because of its total dependence on imports for fossil fuel, Hawaii has been ahead of most states in developing renewable energy such as biomass sources. But more than one-third of Hawaii's renewable generation is also geothermal, facilitated by the volcanic origin of its islands.

The seventh lead-state in renewable energy exploitation is the leader of all, California. By 2006 it was responsible for more than 21 percent of all the non-hydro, but renewably sourced electricity produced in the United States. This was enough to supply 11 percent of California's own needs. Seismically active parts of California enable it to call on geothermal energy for 55 percent of that non-hydro renewable power, followed by wind, wood fuels, and various biomass sources in that order. Despite publicity, California's solar-based electricity in 2006 made up only 2 to 3 percent of its non-hydro renewable power, and still a mere *three-tenths of 1 percent* of all the electricity California itself generated.

Nevertheless, California is a model worth examining more closely. What does the state have going for it as it shows such energy leadership? Can other states follow if they wish?

California appears quite frugal in energy use, but its low energy consumption is undoubtedly due partly to its famously temperate climate. This reduces demand for both heating and cooling in comparison to many other U.S. regions. At the same time, California deserves recognition for both its executive and legislative insistence on energy conservation measures. The state has repeatedly set goals for curbing motor fuel use that it failed to meet, yet the net result has been visible success when judged objectively. This has brought pressure on other states and the federal government to raise CAFE standards.

California's achievements in trying to match supply and demand in electricity have also been heroic, but they speak less to sustainability. California imports more of the electricity it uses than any other state, and it is almost exactly twice as dependent on energy imports of all kinds as the national average.[9] Typically, half of the electricity generated in California uses natural gas as the primary energy input, yet less than 15 percent of that gas is produced within its borders. The state displayed its own competing priorities vividly in 2007 when Governor Arnold Schwarzenegger disapproved an application to build a deepwater structure off the coast of Ventura County to receive much-needed liquefied natural gas in a location he himself had previously favored.

When he killed that project, Schwarzenegger's accompanying statement praised LNG as one of the "cleaner alternatives" for energy supply, and he called it a means of bringing "much needed diversity to California's energy portfolio." He went on to "encourage companies to come forward with a plan that considers the objections raised by state agencies, local officials and communities" and to bring in LNG via offshore facilities.[10] But in the end he said he rejected the plan offered because of less-than-specific "significant and unmitigated impacts to California's air quality and marine life."[11]

Celebrity politics may have played a role too. Film star Pierce Brosnan had led a group of photogenic "name activists" in a "protest paddle-out" against the proposed facility, apparently aimed largely at objecting to a possible marring of the view from shore. In the aftermath, critics distorted Schwarzenegger's action shamelessly, implying that there had been serious public safety concerns and obtusely linking his negative decision to a victory in the fight against global warming—since burning natural gas produces carbon dioxide.

Schwarzenegger was clearly conflicted. While his veto statement boasted that "California continues to lead the nation in efforts to expand renewable energy resources" he added that "guaranteeing a steady stream of *clean-burning* fuel takes on even greater significance" (emphasis added).

If national standards seek to impose renewable portfolios throughout the country they will have to consider the great inequalities among states in respect to both the supply of and the demand for energy. There will also have to be a clear definition of renewable energy. Today, some electric utilities offer their customers green energy of assorted styles at a higher price. They actually manage to provide it in many cases through offsets— by purchasing blocks of generation from suppliers that might be anywhere in the country, and which might never really reach the customer. If all states had to comply at once to a single percentage requirement, buying such credits might be physically impossible if the percentage were too high. Besides, the old laws of supply and demand still work. Those states that have easier access to practical renewable sources would enjoy a windfall; some others could be severely disadvantaged. In any event, the average price of electricity would almost surely rise nationwide.

WHO WILL DECIDE? HOW?

To make rational choices, individuals should establish their own priorities. California's relative success in certain aspects of energy policy has arisen not only from government mandates but also from public acquiescence and even a supportive public spirit. Advertising probably plays some role, as does the interest of celebrities in energy conservation and environmental protection. Emotional appeals succeed where logic, facts, and statistics may fail. A public better informed about energy could also be a dominating factor in policy, but many programs that purport to educate are not objective.

Business and industry will generally follow the primary guidance of supply and demand in making energy choices as to both sales and purchases, and companies that fail to do so will suffer. Successful strategic planners among them will consider short-term, mid-range, and long-term goals and trends. In respect to energy, they will need to measure all economic factors properly and carefully, but also to ponder public perceptions.

Governments at all levels could improve both the wisdom and the success of their manifold energy choices by improving horizontal communication. Governors in each region of the country hold periodic conferences, as do state legislators and regulatory commissioners. In fact, many U.S. groups of this type have similar meetings with their neighboring counterparts in either Canada or Mexico. Energy and environment are frequently on the agendas. While few meaningful interstate compacts evolve from these discussions, they give an opportunity to exchange experiences and to hear different points of view.

To a large extent, players in the energy policy debate have been either reactive or dismissive of diverging views. Accurate information is available but not widely disseminated. Also, it can be ambiguous because there is no such thing as a perfect energy policy balance. Ideally, we might huddle rather than muddle in searching for solutions. But it may take a fresh crisis to coax out that sort of togetherness.

Lobbyists often succeed because they can produce information for officials who lack it and are looking for supporting arguments on behalf of stands they have already half-decided on. Energy companies and trade associations will continue their public affairs campaigns, although perhaps not as narrowly as they have in the past. Greater sophistication in public statements is demanded now that the magnitude and complexity of the nation's energy difficulties are beginning to sharpen in the public focus. Blocs such as organized labor unions and the farm lobby must continue to be numbered among the most important NGOs. By and large, they will have to be satisfied with proposed policy changes—or at least reconciled to them.

The next wild card in the energy policy free-for-all may grow out of the energy-water nexus, because it could bring in additional constituencies and viewpoints in the face of imminent climate change. Drought and excessive rainfall could both occur seasonally, and each stresses our supplies of fresh water—which depend both on surface and sub-surface sources.[12] Water distribution and recycling require large inputs of energy, but energy production uses large amounts of water, too. Just to start with, think of the cooling requirements of thermal power plants and the water consumption involved in unconventional fuel production—including the output of Canada's oil sands, on which both our countries will be increasingly dependent. U.S. agriculture and U.S. industry, each a formidable lobbying sector, are both enormous users of water.

The beginnings of a water supply crunch within five or six years could bring calls for a firm, high price on water. Competing techniques of desalinization would be debated hotly in respect to cost, energy requirements, and environmental effects. The whole chorus of ideas about carbon taxes, carbon ceilings, carbon allocations, and carbon trading could be replayed in a different key—with energy policy being squeezed from a new direction.

Policy problems in regard to energy show no signs of disappearing, although their nature may change. They will continue to affect basic economics. Just remember: The strongest forces of all in the long run are still supply and demand. But don't forget the polar bears either.

ARE WE MASTERS OF OUR ENERGY FATE?

Americans may be reluctant to admit it, but our national energy policy is really "metanational"[13] in nature. It is developed and implemented from both deep *within* this country and well *beyond* it.

As for international inputs, consider the two energy sources that this book has emphasized again and again because of their central roles: electricity and oil. Our most aggravating dilemmas about electricity in regard to environmental effects, cost, and timing emerge from concerns about global climate change. The adequacy, reliability, and affordability of our total oil supply hinges on actions within global markets.

The United States is schizophrenic about oil prices. Some major multinational oil companies are located here, and a sudden plunge in oil price could cause us some economic grief. Yet ultra-high prices were part of the reason for a broad national economic dip in 2008, and this was not the first such experience. What might come closest to satisfying the overwhelming majority of Americans would be some "just right" price—a stable level that is (a) high enough to encourage competitive diversity in energy supply and a deliberate move toward an environmentally acceptable energy mix that promises to balance other goals, but (b) low enough to make energy affordable within a comfortable and growing economy. Nobody can pinpoint that price, and we might not recognize it if it appeared. What irks us, though, is that we seem to be completely helpless even to grope toward it.

But we aren't.

The United States can still achieve a degree of global market power in oil—although not as much as we once held. For one thing, it might involve a different approach to the use of the Strategic Petroleum Reserve (SPR). Instead of allowing releases of its oil only to cope with severe volumetric shortages of an emergency nature, the SPR could be utilized in much the way those who hold private stores use theirs. When oil is relatively plentiful and prices are low, reserves are allowed to build up. When prices are high, oil is released. The size of the SPR is such that it could make a difference, at least smoothing out small price bumps before they roll into big ones.

The SPR holds just over 700 million barrels of oil, of which 60 percent consists of sour grades that could be handled only by certain refineries. It would take about two weeks from the issuance of a presidential order to have oil enter the U.S. market. Official sources state that a maximum of 4.4 million barrels a day could be drawn down from the Strategic Reserve, but some who have been close to its development say privately that this is probably an over-statement. It might also take a while to reach whatever the true maximum drawdown capacity may be.

This particular idea is offered only as an admittedly preliminary example of the sorts of programs a more vigorous and focused policy approach *might* achieve. It is a concept, not a detailed plan, and full analysis and evaluation might reject it also as impractical. Deciding to use strategic government storage as an economic lever would necessitate coordination with both the private sector and the International Energy Agency. The IEA requirement for its members is that the combination of public and private stocks be sufficient to give 90 days of "import protection." The DOE's calculation as of August 2008 was that about 58 days of such supply was on hand in the SPR, and some oil analysts estimated that about the same existed in privately held stocks.

The SPR's value as an emergency stopgap is probably minimized by official accounts, because if it were used to replace a major foreign or domestic oil supply source that had been cut off it's a cinch that conservation steps would be taken simultaneously. Some fairly simple measures could show quick, if temporary, results. For instance, limiting the amount of "storage" in the tanks of vehicle themselves is an action that has been taken before.

There are also a variety of steps on the oil-demand side from such a large importer as the United States that would affect world oil prices.

The EIA's *International Energy Outlook 2008* projected that by 2010 this country will still be consuming 20 percent of the planet's primary energy and North America will be consuming 27 percent of all liquid fuels. A concerted effort to reduce U.S. oil consumption by 10 percent below future projections over several years—if it were believed by the rest of the world—could have profound effects almost immediately on the price of energy futures. This would bounce back to lower spot prices as well. The difficulty is that the prospect of lower prices for oil would dampen companies' interest in pros-pecting for the fuel. That might be compensated for by policy spurs to do-mestic drilling in new frontier areas, cooperation with Canada in resolving environmental problems with its oil sands, and quiet encouragement of Mexico to find some way to reverse the decline in its oil production—a com-plex policy problem of a different sort that is based on Mexico's need for fiscal and energy reforms that the country will have to work out for itself.

Is this a realistic scenario? It is as realistic as almost any other, although it would require a sort of universal political will that this country has not shown in decades and is especially difficult to engender in the complex system described in this chapter. Above all, it would require an understanding of *the need for balance* and a willingness to accept *compromises*.

It's still up to us.

WHY NOT JUST GO ALL OUT?

A chapter on energy policy should not end without addressing the frequent calls for a massive push in one direction or another to resolve the bulk of our energy problems all at once. Such calls are invariably short on detail and lacking any step-by-step approach. They customarily allude to national mobilization in energy and environment matters that would match the scope of the Manhattan Project in the 1940s to develop nuclear weapons or of the 1960s Apollo Project to land an astronaut on the lunar surface and return safely.

We may decide some day to try such an effort, but it would quickly reveal some telling differences between settling energy dilemmas and either building bombs or flying to the moon.

1. In the earlier tasks, the product involved a few weapons or a single system of launch and flight control. Energy and environment are much more complicated, as this book has endeavored to explain.

2. The federal government was in a position in those other efforts to requisition virtually all the talent it needed. That would hardly be the case for energy unless the country was already in a drastic crisis.

3. There was a single customer for those products. A major factor in achieving objectives in respect to energy and environment is that hundreds of millions of customers are concerned.

4. The objectives of nuclear explosions and lunar flight were also simpler, because we knew rather precisely what we wished to accomplish. We are far from consensus about how to assign weights to the five fundamental goals for energy that this book has called out.

5. At best, the time horizon for reaching a largely satisfactory balance in energy and environment policy amounts to more than one decade, rather than a few years.

Al Gore's call in 2008 for the United States to switch all electricity generation to non-carbon-emitting sources in ten years was so bizarre that it attracted little response. A serious effort to achieve such a goal would require dictatorial powers and would wreck the economy.

Even the fully mobilized industrial strength of the nation could not produce that much alternative output in such a short time. Nor could it add sufficient transmission capability to bring power from isolated sites he envisioned for central-station wind and solar installations. They would require continued subsidies to compete. No practical means was considered to compensate the owners of existing generation—including municipalities and coops as well as private-sector companies—for shutting it down. This is to say nothing of the economic disruptions that would take place in the energy labor force, fuel delivery systems, and so forth.

New York Mayor Michael Bloomberg's follow-up proposal to derive all of the city's electricity within a few years from rooftop and off-shore wind turbines died a comparable quick death. Neither the practical requirements nor the side-consequences were thought through before the plan was proposed.

IF NOT THIS, WHAT?

This chapter began by explaining that national energy policy has traditionally evolved rather than been imposed. This does not rule out a role for leadership, but a division of both powers and interests suggests that the most successful path to the future requires shared responsibilities and a constant eye toward consensus-building. This is not a bad point on which to wind down a book about free-market economics, which inherently embodies compromise.

Buyers and sellers both start with a conviction of the rightness of their respective positions on price under various circumstances. If they strike a deal, this proves that both were correct. Neither may be totally happy, or they both may be. The undeniable result is that an "acceptable" solution has been reached.

Just as the conjunction of supply and demand yields price, the reasoned and informed confluence of values and ideas—plus some luck and effort—can lead to solutions for energy and environmental problems that will win general acceptance.

It will take broader knowledge than many people now have. It will take acknowledgment that neither the key questions nor the best-balanced answers are always simple. It will take some sacrifice. It will take political will. It will take *good will*.

Let's hope that the concluding chapter can at least help some readers to move a little way along the pathways of sound economics in finding their own respective paths toward a satisfactory convergence with others.

NOTES

1. I developed this definition in 1997 for an introductory course on energy and the environment, co-taught with Professor Wilfrid Kohl at the Johns Hopkins School of Advanced International Studies.

2. Those who know they won't ever plod through either Adam Smith's *An Inquiry into the Nature and Causes of the Wealth of Nations* or David Ricardo's *Principles of Political Economy* can gain a quick insight into both men's contributions by examining

a survey volume such as Henry William Spiegel's easy-to-read *The Growth of Economic Thought,* 3rd ed. (Durham, NC: Duke University Press, 1991), in this case, especially pp. 243–257 and 328–333.

3. Al Gore, *An Inconvenient Truth: The Planetary Emergency of Global Warming and What We Can Do About It* (New York: Rodale, 2006).

4. Private communication following her presentation at the Center for Strategic and International Studies in Washington on "America's Role in the World: Promoting Environmental and Energy Sustainability," February 13, 2008.

5. *Constitution of the United States*, Article I, section 8.3.

6. *Constitution of the United States*, Article I, section 9.6.

7. Although the book is more than a quarter-century old, contemporary insights into the differential impact of high energy prices can still be gleaned from Hans H. Landsberg and Joseph M. Dukert, *High Energy Costs: Uneven, Unfair, Unavoidable?* (Baltimore: Resources for the Future, Johns Hopkins University Press, 1981). Its Chapter 5 treats "Ways to ease the burden" specifically.

8. Statistics in this paragraph and the next two were derived from data in the EIA's *State Energy Data 2005* and *Renewable Energy Trends 2006*, each of which was the latest composite source of state energy numbers at the time this was written in 2008. They will probably remain indicative of the basic situation for several years to come, but fuller tables are not included here because—as explained earlier—it is best for those seeking the most recent statistics to find them on the EIA's well-maintained website.

9. According to EIA's *State Energy Data 2005: Production*, California produced 3.2 quads of primary energy of all types while consuming 8.36 quads. Thus, 61.75 percent of its energy needs came from imports—including crude oil for its extensive and sophisticated refineries. This compares with overall U.S. statistics of about 31 quads of imports to satisfy its total consumption of around 100 quads.

10. "Gov. Schwarzenegger Rejects BHP Billiton's Application of LNG Project," press release from Office of the Governor: Arnold Schwarzenegger, May 18, 2007.

11. Greg Chang, "BHP Billiton Ponders Its Next Move after California Rejects Its LNG Proposal," *Bloomberg News,* May 21, 2007.

12. Lack of rain lowers the water levels in rivers and reservoirs. Heavy downpours lead to quick runoff, lowering subterranean water tables.

13. I invented this term in my 2004 work, *Creation and Evolution of North America's Gas and Electricity Regime: A Dynamic Example of Interdependence*. It was used there (pp. ii–iii and 316) to explain the nature of the energy relationships among Canada, the United States, and Mexico; but it applies equally well here in a broader context.

Eight

Looking Ahead to "Sustainable Development"

We *can* get it right . . . if we work at it.

This book has tried to apply objective principles of economics to choices about energy, and its emphasis on *balance* presupposes that a workable consensus can move us toward "sustainable development." This increasingly popular phrase implies that *optimizing* sometimes needs to take precedence over *maximizing*. The idea is as solidly grounded in broadly self-interested economics as it is in practical politics. It influences individual choices about energy-related lifestyles or investment decisions, as well as national policy.

The MIT Dictionary of Modern Economics defines "optimum" as 'the 'best' situation or state of affairs." But it speaks also of "constrained optimism," identified as "the best that can be achieved in view of existing limits." Roughly a century ago, Italian economist Vilfredo Pareto described a special case of optimality that consequently bears his name. In a "Pareto optimum," the same dictionary explains, "the economy's resources and output are allocated in such a way that no reallocation can make anyone better off without making at least one other person worse off."[1] That might be a recipe for consensus, but of course these are idealized goals. The U.S. "energy balance" in the first quarter of the twenty-first century is unusually shaky, so a more realistic objective would be some utilitarian variation of "the greatest happiness for the greatest number."[2] But even that formula requires modification. Equity insists that *some* progress be sought toward *all* goals; realism insists simultaneously that not every actor or cause will be equally satisfied.

The main drawback to achieving—or even defining—sustainable development is that it requires an understanding of today's energy outlook, which offers challenges on many fronts simultaneously. Yet attempts to maximize results for the individual goals of lesser order—involving supply, consumption, gross profit, or even avoiding environmental disturbances completely—are *un*sustainable.

The phrase sustainable development was applied initially only to the inter-relationship of orderly economic growth and environmental stewardship, but it can easily be extended to touch on every goal within the energy mobile. Even if energy practices combine what is deemed to be "acceptable" economic growth with what is considered "appropriate" environmental protection, they will not keep peace very long unless they are *also* affordable, reliable, adequate to needs, and achievable in whatever timeframe is available. In short, only a balanced package will sell—in the marketplace and to an electorate, since energy structures depend on both.

This is not altruistic economics. Those two words are contradictory. Totally selfish energy choices can yield short-term gains that may make them seem well-advised, but the long-term interest of almost all individuals within the U.S. economy lies in continuing development generally.

The concept of sustainability was popularized by the publication in 1987 of the report of the World Commission on Environment and Development, *Our Common Future*.[3] "Sustainability" was borrowed quickly for discussions of energy policy, and it has been used wonkishly ever since. As always, how-ever, the devil is in the details.

For a commercial enterprise, development still clearly involves profit. A minimum-wage employee must think of sustainability in part as being able to afford bus fare or gasoline money to get to work. Both parties have legal as well as psychic and health-related stakes in a "clean"—perhaps even a "green"—environment. How does reconciliation among easily diverging goals—that is, optimization—begin?

ENERGY AND ENVIRONMENT
IN KNOWLEDGEABLE PARTNERSHIP

Human beings being human, individuals and associations and govern-ments will continue to aspire to economic growth of some sort. The alterna-tive is stagnation and decline, or ennui at best. So we will continue to produce and use energy. But energy is *change*, impinging inevitably on nature. On an economically globalized Earth, the human species and human society need to handle the interaction sustainably—which involves time and intergenera-tional issues. *Our Common Future* explained sustainable development as "de-velopment that meets the needs of the present without compromising the ability of future generations to meet their own needs."[4]

The easy shift back and forth in this book between references to energy and to environment is more than a coincidence. Energy policy and environ-mental policy are so closely linked to one another that in most cases either will fail unless the two are harmonized. That will not happen generally until the exponents of each learn more about the entirety of both fields of study rather than just the overlapping areas. This might encourage mutual empathy, which is lacking to date.

Earth Day was created in 1970 to awaken interest in protecting the natural environment and resources of the planet, but its annual observances have often spotlighted energy production and use. In March 2007 a new environmental campaign launched the idea of an annual Earth Hour, during which enterprises and individuals in Sydney, Australia, voluntarily turned off all lights to show that concerted effort could palpably conserve energy. Some did this to call attention to the threat of global climate change. Others may have been protesting possible damage to local air quality from power generation, because three-quarters of Australia's electricity comes from coal-burning plants. A few might have even considered it a complaint against electricity rates they considered too high. Regardless of possibly disparate motives, the cogent fact is that they did something, even if it was a simple and essentially negative action. It should be possible to reach consensus on positive social actions, too—even complex ones such as using energy more judiciously.

The "lights out" move attracted publicity and was emulated modestly in dozens of cities around the world the following year. But the *Washington Post* explained to readers that such feel-good gestures accomplish very little compared with more enduring changes in lifestyle. Assuming that each one of the householders joining in the event switched off a total of 10 conventional incandescent bulbs averaging 100 watts each, that avoided the use of a single kilowatt hour of electricity for that year. Replacing those same bulbs with compact fluorescents would save perhaps *a thousand* kilowatt hours or more over 12 months.[5] Energy measurements and simple arithmetic aren't difficult to comprehend. It's just that most people don't bother. They should, in everything from individual purchases to massive investments and government policies.

REVIEWING SOME IDEAS

Trying to apply energy economics comprehensively makes us aware of *multiple* balances.

1. Energy supply and energy demand are interactive factors in establishing free-market pricing, but causality works in both directions. Prices feed back into both future supply and future consumption trends.

2. The energy market within the United States is affected by both conscious and unconscious actions by government and non-government actors, operating domestically and internationally.

3. The policy atmosphere in which supply and demand develop is the result of conflicting interests, many of which make energy market operations less than free. Furthermore, *mis*perceptions of interest carry as much weight as actual facts unless they are corrected.

4. Societal goals for our involvement with energy are sometimes mutually reinforcing, but just as often they conflict. This necessitates tradeoffs. Reducing oil imports, for instance, does not necessarily mean that overall energy expenses or the emissions of global warming gases will be reduced proportionately. The latter two may even go up as a result, depending on what substitutes for the imports.

5. Various energy sources compete for our favor, and a broad energy mix comes closest to approaching multiple objectives simultaneously. In fact, none of the current major sources of U.S. energy supply can be sold short if all legitimate goals are to be pursued. Each has some role.

6. Decreasing Americans' consumption of energy—especially energy from those sources whose supply is most problematic for one reason or another—offers the quickest, easiest, cheapest, and most environmentally benign part of an acceptable "solution." But even this will not suffice by itself. For part of the reason, look back at number one in this list).

Oil and electricity are the energy sources of most U.S. concern today, but they are not ends in themselves. We need illumination, but we now have reasonably acceptable substitutes for incandescent light bulbs. We need modes of transportation for goods and people, but we may be able to get along without as many motor cars, or with different sorts. Energy efficiency is a promising goal across all consumption sectors, but it often comes at the cost of some convenience or short-term outlay. Efficiency enthusiasts may deny or ignore this, but it is generally an economic fact.

Most U.S. consumers have little understanding of such realities in energy economics, so they are baffled and annoyed when confronted personally with unfamiliar or unpleasant choices. There is a difference between opinions expressed about energy in surveys of the public and attitudes revealed in public behavior. Almost half of the respondents to a telephone poll conducted by Deloitte early in 2008 professed that they were "very concerned" about global warming as a result of greenhouse gas emissions. More than another fourth said they were "somewhat concerned." But more than one-third of those surveyed admitted that they would be unwilling to accept *any increase at all* in their own electricity bills in order to curb such emissions. Only about 8 percent said they would willingly pay 15 percent or more above what they were paying now. If an actual choice were offered, it's almost certain that even this limited willingness to sacrifice would falter.

In fact, the positive results of tradeoffs such as "lower emissions for higher utility bills" cannot be guaranteed in advance. As earlier chapters have explained, many factors contribute to residential electricity rates. A direct survey of state utility commissioners carried out by Deloitte at the same time showed that 87 percent expected the *costs* of producing power in their own state to increase the following year, 2009. Almost all of the rest answered that they were "not sure." Here is how they divided in identifying the main reason for escalations they anticipated:

35 percent—increasing fuel costs

23 percent—costs of compliance to environmental regulations

21 percent—higher capital costs

11 percent—inflation

10 percent—other

These were officials involved in actually setting retail rate schedules, so their understanding of energy matters should be well above average. Although their answers were similar for most questions that paralleled the ones put to electricity customers, the regulators overestimated the readiness of retail consumers in their respective service areas to acquiesce in future rate levels that might more realistically reflect costs associated with environmental protection. Fourteen percent of the commissioners (as contrasted with 8 percent in the consumer survey) estimated that increases of 15 percent would be acceptable to residential ratepayers in an effort to mitigate greenhouse gas emissions from electricity generation sources.

The stark truth is that nobody can forecast precisely the end-result of pulls and tugs among cost factors, available technology, operational mandates, conservation and efficiency measures, and prices that are influenced nationally and globally as well as locally. One must be ready for surprises. Flexibility in adaptation becomes a prime economic virtue.

Since none of our current energy sources can be discarded in the immediate future, let's look back at the major ones this book has considered.

SURVEYING THE LINEUP OF SOURCES

As of mid-2008, it seemed all but certain that the United States would join a growing number of economically developed nations in internalizing the environmental costs of global-warming-gas (GWG) emissions by somehow associating an offset cost with such emissions. Possible ways of doing this were touched on in Chapter 5, and the following discussions assume that a "carbon price" of some sort will be in place henceforth—or at least that such a price will remain a sufficiently firm prospect in every form of energy production and every energy consumption sector that it should be weighed in making choices. This assumption seriously affects what have long been the two most troublesome elements in our national energy picture—oil and electricity.

OIL AND ITS SUBSTITUTES

Professional long-range energy forecasters increasingly project our national requirements for liquid fuels rather than for oil. This admits uncertainty. In projecting to 2030 and beyond, there are too many variables to have confidence in even the most expert estimates of how much demand for commercial and personal transportation—our largest oil consumer by far—will or can be satisfied in 2030 and beyond by petroleum products rather than other liquid fuels.

In all likelihood, petroleum will remain the largest single component in our consumption of energy sources for the next couple of decades. However, its use will become a function of negative rather than positive attributes. The choice of petroleum in any specific application will be questioned on the basis of the problems it raises for the five policy goals that have been discussed throughout this book: affordability, adequacy, secure availability, environmental acceptability, and ability to satisfy the first four goals on a reasonable timetable. The same criteria ought to be applied to petroleum substitutes.

Logically, a U.S. price on carbon emissions should impose almost as much of a burden on petroleum—our energy mainstay in transportation—as it does on coal, which dominates the nation's electricity sector. Combustion of oil produces more than four-fifths as much CO_2 as coal in relation to energy content. If public concerns about climate change have been directed somewhat more toward electricity than to petroleum, there are several possible partial explanations:

1. Reaction to the steepness of the rise in oil prices during 2008 pushed *environmental* discussions about oil into the background temporarily.

2. When crude oil and gasoline prices are extraordinarily high, politicians play down the prospect of boosting them even more through what voters would regard as a carbon tax, regardless of the collection mechanism to be employed.

3. Measurement of carbon dioxide releases from mobile sources is more difficult and indirect than those from fixed emitters, such as factories and power plants.

4. Consumers might think that a carbon price on energy inputs to electricity generation wouldn't be passed along to them as easily as one on motor fuels.

5. The decision to phase in higher mileage standards for the U.S. vehicle fleet relieves some public anxieties about GWGs, especially since it promises relief down the road for high fuel outlays.

If Americans wish to be serious about halting the increase in emissions of global warming gases, the respite cannot last. A collision between the reduction goals being publicized and the desire—even the economic need—to keep transport fuels affordable will necessitate further compromise.

Alternatives to oil were discussed earlier in respect to various goals. Some synthetic fuels cost more, or release more GWGs, than does oil. The experience of corn-based ethanol gobbling up one-third of our national crop and raising prices for both meat and grain has brought cries to speed up the development of cellulosic ethanol, although merely pouring money into research and development won't guarantee results. Arguments over cost and convenience continue on choices among electrics, hybrids, and other new vehicle technologies. If any were close to perfect, the competition would be over. It isn't. Those and other innovative energy sources bear close examination in regard to *all* factors: short-term and long-term dollar costs, their life-cycle net energy inputs, environmental impacts, timely deliverability, and volume needed to make a difference. Frustratingly, the evidence on each point will change as experience grows.

As oil prices soared, more of the U.S. public discovered a few other things about oil:

- Nonenergy uses of oil matter. Petrochemicals are in products everywhere. When oil prices rose, prices rose accordingly for everything from diapers to detergent. Procter & Gamble announced that oil-based raw materials would add $2 billion annually to its manufacturing costs for fiscal year 2009, and began to compress the volume of plastic containers to save money in packaging. This reversed the earlier trend toward enlarging containers to give the illusion that products were "super-sized."[6]

- For ages, truck drivers have exceeded posted speed limits because it was generally in their economic interest to deliver loads more quickly. They began to ask themselves: "At what price for diesel fuel might it make sense to slow down by 5 or 10 miles per hour and get more miles per gallon?"

- Flex-fuel vehicles that are capable of using either gasoline or a blended fuel that is 85 percent ethanol get preferred treatment of various kinds, but they don't necessarily reduce oil consumption. Because E-85 pumps are not easy to find, owners of such cars find it easy to ignore the flex option and simply fill up regularly with gasoline. This behavior only points up how difficult it is to curb widespread tendencies for people to be free riders when economic regulation of any sort has practical loopholes.

Not all the answers can be found domestically. Global diplomacy will have to play a role in reaching balanced solutions, complementing the contributions of economics and technology. The price of oil in the world market and the buildup of GWGs in Earth's atmosphere are both clearly influenced by international cooperation or the lack thereof—especially between developed nations and fast-growing countries of the developing world, as well as between the OECD and OPEC. Finding some way to let China and India participate in the OECD's energy deliberations could be an opener. Reviving the old idea of multilateral negotiations between oil producers and oil consumers may sound quixotic at this point, but it is also worth considering.

Similarly, a truce needs to be declared among warring factions within our own country. A windfall profits tax[7] on oil companies is counter-intuitive if we assume that investment by the private sector in both domestic oil production *and* alternatives to oil is highly desirable. Continuing to block *exploratory* drilling in the ANWR and some areas far offshore does little more than waste time by perpetuating ignorance about resources that the nation may find essential before long. By the same token, denying that enough evidence of anthropogenic climate change has been found to justify anticipatory counteraction—or that renewable energy forms need to be encouraged even before they are fully self-supporting—is similarly ostrich-like.

When time is taken into consideration, there are few proposals for internalizing externalities in energy production, delivery, and use that do not merit examination. This is especially apt in respect to measures that can reduce the per-capita and the per-dollar-of-GDP consumption of energy—and of oil in particular.

The only other caveat that might be included in this final brief summary involves the "efficiency dilemma." As demand for any product decreases, prices should fall and the offerings of that commodity will also tend to diminish. Investment in production is discouraged. Additional supplies of oil are not brought to market smoothly, especially when spare production capacity is tight. That can reintroduce short- to mid-term shortfalls and force prices back up. Sad to say, there is no magic policy formula that can control risk in the volatile oil markets still ahead. There is no insurance that government interventions of any sort, no matter how benignly intended and whether they come on the supply side or the demand side, will not bring unintended and undesirable consequences.

Balance is necessary, but it isn't easy to reach.

Aside from oil, the other huge problem facing the United States in years to come will be to make sure that electricity supplies meet the five goals.

Coal

Coal is so plentiful in the United States and so important in delivering baseload electricity from existing generation capacity that it must remain a significant energy source for the foreseeable future unless we are willing to risk chaos. Yet the conventional technique of burning pulverized coal to produce heat and generate electricity produces more carbon dioxide per unit of power output than the employment of any other form of primary energy.

Over the next few years, uncertainty about future regulation will discourage the selection of coal as an energy source in any *new* U.S. installation, except in three modes: (1) as a feedstock for liquid or gaseous synthetic fuels that can be burned more cleanly, taking into account GWG emissions during production;[8] (2) in small or mid-sized units intended primarily as tests or demonstrations of competing technologies to capture CO_2; or (3) in isolated instances where local circumstances make coal plants competitive, even with the added burden of a carbon price; for example, being adjacent to mining operations where adequate transmission links for delivery to power markets exist or can be added with minimum difficulty.

Technologies that might utilize coal in the longer term are still under development, and the exact timing of their emergence cannot be predicted. In June 2008 the World Resources Institute, a nonprofit think tank that is normally sanguine about technological progress, was ambivalent whether carbon capture and sequestration would require government support for twenty more years or fifty.[9] Thus, it would be self-defeating to impose a flat ban on new coal facilities that do not capture carbon and prevent it from escaping into the atmosphere—or which cannot specify a *certain* future time when they will be capable of doing so. On the other hand, it seems fair to insist that all new coal plants allow space and take care to position equipment so capture systems that are not yet available might be backfitted eventually.

There are strong incentives for venture capital from the private sector to search for the missing elements in future coal technology, although public-private partnerships that share development costs and encourage the exchange of new information will probably be necessary to reduce risk in building demonstration units.

Demand for power is still rising year-round, which means that baseload capacity cannot be sacrificed. Despite a steady surge since 2003 in generation by units using natural gas, coal-fired units still produce almost half of all U.S. electricity (48.6 percent in 2007). Thus, phasing out conventional coal plants as the prime U.S. source of electricity will likely take many decades. They comprise more than 300 gigawatts of capacity; an average of only 20 gigawatts or so of all new non-nuclear generation combined can be expected to come on line each year, including intermittent sources such as wind and solar.

Despite a slowing economy during 2007, U.S. generation from all sources rose by 2.3 percent over the previous year. The only time in recent years that demand has failed to grow was between 2000 and 2001. It would benefit the nation in a variety of ways if efficiency and conservation measures could turn the trend in U.S. use of electricity around (perhaps even *declining* at an average of 1 or 2 percent nationally each year). Yet at that rate it would still take longer than most coal foes realize to replace enough of the coal-fired capacity in existing units for new alternative electricity-supply systems to complement the rest meaningfully in matching demand.

Like all projections in energy economics, these are only estimates. It is tempting to try to illustrate all this with a pretense at more mathematical precision, but that would involve so many assumptions that the numbers would be meaningless. For example, wildly varying guesses at the rate and degree of market penetration by electric vehicles skew forecasts of future electricity demand.

Some voluntary or market-forced retirements of existing coal plants are bound to occur, but the pattern of those shutdowns will depend mainly on carbon prices, which are unlikely to remain stable. Nor is it certain that candidates for plant retirement will line up in the order of their tendency to emit CO_2. Their owners will look first at how much it might cost to continue operating older plants, even the most inefficient and/or polluting ones. Investment in them may have been fully depreciated. It might be worthwhile to hold them in reserve to meet occasional peaks in demand. Some plant-by-plant economics are also affected by special considerations in state or local legislation.

The flight from coal in this country may have begun, but it isn't a headlong one. We should remember that this has happened before to King Coal, only to have him double back for reasons that have good economic foundations in retrospect. With inputs from those who are as much concerned with energy security and marginal production costs as environment, government interventions in one direction or another will be attempted and should be anticipated. But the market will decide the actual timetable.

NUCLEAR POWER

A new U.S. nuclear era finally seems imminent.[10] It follows an effective hiatus of three decades after a single disturbing accident near Harrisburg, Pennsylvania, in 1979—in which, incidentally, no lives were lost. The economics of new nuclear designs and regulatory procedures remain to be proved, but fresh orders will make it possible to start adding nuclear electricity capacity in large discrete increments again while releasing relatively small amounts of either GWGs or any other pollutant to the atmosphere over plant life cycles that should on average exceed half a century. This is the case even if one includes the short-term effects of producing large amounts of reinforced concrete for the protective containment shell that envelops the guts of each reactor and small amounts of diesel fuel that might be used as backup power for relatively short periods.

Nuclear power can make no difference in the short run, however, and not much in the mid-term. Total U.S. baseload capacity might grow by as little as 10 gigawatts from new nuclear plants before 2020.

Licensing requirements appear to have been greatly streamlined since the days when half a dozen or more new nukes in the production pipeline might enter commercial operation in a single year, but nuclear power plants still take longer to build than any other kind. Federal legislation in 2007 contained inducements for the private sector to resume building reactor units, and they are so structured that the first half-dozen new plants can be expected to come in a rush. Then we can expect a pause of at least five years or so while the modern processes of modular construction are proved in practice and initial operating experience builds up.

A new wave of nuclear plants should be a boon locally to certain types of construction jobs, but supply and demand within the labor force will probably raise costs—perhaps even beyond the contingency factors that competent planners include. Competition for the necessary stable of special professional skills, ranging from health physicists to control room operators and persons with engineering specialties, will signal even more of a problem.

When U.S. utilities stopped ordering nuclear power plants long ago, those specialties fell out of favor in the nation's colleges and universities. Trained personnel leaving the U.S. nuclear Navy have long helped to fill some jobs in existing plants and enterprises, but that source is limited. Even with active encouragement from the federal government through directed scholarships, it will take a long time for faculties to rebuild and for student interest to reawaken.

Similar difficulties will arise from the dearth of domestic production facilities for some reactor system components. New U.S. plants coming on line between 2015 and 2020 will have to obtain some equipment from overseas suppliers and thus compete with foreign buyers. A particularly serious problem exists for the thick-walled reactor vessels, a dilemma shared by countries around the world. At present, heavy forgings of this type can be supplied by only one manufacturer, Japan Steel Works.

The two biggest barriers to a full-fledged nuclear renaissance both relate to time. They are the high initial investments that take decades to recoup and the need to convince a large enough segment of the public and officialdom at all levels and in all parts of the country that it will be safe and prudent to continue building commercial power reactors for at least a couple of decades without a demonstrated method to dispose permanently of high-level nuclear waste (HLW)—including plutonium and other transuranic elements—with radioactive half-lives in the tens of thousands of years.

Time has not been on our side, and no quick solution is in sight. By repeatedly finding excuses to delay a deep subterranean repository at Yucca Mountain (Nevada) for many years into the future, the United States has limited its options for HLW while inventories of it grow. Germany and several other nations are finding that their earlier legislation to phase out existing nuclear plants within a few years cannot be carried out because adequate replacement power is unavailable for various reasons. With nuclear generating capacity of 100 gigawatts in this country, such an effort would be even less practical here. Formal approval to proceed at Yucca Mountain was finally requested in 2008, but it is entirely possible that it will not have begun to accept HLW shipments by the time the first new nuclear power plants are ready to discharge additional spent fuel.

Consensus for *in*action almost always emerges more easily than for action, so we can expect spent fuel bundles from commercial nuclear power plants to remain where they are for the indefinite future. This would certainly not have been the best conceivable solution, and both Congress and successive presidents can be blamed; but it is the situation we are stuck with and one we can live with. It does not seem to be building toward a crisis. The fuel is well protected and monitored in isolated, passively cooled storage facilities at plant sites. Complaints about the unresolved problem will surface occasionally, but they are largely futile. Until a permanent repository is licensed and ready, the only alternative is to move the fuel across other states to other temporary locations. That would arouse even stronger opposition.

There are some reasons to keep spent fuel in places from which it can be *retrieved* whenever its longer-term fate is decided. The Global Nuclear Energy Partnership (GNEP), established during George W. Bush's administration, envisions reprocessing of used bundles in ways that would discourage diversion of fissile material to weapons use. Even if the GNEP falters in a new administration,[11] another generation may reverse President Carter's 1977 decision to end U.S. reprocessing plans. Reprocessing could reduce the volume and form of HLW to facilitate its interim storage or permanent disposition while recycling part of the residual fissile material. Like some other forms of material recycling, this costly process cannot be justified now on the grounds of the recovered fuel value alone. At some distant future date, the price or scarcity of fresh fissile material might change the cost-benefit equation.

In a very-long-term endeavor to make fuel for U.S. nuclear fission reactors essentially inexhaustible, we might even resume work on breeder reactors that would complement reprocessing. Breeders produce slightly more new fissile material than they consume as they operate. France, Japan, and Russia have continued to pursue them with mixed technical and economic success. Regrettably, a plutonium cycle increases risks of diverting material that can be used for nuclear weapons.

Beyond 2025, continued concerns about climate change and the imposition of higher and higher carbon costs on fossil fuels could revive U.S. interest in breeders; but their long-term net savings are usually oversold to the public. Despite their popular image as fuel factories, the fact is that almost every breeder design has a "doubling time" of many years. This means that any given reactor will not replace the equivalent of its original fuel loading until it has gone through a number of refueling cycles. As Chapter 6 stressed, it seems that everything takes time.

Undoubtedly, nuclear power is still a problematic part of the U.S. energy outlook. Nevertheless, assuming that new plants will make nuclear power economically competitive once again in this country, they are—along with coal—an indispensable segment of a balanced energy mix for the country. Unlike coal, they will prosper if carbon-emission costs rise. Neighboring Canada is a reliable source of abundant uranium, and the domestic enrichment facilities available now can be expanded as needed. Because existing nuclear power plants have been upgraded and their operation has been improved steadily, they continue to supply roughly one-fifth of all U.S. electricity each year. But nuclear power should not be counted on to increase that share of generation more than marginally before 2025 or 2030.

NATURAL GAS

Natural gas is sometimes touted as "the clean fossil fuel." One of its original selling points when long-distance pipelines began to introduce it from coast to coast was that it could eliminate the dirty emissions from municipal gas works whose chemical synthetics of various descriptions had provided illumination from the early 1800s onward and were still energizing cookstoves and home heating units in many parts of the country about a century and a half later. But times and perceptions change. The combustion of natural gas typically releases almost half as much carbon dioxide as coal with identical energy content, and CO_2 is now classified generally as a pollutant. Methane, the basic constituent of natural gas, can also contribute to global warming itself. Of course, the latter complaint ignores the fact that economics as well as U.S. environmental and safety rules have virtually eliminated the once-common releases of unused natural gas into the open.

Some purists recoil at the thought of natural gas as a "bridging fuel" for the United States from more carbonaceous fuels to a visionary energy future relying only on super-abundant sun and wind. They are wrong, because natural gas satisfies *most* of the criteria for such a mission—if, indeed, *any* energy source can.

Natural-gas-fired combustion turbines release only minimal amounts of the gases and particulates that contribute to acid rain, haze, or smog. They can be installed fairly quickly at relatively low capital expense. Combined-cycle systems are about one and a half times as efficient as conventional coal-fueled generators, and they can be useful either for baseload or peaking operation. In 2006, natural gas surpassed nuclear power as a source of U.S. electricity for the first time since the 1980s, and it will remain in second place behind coal for many years to come.

The United States is one of the largest producers of natural gas on Earth. Its known reserves are the sixth largest in the world. They exceed those of prolific oil suppliers such as Saudi Arabia and the United Arab Emirates, although they fall well below those of Russia, Iran, and Qatar. U.S. gas resources and potential reserves are both probably greater than now estimated because moratoria against exploratory drilling have delayed learning more about offshore deposits. Uncertainty about being able to bring natural gas to market from some parts of the Rockies have made companies reluctant to develop geologically promising domestic deposits for fear of producing "stranded gas."

For years, the installation of new gas pipelines in this country has been challenging. Practical siting has been blocked in some areas, even though eminent domain rights have made it easier to clear routes for them than for high-voltage power lines. Now the delivery clog has finally begun to loosen.

The Rocky Mountain region of the United States contains more than 22 percent of our proved reserves of natural gas, yet it has been trapped there for lack of pipelines to deliver gas to the more populous parts of the country where it would be welcomed. In September 2007, the supply-demand balance in the Rockies was so out-of-kilter that the wellhead price of gas bottomed out at essentially zero per million British thermal units—anything to get rid of what was being produced. The average "city gate" price in Wyoming that month was only $3.64. Prices at the same time at Louisiana's Henry Hub hovered around $6 and in the Northeast they were over $10.

On Valentine's Day 2007, a new pipeline went into service to assemble gas from Colorado and Wyoming to a market hub in Cheyenne. In May 2008, a 42-inch-diameter pipeline began to carry gas from there to Missouri. A few weeks later, the Federal Energy Regulatory Commission provisionally approved the 639-mile third leg of the east-west system to deliver gas all the way to Ohio, from which multiple connections already in place will be able to relay it to the Northeast and Middle Atlantic states. FERC's authorization was conditioned on almost 150 actions by the builders and operators of the REX-East Pipeline to avert or soften environmental impacts, but the urgency of filling the delivery gap prompted the commission to order that its construction be completed by the end of 2009.[12] This single new Rockies-to-the-Atlantic pipeline system will be capable by itself of increasing U.S. access to its own gas reserves by about 3 percent—an impressive one-time jump.

In almost any scenario between now and 2020 that tries to satisfy the multiple criteria recited so often in this book, more natural gas will be needed. Utilizing it optimally in North America depends on a combination of new technology, bold financing, a paradigm of higher prices, and adaptive government policies. Nearly half of all domestic U.S. gas now comes from unconventional sources. Some originates in coal seams in the form of coalbed methane (CBM) rather than from conventional wells. An increasing percentage is produced by sophisticated drilling and fracture methods from gas shale in regions that were considered devoid of economical gas prospects only a few years ago.

Articles in the mass media have left a widespread impression that the relatively clean combustion properties of natural gas and its popularity as a quick, less capital-intensive substitute for coal in the electric power sector have enabled the use of gas to grow steadily in this country. This is not true. Annual U.S. consumption of the fuel has seemed to be locked between 22 and 23 trillion cubic feet since the early 1990s. Yet there should have been no difficulty in matching demand with rising supply potential.

Gas prices over this entire period have bounced up and down, although the trend has been steadily upward since 2003.[13] While these more recent price rises have forced both inter-sectoral and intrasectoral adjustments, they have proved to be "sustainable" by broad national criteria. Both U.S. consumption of natural gas and its adequate and reliable supply to the nation can afford to increase. At least one major new gas pipeline from Alaska and northern Canada will be needed soon, along with fuller utilization of LNG ports and improved storage facilities.

Integrating an environment-sparing price for carbon dioxide emissions by electricity producers will tend to restore the competitive cost-advantage natural gas held earlier over coal in the generating sector. A complex of advantages for gas over oil as a source of heat for buildings should enable natural gas to increase its market share in both residential and commercial energy consumption. In itself, this need not push seasonal gas costs higher in those sectors, since warmer winters nationwide could reduce total requirements for space heating.

In surface transportation, the tendency will continue to replace fleets of buses and short-haul trucks gradually with new vehicles fueled with compressed natural gas. Stock turnover in this important sub-market is rather slow, however, and CNG will face growing competition from other technologies—including electric vehicles, hybrids, ands some dedicated to a regionally suited assortment of biofuels.

The most inviting U.S. possibility for expanded use of natural gas is in industry, where repenetration will be almost purely a matter of overall cost comparisons in both energy sources and equipment. We have not fully exploited a number of direct applications of natural gas in industrial functions that had long been assumed to require electricity. These include the ability to produce extremely high temperatures, focus heat very selectively on limited areas, and even heat liquids from the inside rather than through the walls of containers.

During the final years of his tenure as Chairman of the Federal Reserve Board, Alan Greenspan spoke often and insightfully about the realities of the

U.S. natural gas market and the importance of the fuel to the economy.[14] More recently, the most vociferous spokesman for gas has been veteran oilman T. Boone Pickens, but his 2008 advertising push to use wind power as the replacement for natural gas in the U.S. electricity sector so that motor vehicles could switch en masse to CNG fuel was unfortunately filled with egregious inaccuracies and miscalculation. Mentioning a few should bring home the point that "simple" energy solutions should always be dissected before declaring victory.

A glance back at the spaghetti chart in Chapter 1 (Figure 1.4) shows that *all* of the natural gas now used to generate electricity would be the energy equivalent of only a minor fraction of what U.S. petroleum supplies to the transportation sector. The chicken-and-egg problem of simultaneously introducing new-fuel vehicles and the filling stations to serve them—discussed in Chapter 4—would be unusually tough for compressed natural gas because there are some areas of the United States that are practically devoid of gas pipelines.

It should also be noted that Pickens owns a company dedicated to exploiting compressed natural gas vehicles in the transportation sector—and has said he contemplates building the largest wind farm in the world by 2011. It would add 4,000 megawatts from the Texas Panhandle to that state's grid.[15] But, while justifiably lauding natural gas as a domestic product, the fabled oil entrepreneur failed to note that all of North America will still require growing imports of LNG to match currently projected demand. His boasts that U.S. gas equaled the oil holdings of Saudi Arabia showed confusion between reserves and resources—an equivalency debunked in Chapter 2.

There were other mistakes in Pickens' television and newspaper campaign too, some related to the wind portion of the scheme. For example, it says nothing about the difficulty posed by Texas's deficiency in electricity connections with other states. Most of the errors should have been obvious to anyone who has read thus far in this book, but the hardest to explain was the mis-statement of what this country spends on imported oil. The true figure *is* way too high and ought to be cut, but the figure of $700 billion annually given in Pickens' ads was wildly overstated and must have been based on exaggerated projections of some sort. Such errors should have been enough to make even a billionaire in the energy business blush and bite his tongue.

WIND

Enthusiastic exaggerations aside, U.S. windpower *did* seem to mature during 2007. At a cost of roughly $9 billion, developers brought more than 5,300 MW of new capacity on line that year. The Office of Energy Efficiency and Renewable Energy of the Department of Energy noted with pride that this was more than twice as much capacity as had ever before been added annually.[16] It surpassed additions of coal capacity for the year and wasn't far behind the 7,500 MW of new gas-fired generating capacity. Wind now exceeds geothermal installations as a source of U.S. electricity, and it has finally justified projections dating back to the earliest days of the DOE that it had the greatest potential among renewables to become a credible source of electricity for the nation.

Statistics for 2007 can be misleading, however, in respect to what new windpower units might contribute to U.S. electricity needs over a longer span. As explained earlier, generation *capacity* does not equate directly with generation *output*. At one extreme, baseload coal plants pump out power all year long, operating around the clock. At the other, because fluctuating wind velocities do not correspond to up-and-down demand for electricity, wind output may be available less than 10 percent of the time when demand is peaking. During 2007, an apparently more favorable yearlong comparisons of electricity production between new wind turbines and those using natural gas may have been atypical.

The DOE data show that wind units represented about 35 percent of all new capacity, and it was calculated that they produced an almost identical percentage of the increase in electricity produced. This was undoubtedly influenced by the fact that utilities were obliged to accept wind output whenever offered. Furthermore, the production tax credits available to wind turbines encouraged operators to maximize their output, regardless of comparative economics in basic costs. At the same time, because gas prices were relatively high during 2007, many of the combined cycle combustion turbines using that fuel were operated only as peakers or intermediate suppliers rather than baseload plants. There were even some cases where older, boiler-type generating units switched from gas to cheap residual oil. This situation should not be assumed to persist indefinitely.

To its credit, the DOE's *Annual Report on Wind Power for 2007* is full of careful footnotes and explanatory interjections. At one point (p. 20), the text even cautions that "comparing wind and wholesale power prices in this manner is spurious, if one's goal is to fully account for the costs and benefits of wind relative to its competition." State tax and financial incentives are not uniform. The timing of wind patterns varies enormously, even over short distances. Installation costs differ across the country, as do the costs and difficulties of connecting to grids and thus reaching customers who can benefit most.

Some reports suggest an average capital cost of around $1,700 per kilowatt of capacity, but this undoubtedly is subject to considerable variation. Like most energy sources, wind has profited to some degree from economies of scale. The overall size of wind projects has increased, but the DOE report

notes that it is too early to count on specific savings in operating and maintenance costs from larger sites using more wind towers.

Offshore wind turbines are common in Europe, but few have survived the
protests of Americans who object to them as visually undesirable despite considerable distances from shore—or as threats to fishing and boating. On land,
a few dozen individual turbines on the order of 3 megawatts each had begun
to operate in this country by the end of 2007, but the largest have averaged
about 1.5 MW for several years or more. Since wind-turbine towers and
blades are already quite large, there is probably an upper limit to unit output.
But it obviously has not been reached, since there is talk of 5 MW machines
and perhaps even larger ones. There is no reason to exaggerate the impressive
growth that has taken place in capacity, yet even the latest DOE report mean-
inglessly swells the *number* of wind turbines by officially defining as "large-
scale" any wind machine with a capacity of more than 50 kilowatts—that is,
0.05 MW. The tendency of proponents for any specific energy source to make
its performance look as good as possible is hard to discourage.

Wind is still primarily a regional energy source. By the end of 2008, the
United States had built somewhat more than 20 gigawatts of modern wind
generation capacity, but about 40 percent was in just two states—Texas and
California. Another 30 percent was operating in Washington, Minnesota,
Iowa, and Colorado.

Just as natural gas availability has been cramped by delays in pipeline construction, so the potential of remote wind sites has suffered from a lack of
transmission capacity. Here again, however, barriers are being attacked. Texas
and other leading wind states have started to consider setting up discrete
"renewable energy zones" where transmission planning would be undertaken
regionally. The Western Governors' Association (WGA) is pushing a multi-
year project to extend the idea to eleven states, two Canadian provinces, and
areas in Mexico that are part of the Western Interconnection. This fits into a
very ambitious WGA target to add 30 gigawatts of "clean and diversified
energy by 2015," but indications are that the progress of transmission zones
beyond the conceptual stage depends on federal financial support.[17]

Wind parks have lured substantial interest from the private sector, even
including foreign investors; and new projects for more than a dozen times the
capacity that existed at the end of 2007 are being explored. Apart from Boone
Pickens' announced plans, Shell's wind-energy arm and Luminant are focused
on a 3 gigawatt wind project in Texas. Some serious efforts will undoubtedly
be carried out, but many companies are just testing the waters. In actions
paralleling announcements of "planned" LNG receiving facilities, many in the
large "queue" of wind projects described in the press will never be undertaken.

An overwhelming 83 percent of wind-turbine capacity already installed is
owned by independent power producers, with only 11 percent belonging to

investor-owned utilities and less than half of that to publicly owned utilities. Costs are rising—especially for the turbines themselves, which were expected to remain in short supply through 2009 at least. Installation costs have risen. Power purchase agreements of 20 years, more or less, for the electricity output are common, but owners and power marketers are increasingly willing to assume some merchant risk by selling some portion of their product output through the spot energy market or via short-term contracts. This is a hopeful sign.

The fuel costs of wind are zero, but this energy source is capital intensive and thus sensitive to interest rates, depreciation allowances, and ultimately the practical life of the equipment as compared with coal or gas facilities. U.S. wind projects for the near term are more contingent on developing innovative financial structures than on any kind of technological advance. Many depend on project-level debt, third-party investors, income tax liabilities, and rulings by the Internal Revenue Service. Since conditions for such ventures can change quickly, a wise idea is to seek current information that applies regionally.[18]

"Big wind" surely offers good investment possibilities, as well as a chance for financial pitfalls. But wind is still only a complement—rather than a replacement—for the bulk of the U.S. plants that will continue to use coal, nuclear fuel, and natural gas as primary energy inputs.

Small-scale wind units make for interesting feature stories and a growing niche market. They lack the federal tax credits enjoyed by residential solar installations. Small turbines in wind-rich rural areas help to encourage public appreciation of energy requirements and the need for cooperative approach to matching all types of energy supply with demand, but they have little significance nationally. They may be useful to replace LPG and small diesel generators, but they are not usually an economic bargain, despite generous state incentives that may cover 30 to 40 percent of a project's initial cost. An estimate by Joe Schwartz, editor of *Home Power Magazine* and thus assumed to be a friendly voice, was cited by the *New York Times* as indicating that even with subsidies it could take 20 years to pay for an installation.[19]

Government support for wind at the level of small consumers and self-generators may also carry some small hidden costs to the economy and/or taxpayers that are not usually mentioned. If owners of such small wind systems are also connected to a grid, net-metering laws effectively require utilities to deduct any electricity supplied by wind generation from regular utility bills. Thus, companies are buying this excess power at the retail price rather than wholesale, and charging customers accordingly. The same applies to home solar units.

Solar Energy and Other Renewables

Solar energy is a hole card in the poker hand this country must play for the high stakes of a successful energy future. Realistically, however, its chances of winning the pot by itself now seem akin to those of drawing to an inside straight.

Discussions of solar energy's potential are muddied by ambiguities in its very definition. A few advocates of renewable alternatives go so far as to include wind and biomass in their solar projections, since winds result from solar heating of our planet, and trees grow in response to photosynthesis traceable to the sun. Some even take credit for hydroelectricity—which is alternately condemned as doing violence to Nature and implicitly saluted. They make statistics for our use of renewable energy seem more impressive than they are, by always incorporating hydro's contribution.

When ordinary folks refer to solar energy, they almost certainly think they are talking about either (1) photovoltaic cells, which convert various wavelengths of solar radiation directly into a flow of electrons that we recognize as electricity, or (2) solar-thermal systems, in which heat produced by absorption of the sun's rays is utilized somehow—in anything from swimming pool heaters (which make up the bulk of the large number of "solar installations" credited to the state of California) to spread-out heat-collecting arrays that can reach the multi-megawatt range in generating electricity the old fashioned way via turbines.

Photovoltaics and solar-thermal systems will become increasingly important, so both deserve investment and appropriate government support. But how long will it take for the combination of these two to exceed 1 percent or so of our national energy supply? The question brings a diversity of opinion from witnesses with some credibility that is so wide as to verge on the comical.

BP is the oil company that invented "Beyond Petroleum" as a slogan and features the sun in its ads. But Steve Westwell, the company's executive vice president and group chief of staff, told the OECD Forum 2008 that he has become less optimistic during the past five years and now believes it will take decades to develop solar energy on a wide scale. He saw perhaps a century elapsing before the still-costly solar devices of today would become *the* major energy source.[20] By contrast, Ray Kurzweil is one member of a blue-ribbon panel convened by the National Academy of Engineering that reported its findings on engineering challenges at virtually the same time; he contends that "a crossing point where solar energy will be cheaper than fossil fuels is definitely within 5 years, maybe sooner."[21] Obviously they both aren't correct.

Kurzweil is a member of the National Inventors Hall of Fame and has received prestigious national awards for his technical innovations. Nevertheless, he bases his solar-cost projections rather loosely on the simultaneous early convergence of *numerous* technological breakthroughs.[22] Many relate to a revolution in nanotechnology, a relatively new field that involves working with materials at the molecular level. Kurzweil foresees reducing the cost of solar panels by a factor of 10 to 100 while doing the same for fuel cells and improving the storage density of batteries and super-capacitors by like amounts. He counts on using transmission systems in which carbon nanotubes have been woven into long wires, at least until long-distance wireless transmission by microwaves appear and we can eventually augment terrestrial systems by giant solar panels in space. At the same time, he assumes huge reductions in energy *requirements*, envisioning tabletop devices that could manufacture finished products ranging from computers to clothing while using very low power.

When one recalls the speed with which developments such as cheap Black-Berries invaded the market, it is hard to dismiss completely what Kurzweil calls "the law of accelerating returns"; but the likeliest future for solar energy probably lies somewhere in the vast gap between him and the disillusioned BP executive. Meanwhile, the boom in solar power—amounting to some 148 megawatts of new capacity in 2007—is being driven at least as much by what the *New York Times* once called "financial engineering" as by new technology.

Power-purchase agreements have found a way to reward solar equipment manufacturers with the up-front incentives offered by the federal and state governments while allowing electricity consumers to spread their costs over 20 years or more. These schemes are being pushed by reputable firms such as Morgan Stanley, Goldman Sachs, and Wells Fargo, who should be able to supply details of various arrangements as they evolve and are tested. Cautious companies such as Wal-Mart have discovered that generous local ground rules in states as different climatically as California and New Jersey can now justify switching to solar power to some extent. Yet residential consumers should read the fine print in any plans offered and weigh the economic pros and cons carefully. A municipal program in Berkeley, California, pays homeowners to install solar systems, but plans to recoup the city's costs by annual increases to the property taxes of each household for 20 years.[23]

With all this in mind, one must still compare the tiny total annual additions of solar capacity nationwide with national demand and note that actual generation from 148 megawatts of capacity amounts to far less than the steady output of a single gas turbine.

Meaningful solar penetration of U.S. markets may well depend on either (1) incorporation of photovoltaic converters into building materials such as facings and windows; or (2) an all-out effort to connect remote "sun farms" to urban areas. In either case, both federal and state governments could hasten this by dedicated procurement of such systems.

On the off-chance that optimistic technological visions will prove closer to being correct than more pessimistic ones, it would be frivolous to give up on the "solar hole card" until the entire hand is turned face-up. It goes back to an observation in an earlier chapter: With our present outlook, we need *all of the above*.

PUTTING IT ALL TOGETHER: THE LONG VIEW

The view throughout this book has been that energy independence—even if forgivingly redefined as "independence from oil imports"—is a foolish and impractical goal. Nevertheless, if the United States determined at all costs to become "energy independent" in that more limited sense, could it do so? Perhaps . . . by 2060 or so.

But, what would it take? The fact is that there is no certain, clear path.

Energy independence would probably not be made possible by relying almost exclusively on coal, unless the surface transportation sector switched entirely to some form of electric propulsion. Unless technical problems that have already stymied humankind for more than half a century in approaching commercial fusion are resolved within the next 50 years, nuclear energy could not do the job alone. Independence is unlikely to be achieved via a hydrogen economy either, because of the huge new production-and-delivery infrastructure that would have to be developed. Various forms of renewable energy might lead us toward national or continental energy independence *some day*, but only if major breakthroughs came first in the storage and delivery of electricity *and* in the biochemical production of easily storable synthetic liquid and/or gaseous fuels.

There is little doubt that this country faces one type of energy crisis after another as the delicately balanced mobile of goals trembles in every shifting breeze. For example, to adapt one of Abraham Lincoln's most famous phrases, one wonders if the natural gas and electricity industries can survive, half-controlled and half-free. The likely answer is that they must, so they will.

Energy economics offers us a menu of choices. Some choices are made by individuals, some are made by businesses or government officials, and some are forced upon each of them by changing circumstances.

All this involves more than asking how much it costs in dollars and cents to satisfy requirements for a million British thermal units in various ways. The energy picture changes completely when choices are evaluated from the perspective of trying to balance U.S. policy goals.

From the standpoint of energy adequacy alone, coal cannot be dismissed. The United States has enough coal to last the nation for hundreds of years at current rates of depletion. It has long been our largest source of primary energy to generate electricity, and it could remain so. Chemically, coal can also be converted into liquid or gaseous fuels, although the processes to accomplish this subtract from coal's advantage over most other sources in current prices per unit of raw energy.

Because the costs of producing and delivering energy generally seem destined to remain high, our best single hope in keeping our requirements for it affordable is to use less. This doesn't have to mean deprivation. The best answer here involves reducing energy intensity in getting things done, especially in the residential and transport sectors.

Improved reliability of supply starts with preserving a good energy mix—including nuclear power and wise use of North American natural gas; but it also necessitates closer attention to developing delivery infrastructure in the form of pipeline and powerline networks (along with LNG import facilities). All should be geared to changing supply and demand patterns, and distributed generation can also play a role.

Environmental concerns might be met a long time hence by a source such as solar energy, but there must be multiple bridges to that future. Natural gas and windpower are already complementary sources that help serve this purpose, since gas turbines are commonly used to fill in for intermittent supplies of wind. But the natural advantages and limitations of each need to be better understood.

That brings us to the final key factor—Time. This may be the toughest of all to cope with in the United States, because we do not have—and don't wish to have—a centrally planned economy and society. Our alternatives to central planning in ensuring that there will be sensible targets in the short-term, mid-term, and long-term are leadership . . . and patience. It is in our individual interests to make prudent choices as consumers. It is up to businesses, industry, and government at all levels to do the same.

We need to get over any idea that our energy future will be easy or perfect.

Even if many of the new things we try fail to meet full expectations we can still be ahead of the game. If individual U.S. citizens and our leaders act wisely—which involves a big "if"—the picture seems to brighten toward 2020. So . . . don't be discouraged; be realistic.

What should we do about all the dilemmas we face? Thomas J. Watson of IBM posted a slogan all over the giant firm he headed. It is the most basic principle of energy economics as well: *Think!*

NOTES

1. *The MIT Dictionary of Modern Economics*, 3rd ed., David W. Pearce, ed. (New York: Macmillan, 1986).

2. For the philosophical underpinnings of this economic/ethical approach, consult the works of the eighteenth and nineteenth century's Jeremy Bentham and John Stuart Mill (see Spiegel, op.cit., pp. 340–345). For modern applications, see contemporary campaign speeches.

3. Often identified as "the Brundtland Report," eponymously recognizing Norwegian Prime Minister Gro Harlem Brundtland, who chaired the commission established by the United Nations. The report is generally credited with inspiring the 1992

Earth Summit in Rio de Janeiro, which produced the Framework Convention on Climate Change . . . and ultimately the Kyoto Protocol and efforts following it.

4. *Our Common Future*, Report of the World Commission on Environment and Development (New York: Oxford University Press, 1987), p. 19, and Chapter 2, "Towards Sustainable Development," *passim*.

5. "Switching off or Switching Bulbs," a box accompanying Shankar Vedantam's article, "On Climate, Symbols Can Overshadow Substance: Lights-Out Event More Showy Than Practical," *Washington Post*, May 17, 2008, p. A-1.

6. Louis Uchitelle, "Oil Prices Raise Cost of Making Range of Goods," *New York Times*, June 8, 2008, p. 1.

7. A true "windfall profits tax" on oil companies would be a special levy on profits resulting from exogenous sources unrelated to costs of production and the costs of doing business, including the assumption of risks. In view of how oil prices are formed, it is probably impossible administratively to *measure* that amount—which must vary from company to company anyway. What is usually recognized as a WPT is any extraordinary rate or form of taxation that applies to the difference between the market price during a given period for some stipulated form of crude or refined product and a lower, "normal" price level set arbitrarily through reference to history and a compromise reached by legislators. A WPT also introduces disputes over how the revenues it produces should be expended, with possibilities ranging from deficit reduction or redistribution in some formula among "ordinary" taxpayers to designation for such special projects as energy R&D or subsidies to producers and consumers of competing energy sources.

8. This possibility is intended to embrace integrated units in which coal is gasified and then combusted to generate electricity as well as the option of converting coal into fuel for other uses.

9. Debra Kahn, "Technology: Carbon Sequestration Will Need Government Support for 20–50 Years—Report," *Climate Wire*. June 4, 2008. The excellent WRI report itself is Hiranya Fernando, John Venezia, Clay Rigdon, and Preeti Verma, *Capturing King Coal: Deploying Carbon Capture and Storage Systems in the U.S. at Scale* (May 2008).

10. An interesting signal to this effect was sent in mid-2007 by the publication of the *Nuclear Power Joint Fact-Finding Report* by The Keystone Center, a non-profit organization that for more than three decades has facilitated cross-sector dialogues on pressing environmental, energy, and public health issues. This initiative brought "general support" from members of such diverse groups as the National Wildlife Federation, the National Association of Regulatory Utility Commissioners, the Natural Resources Defense Council, the National Commission on Energy Policy, the Union of Concerned Scientists, and companies from the nuclear industry itself, as well as consultants and academics. Although unanimity was not achieved and although the individuals involved were not representing their organizations in official capacities, the findings and recommendations suggest that consensus is possible.

11. The Global Nuclear Energy Partnership continued its ministerial-level meetings right up to within a month of the 2008 presidential election. Russia and China are both among more than a score of partner-nations in GNEP, and it is conceivable

that the forum it provides could complement ongoing but sometimes frustrating consideration of non-proliferation matters within the International Atomic Energy Agency (IAEA).

12. "FERC authorizes REX-East pipeline to transport Rockies Gas to Eastern Markets," FERC News Release, May 30, 2008.

13. The year 2002 was aberrant in many respects because of the attack on the World Trade Center near the end of the preceding year and subsequent economic turmoil from a variety of causes. In this case, gas prices would fit the argument put forth in the text, but they were deliberately excluded to reinforce a point made in Chapter 1—namely, that a span of years chosen to diagnose a trend should if possible avoid beginning or ending with a year that is probably atypical.

14. Even though the numbers have changed and some issues are evolving, several texts from Greenspan's periodic testimony before Congress in 2003 and 2004 are worth re-examining. For example, see his discussion of natural gas supply and demand before the House Committee on Energy and Commerce of June 10, 2003.

15. "T. Boone Pickens: His Life. His Legacy," website at http://www.boonepickens.com/helping

16. U.S. Department of Energy, Energy Efficiency and Renewable Energy, *Annual Report on U.S. Wind Power Installation, Cost, and Performance Trends: 2007* (May 2008). This was only the second year for what was promised to become an annual series. Observations in this section are based largely on the data it contains, but it was occasionally necessary to supplement those with information from broader reports by the Energy Information Administration to provide comparisons or analytical context.

17. Western Governors' Association website, http://www.westgov.org.

18. To get started, see Lawrence Berkeley National Laboratories, *Wind Project Financing Structures: A Review & Comparative Analysis*, Report 63434 (September 2007).

19. John Casey, "Technology Smooths the Way for Home Wind-Power Turbines," *New York Times*, April 15, 2008.

20. "RENEWABLES: World unlikely to cut CO_2 significantly before 2050—BP executive," *Climate Wire*, June 4, 2008.

21. "Are we near a solar energy tipping point?," Program #5523 of the Earth & Sky Radio Series, with hosts Deborah Byrd, Joel Block, Lindsay Patterson and Jorge Salazar, available at http://www.earthsky.org/radioshows

22. See Ray Kurzweil, *The Singularity Is Near: When Humans Transcend Biology* (New York: Viking Penguin, 2005), pp. 243–250.

23. Peter Maloney, "Pay for the Power, Not the Panels," *New York Times*, March 26, 2008.

Index

ABOUT THE AUTHOR

JOSEPH M. DUKERT, Ph.D., a political economist, has been an independent energy analyst and consultant for more than forty years. He is regarded by many in the field as the outstanding authority on the interdependent North American energy market. His expertise covers both technical developments and economics in all energy sources as well as energy efficiency. An adjunct fellow at the Center for Strategic and International Studies, he was named several years ago as a Senior Fellow of the U.S. Association for Energy Economics. He has also served as Senior Advisor to the North American Commission for Environmental Cooperation and as a consultant to the International Energy Agency of the OECD.